THE COTHILL STORY

THE COTHILL STORY

GEORGE PIKE

COTHILL HOUSE
OXFORDSHIRE
1991

To Gabrielle
who has helped me enjoy it all

First published 1991 by
Cothill House, Frilford Heath, Abingdon,
Oxon OX13 6JL

British Library Cataloguing in Publication Data
is available from The British Library

ISBN 0 9518 2880 0

Designed by Humphrey Stone
Typeset in Monophoto Sabon by
August Filmsetting, Haydock, St Helens
Printed in England by Henry Ling, Dorchester
Bound by Green Street Bindery, Oxford

CONTENTS

Foreword by Eric Anderson 7

Preface & Acknowledgements 9

Introduction 13

PART I · 1870 – SUMMER 1962

C. W. Carles – M. J. Daughlish / F. Knowles
M. J. Daughlish / R. Tomkinson – S. A. Pike

1. Origins 17

2. Early days 24

3. A small school, a Great War 41

4. The arrival of the Pikes 57

5. The Thirties 71

6. World War II and back to peacetime 99

7. Apprenticed as assistant master 121

8. Farewell to S. A. P. 147

PART II · AUTUMN 1962 – 1990

G. L. S. Pike – A. D. Richardson

9. New broom 181

10. 'The World of a Child' 203

11. Cothill House School Ltd 228

12. New directions 258

Appendix I:
Numbers of Cothillians at public schools, etc., 1894–1989
295

Appendix II: Awards – scholarships and exhibitions – to Cothillians, 1895–1989
297

Appendix III: In Memoriam, 1914–1918/1939–1945
299

Appendix IV: School Song 301

Bibliography 302

Index of names 303

Subscribers to the book 313

FOREWORD

'Come in and have tea.' That was my introduction to George and Gabrielle Pike. I was the new Head Master of Abingdon School to whom, characteristically, they were showing kindness. It was a glorious October afternoon with the sun shining over drifts of golden leaves; there was a fire burning in the drawing-room, deep chintz armchairs, a wonderful tea and above all the warmth of two people very much in the right place and running, quite obviously, a superb school. Small boys kept appearing at the door with requests for this and that, all of which George decided with friendly expedition and I remember being impressed by how easy and yet courteous the boys were.

That was my first introduction to Cothill and nothing that I have seen of Cothill and Cothill boys since has altered the essentials of the picture. As this delightful book, which traces the school's history from the beginnings, well illustrates, it deserves the confidence that generations of parents have shown in its various headmasters, for it has done a most important thing: educated sensibly, firmly, but with flexibility and humour, hundreds upon hundreds of keen young boys who have gone on to the best schools in the land and after that to careers in every walk of English life.

What I like about the book is the picture it gives from the inside of that quintessentially English phenomenon, a prep school. Nothing like Cothill exists in other countries, but the history of the school and the anecdotes with which it is illustrated show exactly why so many Englishmen look back with such affection on their early schooldays. All prep school life is here.

Its other fascination is its picture of quiet, evolutionary change. There has been change within the school over the years and change, on the whole, for the better; but there has been change, too, outside, to which the school has responded. It was interesting for a former Head Master of Abingdon to see that school and other good rising schools beginning to figure in later years among the list to which Cothill sent its brightest and best. It is that ability to combine continuity and change which has been the secret of success in independent schools in this country. This very readable book gives a fascinating glimpse of that dual process at work. It will appeal, I hope, to a wider audience than to loyal Old Cothillians, although they above all will find much to delight them in these pages.

ERIC ANDERSON
Eton College
June 1991

PREFACE & ACKNOWLEDGEMENTS

No book has previously been written about Cothill, and since my father and I have spanned fifty years as successive Head Masters I felt it was time that a history should be written. I have tried to tell the story of the school's development from memories of individual Old Boys, parents, members of the staff, family and friends, but as I have myself lived in the orbit of the school since 1927, this account is, to some extent, autobiographical.

It may be helpful if I explain the line I have taken in dealing with some of the 'mechanics' of the text. First of all, in order to avoid any confusion between boys and masters, I have made a distinction in the way that I refer to them. I have used Christian name and surname for a boy (or Old Boy); initials and surname for a master (with Christian name usually recorded at some stage). I have relied on initials alone for the principal figures among the masters, once they have become established. When in doubt, refer to the Index.

I have introduced contemporary quoted memories in the present tense, even though some of the writers have died during the preparation of the book (as recorded below). This distinguishes these quotations from those taken out of the *Magazine*, where the lead-in is in the past.

In choosing pictures, I have thought it invidious to single out and caption by name a necessarily unrepresentative selection of boys. Instead, I have chosen illustrations largely of a general nature and kept the boys anonymous. Boys and Old Boys anyway hold sway in the text. Staff have been captioned by name, informally in more latterday snapshots, formally in the groups.

There is at least one deliberate inconsistency: I have stuck to 'Great War' – so instinctive to someone of my generation – and paired it with 'World War II'. Also – brought up alongside RAF Abingdon – I prefer the use of 'aerodrome' to 'airfield'.

I wish to thank everybody who responded to my appeal for written contributions, photographs and ephemera. I have gratefully drawn direct on material from the following, some of whom wished to be anonymous:

Alastair Aberdeen, Mark Aldous, Christopher Arnander, Nick Assheton, Mike Atkin-Berry, Ian Aylesford, Richard Bailey, the late Tim Bailey, Jack Banks, Johnny Banks, Tim Barker, Chris Barnett, Oliver Barnett, Hugh Barrett-Lennard, Daniel Beazer, May Bedwell, Jim Bellew, Anton Bilton, Richard Bird, Simon Blackmore, Charles Bland, Chris Boothroyd, Oliver Braybrooke, Christopher Brett, Kemmis Buckley, Julia Budworth, Francis Burkitt, James Calvert, Roger Carrington, Vi Carrington, Peter Carter, John Cartwright, Bromley Challenor, Roderick Chamberlain, Stanley Chattey, Scottie Cheshire, the late Charles Close-Smith, Mike Cocks, Tim Collins, Peter Cooper, Brian Costeloe, Clive Craigmile, Nico Craven, Nick Dawson, Tim Dawson, Dick de la Hey, Alan de Piro, Elwes Duffield, John Duffield, Philip Duncombe, Louise Dunmore, the late Catherine Eastwood, June Esau, the late Tony Farnell, Donald Fergusson, Tony Findlay, Marigold Freeman-Attwood, David Gardiner-Hill, Nick Georgano, Anthony Gill, Peter Glazebrook, Charles Gooch, John Goodrich, Daphne Gough, Mike Gover, the late Basil Greenwell, Barbara Hall, the late Guy Halsey, the late Pat Halsey, Gerald Hamilton, David Hannah, John Hannah, Rosie Harley, Tom Harley, Rosemary Hatch, David Heaton, Mark Hely-Hutchinson, Diana Heyman, Peter Heyman, Fergus Higgins, Hyla Holden, Tim Holland, Tony Holland, Paul Holmer, Tom Holmer, James Holt, the late Jack Hooke, the late Philip Hudson, the late Evelyn Hulbert-Powell, Tom Jackson, Jonathan Janson, Bapji Jodhpur, Gay Kindersley, Michael Knutsford, Maggie Laing, Robin Langhorne, Bill Lanyon, Robin Leanse, Shirley Leggett, Roger Leigh, the late Godfrey Llewellyn, Andrew Loyd, Sue McArthur, Jeremy Malim, Dan Massey, Jane Matthews, the late Waltsham Maynard, Simon Moffett, Guy Neale, Ran Ogston, the late Jack Paine, Raphe Palmer, Wold Palmer, Chris Palmer-Tomkinson, Audrey Parry, Johnny Peel, Robert Peel, Marc Piercey, Margaret Porter, the late Richard Porthouse, Toby Pryor, Francis Pym, John Rambaut, Duncan Rawson-Mackenzie, Graham Rogers, Harry Rogers, John Rogers, Nicky Rootes, Peter Rowley, John Rucker, Richard Ryder, John Saunder, Patrick Savage, Claude Scott, Franko Seymour, Nicholas Scott, Peter Shakerley, Robert Shaw, Hugh Shelton, Julian Shuckburgh, Michael Snow, Chris Somers, Jack Somers, Walter Somers, John Stainer, Bev Stanier, Jonathan Stedall, Daphne Stewart, Paul Stibbard, Bill Stockton, the late Hugh Stockwell, Humphrey Stone, Janet Stone, Michael Stourton, Michael Stratton, John Stubbs, Joan Swinbank, Leonard Swinbank, Mark Swinbank, Robin Swinbank, Richard Symonds, John Thomson, the late Ken Tomkinson, John Vassar-Smith, Louisa Vincent (Vivian), Richard Vivian, the late Vincent Waite, Bill Waller, David Way, Ken Welby, Anthony Weld Forester, Robin Wellesley, Charles Whitbread, Mike Whitbread, Paul Whitfield, Desmond Wigan, Nishy Wijewardane, Kit Wilson, Mark Wordsworth.

I am also most grateful to those who have read the manuscript – some of them in more than one draft. Donald Leinster-Mackay has carefully read a late draft in Australia and produced many helpful suggestions from his wide knowledge of the history of prep schools. Detailed comments and advice have also been forthcoming from Marigold Freeman-Attwood, Tom Jackson, Jeremy Malim, Stephen Ryder, Leonard Swinbank, Raymond Willis and Robin Woods. My two sisters, Diana and Audrey, have also read the text and jogged my memory. Gabrielle has helped with the book from the beginning.

I have been fortunate in the professional help which I have received from two Old Boys, Humphrey Stone and David Way, and Rosie Harley, the mother of another Old Boy: between them they clock up about seventy-five years of publishing/printing experience. David has given overall editorial advice and support, while Humphrey has designed the book's form; in addition, they have jointly handled the final production operation for the school. Rosie's contribution, in co-ordinating work on the project, has been absolutely crucial over eight years. Not only has she done most of the typing, but she has been tireless in her diligent approach to the text and picture research; she has deciphered my handwriting and corrected my mistakes in a continuous editing process; she has also compiled an Index. I owe her a great debt of gratitude for her patience, enthusiasm and encouragement. I am also grateful for additional typing assistance from Binky Aylmer and Sybil Fox, while Lulu Phelps has made the photographic prints.

The *Magazine* has been the source of many of the photographs, and among its photographers to whom I am indebted are John Burbank, Tim Hodgetts, Hyla Holden, the late Noel Lachlan and Jeremy Malim. Tim Hodgetts took the aerial view of the school, and for this our thanks are due to the Commanding Officer of the Army Air Corps, Middle Wallop.

I have received generous help from the following, who have given permission to reproduce school groups and other illustrations: Cotswold Portraits (T. J. E. Ashwin), Gillman & Soame (F. M. Douglas), B. J. Harris (Oxford) Ltd, Hills & Saunders (Richard Shymansky) and Alan Spence Photography.

Last but not least, I want to thank Adrian Richardson for giving the venture his blessing and support from the start in 1983, and to express gratitude to the Governors for their willingness to allow the school to be my publishers.

G. L. S. P.

INTRODUCTION

Cothill has always been a school for the average boy. There have been many highly gifted pupils, but relatively few scholars. The hundred or so awards to public schools gained in the 95 years since records were kept cannot compare with the academic achievements of such rivals as the Dragon, Summer Fields and Horris Hill. No special pressure has been applied to ensure that a boy gets a scholarship. The exceptional scholar has, as it were, 'taught himself', in a top class kept as small as possible to provide a maximum quality of competition. Academic excellence has run in certain families, as can be seen from the list of awards in *Appendix II*. Members of the staff over the years have been generally very competent, often devoted, at times outstanding.

Henry Marten is said to have remarked to his boys at Eton in the early years of the century: 'Gentlemen, we have everything to offer; take it or leave it.' Of course not all have taken full advantage of what Cothill has had to offer, but the majority of Old Cothillians seem to have profited by the habit of happiness which successive Head Masters have tried to inculcate. A few boys have been very unhappy, either because they were bullied or because they were temperamentally unsuited to life in a boarding-school. But most prep-school boys are gregarious, many are clubbable, and want nothing better than to be accepted by their peers for what they are: lively, amusing, appreciative individuals with more virtues than vices, capable of unkindness, but fundamentally thoughtful for others. They enjoy the bustle of school life, being organised for most of the day, being kept up to the mark by a discipline which is strict but just. A new boy learns how to cope within days of his arrival. Of course it helps if father has been at Cothill or a similar school, where man-to-man talk can soften the shock of leaving home for the first time. But the young boy has, in the last resort, to find his own feet, and the hope of all involved with Cothill is that he finds them in a civilised atmosphere.

PART I

1870 – *Summer* 1962

C. W. CARLES

M. J. DAUGLISH / F. KNOWLES

M. J. DAUGLISH / R. TOMKINSON

S. A. PIKE

I

ORIGINS

Dr Donald Leinster-Mackay, in his *The Rise of the English Prep School* (1984) – the first ever academic book on English prep schools – listed Cothill House in his Appendix I as a nineteenth-century foundation now defunct. The error of this unfortunate miscategorisation was compounded by there being no further references in his otherwise very informative book.

Whatever the reason for this omission, this history of Cothill seeks to put the record straight. Cothill is certainly not defunct; it is very much alive, with a creditable all-round record, respected by its peers and by public schools, and occupying a high position in the Preparatory School League Table. This book tells the story of the development of the school from its small beginnings under its founder in 1870, through Edwardian prosperity and the Great War of 1914–18 under Dauglish, on to the Pikes, father and son, from 1927 to 1976, to the present tenure of the Richardsons. Since 1870 there have been only seven régimes of Head Masters; under some of these there have been considerable building programmes; the number of boys has risen to over two hundred and is still increasing.

Most English prep schools were founded after 1864, the date of the Clarendon Report on the eight leading public schools, in which the need for the separate treatment of younger boys was recognised. At Eton, for instance, the Report recommended that Lower School should be separated from Upper School, adding that 'the care and instruction of little boys is as important, and, in some cases, as difficult as the care and instruction of older boys'. In the eighteenth century private classical schools for older boys had competed with the public schools and grammar schools for entry into the universities. These schools were mostly boarding and were run for profit. By the mid-nineteenth century their function had changed and they prepared younger boys for the public schools. The demand for places in both public and prep schools increased rapidly with the rise in population, the need to educate the children of expatriates serving the expanding Empire, and the desire of the newly rich middle classes to give their sons some gentlemanly polish. The expanding railway system made possible a big increase in the number of preparatory schools throughout the country during the 1860s and 1870s. These developed strong ties with certain public schools through the scholarships offered to the most able and by the entrance examinations for the majority. Thus Summer Fields in Oxford has had a particularly close association with Eton since 1864, while Windlesham House was Harrow-orientated as early as 1837. Horris Hill, founded in 1888, sent the majority of the boys to Winchester. Unique among prep schools, the Dragon School, founded in 1877, with its six hundred-odd boys, and a few girls, has supplied almost every public school in the country, producing top scholars at Eton and Winchester with enviable regularity. It was the close association with the public schools that distinguished prep schools from other private schools of the last quarter of the nineteenth century and gave them such a great advantage.

During this heyday of Empire a transformation occurred in the conditions of the best prep schools; they became less spartan, more humane; boys were no longer taught by hack ushers – such as the poet Verlaine in Eastbourne – who were paid a pittance. Games were becoming more organised, especially cricket, thanks to the influence of W. G. Grace. The curriculum was still based on Classics, but more time was spent on the teaching of Mathematics and French. At Cothill early time-tables referred to English as Modern, while the term English covered History, Geography and Scripture. Little Science was taught in the majority of prep schools, though from the Dragon Archer Vassall advocated it strongly in the pages of the *Preparatory Schools Review* of 1898. Of the public schools in the late nineteenth century only Oundle developed a strong scientific bias and prep schools provided what the majority of public schools asked for. There was, however, a close relationship between prep schools and the Royal Navy. Spenser Wilkinson, in his book *The Nation's Need*, published *c.*1903, wrote: 'Whatever the Navy requires for entrance to the *Britannia* the preparatory schools will do. There are no schools in the world where boys are better looked after or more carefully taught.' By 1924 there were 230 prep schools preparing boys for the Navy, though Osborne had closed in 1921. In 1948 the 13-year-old entry was abolished.

In the history of English education, 1870 was an important year. Forster's Act ensured compulsory elementary education, and this coincided with the start of a school in Meriden, Warwickshire by C. W. Carles, graduate of Lincoln College, Oxford. Little is known about the school in its earliest days, though according to *White's Directory* of 1874 the building was Darlaston

Cothill House, south-west view, c. 1870.

Hall, formerly the Bull's Head, a coaching inn, 'famed from time immemorial for its excellent malt liquor'. The house, during the eighteenth century, had belonged to Lord Aylesford, and by coincidence a descendant of his, Charles Guernsey, was a boy at Cothill in the 1950s. C.W.C. is described as aged 28 and unmarried in the Census of 1871, which must have occurred in the holidays, as the only other people mentioned are a 19-year-old unmarried(?) pupil, a housekeeper and two female general servants.

In 1879, when larger accommodation was needed, the school moved to Cothill House, near Abingdon, then in Berkshire. This had been the parsonage occupied by the first Vicar of Dry Sandford, the Rev. H. C. Adams, who had founded Dry Sandford Village/Church School in 1870, and was an author of adventure stories for boys. It was he who sold Cothill House to C.W.C., for £2,900. Photographs of the period show a three-gabled, substantial house which formed the private side of the school until the 1980s.

The hamlet of Cothill was originally called Cotwell. It stands on a small saddle, near a well. It consisted of half-a-dozen cottages, the Fleur de Lys inn and the Baptist chapel, built in 1830. Next door is the Masters' Cottage, which was originally the Baptist Minister's house. The story goes that he and Adams disliked each other so much that Adams built the stone wall between

Cothill House, west view, c.1909. *This postcard was sent by a boy in the school to his younger brother in* c.1920. *'Angus', he wrote, 'Plese send me a postcard some time for about the hundredth time.'*

his house and the chapel. Whatever the truth of the story, walls made of the local stone are a feature of the neighbourhood and add greatly to the character of the school. The view south towards the Downs is still a beautiful one, for even the Didcot Power Station, five miles away, has its own grandeur and the Harwell Atomic Station chimneys are now part of the landscape. To the north is an alkaline fen, the well-known nature reserve of Parsonage Moor, the whole well-wooded and known as the Marsh. Before Dutch elm disease altered the character of the landscape and before an unsightly bungalow development grew up to the west, and the increased motor traffic made walking on the roads dangerous, Cothill was for nearly a hundred years a quiet community in an attractive backwater. Here C.W.C. conducted his custom-built school. He must have been unusually confident having moved the school to Cothill for he doubled the size of the house by building six dormitories, the Dining Hall and the Big Schoolroom. The earliest prospectus states that the new site for the school was 'selected chiefly for its sanitary advantages', and mentions the deep bed of sand and the Berkshire Downs some 12 miles distant. 'The school is therefore perfectly dry, and has the advantage of remarkably pure air. Boys are received as soon as they are old enough to commence the Latin Grammar, and are allowed to remain until they have completed their fifteenth year. A special course is provided for boys intended for the Modern Side.' The fees were £100 per annum (boys under

13, 80 guineas), with the only necessary extras a charge of £1 a term for 'Washing'. Music and Drawing cost an additional £2 and £1.10*s* a term respectively. The 'Course of Instruction' included 'Latin, Greek, French, German, Mathematics, History, &c., and Singing'.

We have no written records of this first Cothill régime and therefore have to rely on photographs. Luckily school groups have survived from 1879, and from these we can get an idea of those early days. Originally there were 29 boys, and the first year shows them wearing Eton collars and tiny caps. C.W.C. has Dundreary whiskers and wears a billycock hat. Two 'ushers' stand with him at the back of the group, in similar hats and with drooping moustaches. Their names, recorded in the 1881 Census, were William B. Dalby and Walter F. Morley. Midsummer 1880 shows the group in front of the dark front door, which is obscured by a large laurel bush. There are now 36 boys, mostly bare-headed, though some wear or carry straw hats. According to the Census, four boys were aged 15, ten were 14, five were 13 and 12 respectively, seven were 11 and five were 10. Three maids in caps look out of a ground-floor window. In 1881 the school group numbered 40 boys, and

*First school group, Michaelmas 1879. C. W. Carles (*left*), with ushers W. B. Dalby and W. F. Morley.*

there was now a lady, wearing a flowery hat and long-sleeved dress buttoned up at the neck with a choker. The Census states that she was C.W.C.'s widowed sister, and there was mention of his mother, also a widow. The straw hats have bands of two colours, and there is a general air of increasing prosperity. Although the photographs are taken at 'Midsummer', everybody is dressed in thick, uncomfortable-looking clothes throughout the Carles headmastership. He himself is seen as a somewhat fleshy figure, with the eyes of a bloodhound.

At some unknown early period the present cricket ground was acquired, with a football field – small, with a notorious slope – where the classroom Complex now stands. The brick clock-tower probably dates from the 1880s; together with the stone-built rooms on either side, it was originally separated from the main building and remained so until the present kitchen block was built in the 1930s. These rooms were used as classrooms until the late 1970s, and are now music rooms and a school laundry. Outside, the playground was probably developed from a stable yard. Surrounded by walls or buildings, it became the scene of two special Cothill games – 'Snob' and yard-game football. According to the prospectus, two good cricket and football fields were included in the grounds, and there was a small thatched rustic cricket pavilion, in front of which the school group of 1888 was photographed.

We know that 'the Inter-School Sports took place at Reading on 27 March 1889, the results being: Park House 38 pts, Cordwalles [later St Piran's] 26½, Hartford House 24, Cothill House 8½'. This information comes from the history of St Piran's, Maidenhead, entitled *The Millstone Race*. Clearly Cothill was outclassed, perhaps because it did not take athletics very seriously. At cricket, on the other hand, there were signs that the school could compete on more equal terms with its local peers. Thus we learn from a Dragons' magazine of 1890 that the Young Dragons Cricket Club (YDCC) played Cothill. The complete scores show that Dragons made 102, Cothill 16 and 21 for 4. The following Summer, in another two-innings match, Cothill CC scored 26 and 67, YDCC 8 and 67. A Cothill bowler called Harding took 7 wickets in the first innings, and a Lubbock showed up well as an all-rounder. The prospectus also mentions that 'a good bathing place has been constructed close by' and that 'there are also excellent golf links (private) within a short distance'. Wherever the links were, presumably the boys were allowed to play on them.

One gets the impression of a small, flourishing school, until 1894 when the number of boys in the school group had declined to 15. C.W.C. looked ill and his sister grim. By then arrangements had been made to sell the school to Messrs Dauglish and Knowles for the sum of £3,000. I remember seeing, many years ago, a 'jellied' (cyclostyled) letter from C.W.C. to all parents, explaining that he was retiring for reasons of health and thanking all for their loyal support. Unfortunately this letter has disappeared, but C. W. Carles himself did not entirely vanish from the scene. In 1899 he wrote a letter to the *Preparatory Schools Review*, in defence of King Edward's School, Bromsgrove. The *PSR* had published an allegation from a correspondent that 'no respectable preparatory schoolmaster would send a boy there if he could help it'. Describing himself as 'Late Head of Cothill House School', he wrote that for 23 years he had recommended Bromsgrove to parents: 'If you desire the best teaching available anywhere . . . you will find it there . . . and a moral standard of the highest and a vigour and earnestness pervading the life of the school . . . imparted by great moral and intellectual force in the Head.' This letter was duly circulated by all preparatory school headmasters with their end-of-term reports.

2

EARLY DAYS

The two new Head Masters, M. J. Dauglish and F. Knowles, had been prominent athletes at Harrow. M.J.D. had captained the cricket XI in 1886, when as wicket-keeper, according to R. H. Lyttelton and Arthur Page in *Fifty Years of Sport*, he 'doffed his pads and gloves and had a turn with lobs', taking a wicket in his second over. He had gone on to play cricket for Oxford in 1888 and 1889. After going down he had been an assistant master at Evelyns, near Uxbridge, and having bought Cothill House with Foster Knowles, he evidently became the dominant partner. He was described in his obituary notice in the *Preparatory Schools Review* of December 1922 as 'not a great scholar nor a great athlete, . . . a very considerable personality, . . . extraordinarily direct; he said what he thought; . . . a wonderful judge of character, especially of boys' character, but did not know how to flatter. Absolutely devoted to his work, he was quite incapable of advertisement either of his school or of himself. His nickname "Doggie" seemed to fit in with the character of a watchful friend.'

To many Cothill boys M.J.D. was a most kindly man for whom nothing was too much trouble. An interesting teacher of History, he also had a touch of genius at coaching the boys in cricket and football, spending hours at the nets and hitting balls for boys to catch. He was a strict disciplinarian. Hugh Stockwell, who was to command the British troops at Suez in 1956, has observed, 'he would beat you if he thought you deserved it – idle, scruffy or lazy. I was devoted to him, and he had a great influence on my life.' On one occasion he asked a boy batsman if he had cleaned his teeth that morning. 'No, sir.' 'What! How can you expect to make runs with dirty teeth?' Charles Close-Smith writes that 'Doggie was a born leader, whom parents and boys both loved and trusted, and boys obeyed. He had that rare gift among schoolmasters of knowing when to turn a blind eye, so that boys always felt that he was a little bit on their side.' An unathletic boy like Tony Farnell was not so appreciative. 'Doggie rushed up and down the football field like a rather stout terrier, blowing his whistle and barking "Fool" at us when we kicked the ball to the wrong person. . . . He was only really keen on two things: taking us in cricket and football. That, he loved. It was not easy to see

*The Summer group in 1900. F. Knowles (*centre*), with M. J. Daughlish (*left*).*

M. J. Dauglish, Summer 1902.

that he loved anything else. Nor did he expect us to love anything else, either. We had to excel in cricket and football, otherwise he washed his hands of us. . . . He was not interested in skating; he couldn't skate and never came to see his school disporting itself on the ice.'

Another of Doggie's blind spots was his attitude to the recently founded Boy Scout movement. He took against it to such an extent that he objected strongly when asked to allow the two sons of the Scout Commissioner for South Bucks to attend the great jamboree in Windsor Great Park. 'Dear Mrs Nickalls, I really must protest . . .', and that was that.

F. Knowles, by contrast, has left little impression. In the school groups from 1894 to 1910, he appears with a large moustache, smartly dressed in a high stiff collar. One gathers that he was in charge of the academic and financial side of the school. He evidently retired early, for he disappears from the group of 1911. According to Robert Shaw, 'he deserted his wife for a sanatorium sister'. His place was taken by R. Tomkinson. F.K. was a good teacher of the Classics, and he reappears in the school *Magazines* of the 1930s as the organiser of a yearly inter-schools Latin competition, in which Cothill performed creditably. I remember being coached by him myself – by correspondence. My efforts were heavily corrected in red ink.

An outing in the straw hats, Summer 1903.

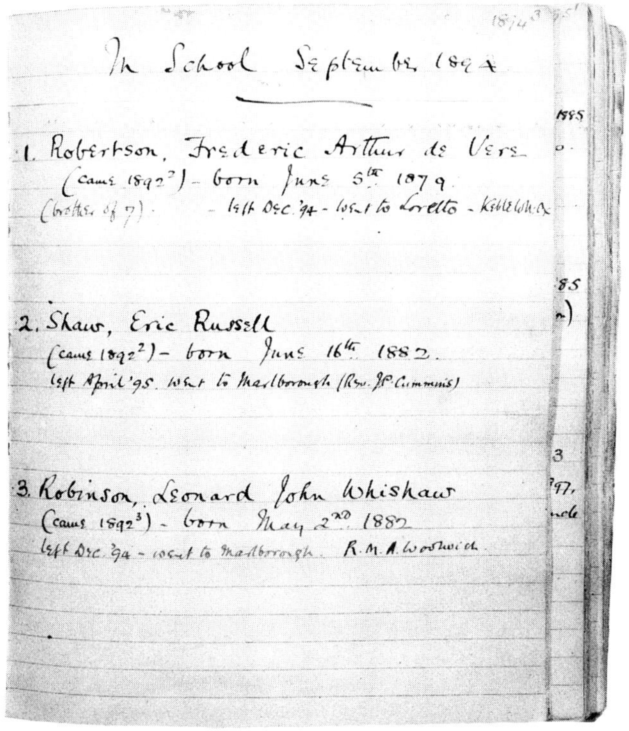

M. J. Dauglish's record book, 1894.

From 1894 begins the first documentation of the school, with the boards in the Dining Hall providing a nominal roll of pupils from then until the present day. M.J.D. kept a bound record book, noting each boy as he came; name, date of entry and the public school he went on to and any award received. In the Autumn term of 1894 there were 12 boys, but numbers had risen to 33 by Summer 1898 and 38 in 1900. Between 1894 and 1902 eight scholarships were won, to Fettes, Charterhouse (2), Harrow, Clifton, Rossall, Wellington and Radley, the last two being 1st scholarships won by H. E. W. Berkeley-Hill and A. C. Longland respectively. Between 1903 and 1914 nine scholarships were won. For such a small school this scholastic record is impressive. The earliest boys recorded by M.J.D. in 1894 had entered the school in 1892. All boys were numbered in the book. No. 1, in 1984, was Frederic Arthur de Vere Robertson, born 1879 and left for Loretto. No. 8, Kenneth L.'Estrange Hamilton Macclesfield Heath, who had arrived in 1893, clearly could not take the new régime, as M.J.D. notes, 'Ran away Oct. 12 1894 – re-captured same day – went home Nov. 13. Went to Littlejohn's next term to cram for Navy. Returned 20 May '95, left July '96 and went to Cheltenham (having failed twice for *Britannia*). Then went to Wellington.'

A. C. Phillips, early 1920s.

In 1903 A. C. Phillips joined the staff. He has been described by so many Old Cothillians during the next 35 years that it is clear that in many ways for them he was Cothill. A tall, thin, Edwardian-looking figure, with a long, nicotine-stained moustache and fair hair plastered back, he invariably wore knickerbockers, except when riding his motor cycle. Then he would encase himself in brown leather, with helmet and goggles, and thus he would appear some days before the beginning of term, having covered much of England as a self-invited guest in as many parental homes as he could muster. Elwes Duffield describes him as 'a popular, conscientious master, who liked nothing better than basking in the adulation of small boys'. One of his great moments was singing 'The Lost Chord' at Saturday-evening sing-songs, accompanied by his sister Fanny Phillips who taught the piano, and his disappointment was obvious if it did not evoke sufficient applause for him to sing 'Spring is Coming' as an encore. He lived in a world of graphs. Everything in the life of the school was recorded. Even the lavatory performance list was carefully checked. Kemmis Buckley recalls, many years later: 'We queued up, . . . marked the result of the occasion, . . . a tick for success, an "o" for a doubtful visit, an "x" for failure. Four "x"s brought punishment: since there are few people who volunteer for punishment, there must have been many constipated schoolboys.'

His classroom walls were covered with graphs showing every boy's performance. From a great pile of matchboxes in front of his desk he would present deserving boys with a daily medal; when a boy collected five medals, 'G.B.' for 'Good Boy' was written on his book in green chalk; if he got 15, he was called a 'Permanent Good Boy' and could wear a blue ribbon. These rewards culminated in a Royal Sovereign pencil complete with rubber, with the boy's name inscribed on it, and a metal-spring pencil-clip to wear in the pocket for all to see. According to Ken Tomkinson, 'the medals were awarded [and lost] on a points system whose very complications were part of its interest to pedantic small boys. They were awarded independently of the school marking system for intellectual or behavioural virtue, and were quite a successful technique of boy management.' Tony Findlay says A.C.P. 'would let out a bellow of dismay at some futile bit of work, which embarrassed the culprit and amused the remainder'.

Tony Farnell, who came in 1917, considered him 'a jolly good teacher. If you were in the top-form French, you did really learn how to form the subjunctive, how to conjugate it, and when to use it. This I have never forgotten.' (Tony later spoke perfect French.) For the less intelligent boy, Kemmis Buckley says he was equally effective: 'Two aspects of his teaching remain in the mind. To those who found Mathematics difficult, his lessons on mental arithmetic have not been forgotten by at least one pupil; and, curiously for someone with a mathematical bent, he was able to give the slower boys some feeling for the composition of an essay.'

A.C.P. was a man of parts. He was a keen photographer, processing his films in a small darkroom and teaching boys to do the same. This no doubt

An entrant for the annual photographic competition (cap reversed), Spring 1903.

A. C. Phillips's study, Spring 1903. '... a clutter of memorabilia ...'.

helped them to participate in the annual school competition, started at the beginning of the century, for 'the best photograph taken with a Brownie camera'. A prize-winning subject in 1924 is captioned 'Blackbird's nest in Minor Game field', most likely snapped as a result of the interest that A.C.P. also generated in natural history. He kept weather records with a rain gauge and barograph. Favourite boys were instructed in astronomy with the aid of a brass telescope in his study, described as 'a clutter of memorabilia of school occasions, photographs of cricket and soccer teams'.

Mike Atkin-Berry gives a picture of A.C.P. in the 1930s, out of school: 'Phillpots in his black, flappy, one-piece swim-suit – thin and tall, white hair and whiskers, is still very much my picture of Merlin in the Arthurian stories. ... Going down the woods, building hides, and drinking lemonade made from crystals which we carried in hip flasks. ... All this was sheer magic for small boys. (Perhaps this is where the Merlin connection comes in.)'

M.J.D. kept a 'Games Book', containing details of school teams, matches played, and Athletic Sports Days. It also contains, from 1907 to 1913, yearly reports of a School Fund he had started 'for the maintenance of a small boy rescued from the slums of London'. Willie Wood and his sister were lodged at the cottage of a Mr and Mrs Pittaway in the village, at a cost of *6s* a week. *£33.19s.6d* was raised from 55 contributors. Willie Wood is described in the reports as a good boy, who liked Cothill very much 'and would not return to London on any account'. In his fifth year the village schoolmistress described him as 'very sharp at answering questions'. Yearly pocket money and a visit to parents in London cost *5s.11d*. In May 1913 M.J.D. reported that the boy, now aged nearly 12, had been returned to his mother and father in Whitechapel. 'I was glad to see that their home was clean and respectable.' The balance of *£23.17s.11d* was put on deposit at the P.O. Savings Bank for a holiday or towards apprenticing to a trade, in consultation with one of the clergy of St Mary's, Whitechapel.

What sort of school was Cothill in the 1900s? Class lists exist from 1902, printed in five columns; Latin, Greek or Modern, Maths, French and English. There was an unusual system of 'setting', whereby a boy could move up or down in any of the main five subjects. 'This enabled him to move ahead where he had aptitude, rather than being held back by his weaker subjects', as one Old Boy has put it. But it meant that everyone was taught the same subject simultaneously and that the masters had to be competent to teach most subjects.

The earliest memories from Old Boys date from 1903. Godfrey Llewellyn gave an account, just before he died in 1986, of how there were 38 boys in the school. He remembered, after being ill during one Summer holidays, that he was not allowed to play games and was provided with a bicycle for exercise and went for rides with one of the masters. He was sent back with a case of claret as a pick-me-up, much to the envy of the other boys. His brother Jack, three years older, brought back a .22 pistol one term and fired it into a barn door. When later it misfired, he kept on pulling the trigger to no effect, handed the pistol to a boy called Hull, who pointed it in all directions in the main classroom, pulling the trigger until eventually the pistol went off into the fireplace. This attracted the attention of a master, who confiscated the pistol, but apparently took no other action.

Jack Paine considers the school was very well run in 1908. Most of the boys went on to Radley. There were two football fields, a cricket field next to the road and a squash court. A feature was the bathing-pool a little way down the road. It was surrounded by trees and the sun seldom warmed the water which was full of beetles and other forms of pond life. 'At the beginning of each bathing season a party of senior boys was detailed to go in first and clear the scum which had accumulated during the Winter; not a very pleasant task but no one was any the worse for it.'

Bathing-pool, c.1912.

Cold water was no rarity. Daily cold baths were supervised by M.J.D., whose bedroom was at the end of the dormitory passage. Each boy had one weekly hot bath. A 'List of Necessary Articles of Dress, etc.' of this period has survived, and from it we learn that a boy would discard his night shirt or sleeping suit, put on vest, drawers or combinations, a flannel shirt with an Eton collar, a suit of knickerbockers, and strong boots. He would play football in grey-flannel knickerbockers, cricket in white-flannel trousers, with a white-flannel coat as a blazer. 'Sailor and other Fancy Suits' were not allowed, but one 'Eton Suit' was obligatory. Should dancing be learnt, a pair of pumps and kid gloves were needed. School caps and straw hats were provided by the school. A number of boys are photographed wearing watch-chains in these early days.

The water supply – described in the prospectus as 'excellent' – was pumped up by a windmill from a well a quarter of a mile down the Abingdon road. Here also was the Sanatorium, a corrugated-iron building containing six or seven beds and presided over by 'a dear, God-fearing old couple, Mr and Mrs Stone'. In an epidemic of measles, 'there were too many for the Sanatorium, so two dormitories in the school were given over to the victims. Sheets were hung over the doors, and the floors liberally besprinkled with Sanitas.' The first Matron mentioned was Miss Hames, known to the boys as

Miss Hames's room, Summer 1903. No 'clutter' here.

'the Hatter', and by all accounts she was an efficient, understanding, if somewhat awe-inspiring woman. She looked after the boys from 1894 to 1925 when she retired. One Old Boy says 'she would always exchange presents of sweets or chocs which weren't allowed for fruit; otherwise I seem to remember being afraid of her'; another, thought that 'she was the careful guardian of our clothes and health and welfare... a thoroughly good influence... kindly, firm, considerate and always ready to comfort the homesick'. In a letter dated 3.5.14 to the mother of a new boy, Pat Halsey, three days after his arrival, she wrote: 'You will be v. pleased to hear that your dear little Pat is settling down quite happily.... He has a sweet little face with such a sunny happy expression.... Thank you so much for the splendid way in which you have sent his clothes.... Would you like him to have weekly fruit... 1/–, *9d* and *6d* each?... Billy is looking after his cousin like a small brother.' As the only woman in a bachelor establishment she was 'splendid when one was ill... and motherly'. Tony Farnell used to have long discussions at home with his elder brother 'as to whether Doggie was going to marry Miss Hames. She would presumably produce lots of little Doggies, which might or might not be a good thing. But we had to admit there was little sign of it. Doggie had rushed up and down the field in my brother's day, he rushed up and down the field in my day (perhaps a little stouter) and we could not see how this

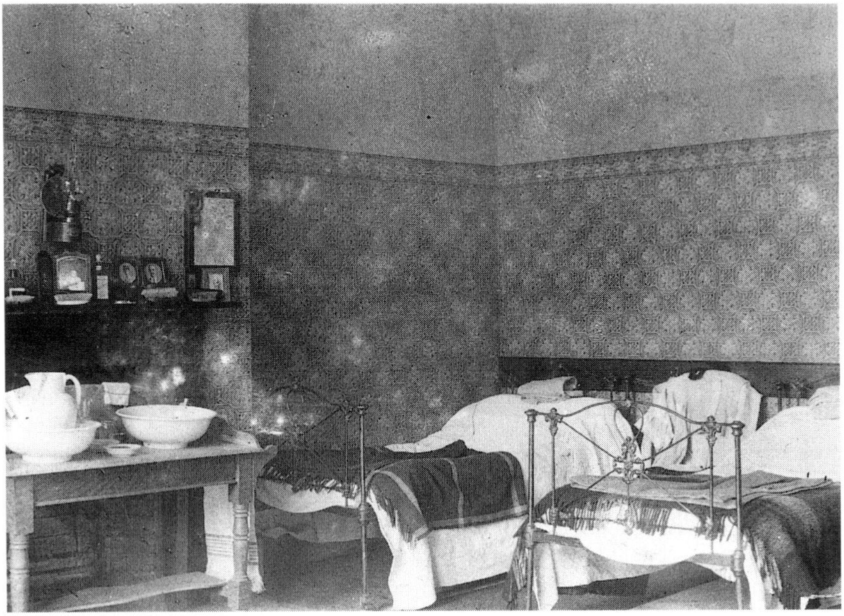

Dormitory V, Summer 1903. Elaborate bed-heads and wide beds contrast with later eras.

rushing might eventuate in his solemnising the sacrament of Holy Matrimony with Miss Hames.'

The day would begin at 7.00, when Enstone, the general factotum known to the boys as 'Piggy', came into the dormitories with two large cans of hot water which he poured into each of the six wash basins. 'In very cold weather, the water in the jugs and tumblers was frozen over. . . . I feel sure that none of us felt hardly done by.' The boys would clatter down the narrow staircase for prayers ('a Psalm, the General Thanksgiving – I've known it by heart ever since') in the Big Schoolroom. This contained six rows of desks, each row having six lockers, with benches to sit on. A sliding partition divided the Schoolroom into two for work purposes, and in Winter blazing fires at each end provided plenty of heat. For breakfast there was porridge, with sausages on Sundays, and very good hot rolls twice a week. The general impression from Old Boys at this time is that 'Cothill fed us very well'. After breakfast a visit was made to the earth closets, emptied daily by Enstone. This was followed by yard-game football in the Winter and in Summer by the unique Cothill game of Snob. According to Michael Snow, 'It was played with a club similar to a baseball bat, and balls somewhat smaller than lawn-tennis balls, but harder and leather-covered. The wickets were wooden triangles placed in front of a brick wall and the rules were simple. As I remember, you could be bowled or caught first bounce, or off a wall or roof.

Big Schoolroom, c.1909.

Dining Hall. This picture can be dated 1909 from the 'boards' on the left.

ABOVE *The yard, c.1909. A. C. Phillips in the centre; Snob in the background; the clock-tower and classrooms separated from the main building.* BELOW *Snob, c.1912.*

Carpenter's shop, Summer 1903. Mr Short, 'a large man with a black beard', is in charge.

Everyone took part and ball followed ball in rapid succession so that, with several games proceeding simultaneously, it appeared quite a mêlée.'

The work programme was in the hands of Messrs Dauglish, Tomkinson, Phillips, Sheldon and Northcote in the Summer of 1914. 'There is no doubt about our being well taught. The smallness of the school certainly helped here, making small classes with plenty of individual attention.' M. J. Dauglish used to give History lectures to the whole school. R. Tomkinson was a good classical scholar, having won the Newcastle at Eton, while A. C. Phillips had his own methods already described, and very effective they appear to have been. In the long break before lunch the carpenter's shop was presided over once a week by Mr Short, 'an impressively large man with a black beard and a resonant voice and pleasing aroma compounded of wood shavings, glue and linseed oil. He was a kindly man, but no sloppy work was tolerated.' Kit Wilson writes: 'He called himself "Jarge Shart". He enthused generations of boys, whether naturally handy or not. I still think of him whenever I put in a screw and take his tip "Gie it a dro' o'eyel".' 'He was known to be a bit of a wag', writes Gully Nickalls in his book *A Rainbow in the Sky*. 'On my first introduction to him he asked what I would like to make. He reeled off a number of possibilities and ended by enquiring "Or what about your own coffin?". At this quip he slapped his thighs and bellowed with laughter. I took him seriously and began to make mental calculations as to my probable dimensions at the time of my demise.'

A. C. Phillips with nearly the full complement of thirty boys, c.1910.

Lunch in the Dining Hall would be plentiful; maids would go round offering beef or mutton. After lunch extra fruit was given out to those whose parents paid for it. In games, the smallness of the school could be a disadvantage. Kit Wilson says 'It meant that all ages were in the same game, which could mean unpleasant experiences for the youger boys competing with 13-year-olds.... After I had missed three catches I was taken round to the Tinneries, as the old earth closets off the playground were called, and beaten.' One wonders who did the beating. There is a story that M.J.D. had beaten a boy for saying that rounders was a better game than cricket. This is presumably apocryphal, but any criticism of cricket was sacrilege to Doggie. For one relatively unathletic boy, soccer taken by the latter was a strain: 'He shouted loudly throughout the game. I always rather dreaded it. He certainly terrified me on the soccer field. I can hear him now exhorting us with apparent fury to "run like a hare". I will always remember the popular end-of-term ditty:

> "This time next week where shall I be?
> Out of hands of M.J.D." '

But another has described how thirty boys aged 8–13 lived happily together, with very little bullying and a high standard of trust. 'There were plenty of fights which were not stopped by masters at once. ... There was never a moment unsupervised. I now look back on that as a good thing, as being the best way to learn the realities of life. ... Only one boy ever stole, and the rest of the boys blamed his parents for not explaining that it wasn't on. ... It was an economically run school, with no waste. ... Cricket bats were oiled and bound as necessary; if a boy's cricket ball was lost, the whole school would search the bushes until it was found.'

The small world of Cothill in the last years before the Great War seems to have been a place of disciplined security and self-reliance. There were few luxuries; amusements were home-made; two Christmas Concert programmes of 1912 and 1913 are pasted, somewhat incongruously, into M.J.D.'s Games Book. He himself recited Kipling's 'If...', Messrs Phillips and Northcote contributed songs, Miss Tomkinson played the violin. The boys played musical instruments and sang. The programme is a cyclostyle written by A.C.P. Weekly sing-songs were the nearest thing to regular entertainment that Cothill boys experienced during term-time. Frivolities belonged to the holidays; work and play were organised by M.J.D. to inculcate self-discipline and the team spirit. Incorrigible slackers were punished, whether in the classroom or on the games field. The carpenter's shop and A.C.P.'s nature walks in the Marsh provided a welcome relief for the unathletic. Boys made their own amusements under his guidance; they also learnt to skate by watching his performance.

R. Tomkinson's Austin motor, 1914.

Pat Halsey's father was an old friend of M.J.D.'s, and Pat's first letter, in May 1914, to his mother mentions his delight that 'the boys call Mr Dauglish Doggie, just like father does. They call Mr Tomkinson "Tomcat".' He goes on to say that 'Latin is lovely. We drill twice a week.' A month later he wrote to his father mentioning that he had made his first run and reached Ex. 23 in Latin, presumably Hillard and Botting. He then describes an expedition to White Horse Hill. 'I went in Mr Tomkinson's motor. . . . We all slid down the hill . . . then we got some sticks and made a fire. . . . I took an hour and a half to get home. When we came up the drive we all cheered as hard as we could it was so lovely.'

This somewhat idyllic picture is in contrast with Pat Halsey's contemporary Kit Wilson, who did not enjoy his first experience of school at the age of nine 'after the freedom of a country upbringing, especially as we shared our governess with neighbours. . . . The journeys back to school, by horse and train, are still about my dreariest memories. The journey finished with a six-mile drive from Oxford Station in a frowstily evil-smelling horse-drawn cab, with the whole of Cumnor Hill done at a walk. . . . I never became any good at cricket. . . . Doggie in an exasperated moment at the nets once burst out, "I thought, when I got a Wilson here, I was going to get a cricketer, and then I got you".'

Expedition to the White Horse by horse-drawn brake, July 1914.

3
A SMALL SCHOOL, A GREAT WAR

To one born in 1916, the Great War was a most important influence on early childhood. Many of my father's friends had been killed, including my godfather, and one of my earliest memories was of the Armistice Day silence in London and being told by my mother to think about him and the others who had died for King and Country. I remember the Victory March of 1919, and how indignant I was that it contained no Germans – in chains presumably. Children of my generation whose fathers had fought were united in pride as we pored over copies of the *Illustrated London News* and other pictures of battle scenes. My family was scornful of anyone who had 'shirked the war' or was a 'war profiteer'. Another reminder of the war was my father's yearly bout of malaria, originally contracted in Salonika, which recurred on almost the same date until the mid-1930s. Even to my childish mind there was no doubt that a curtain had come down on 4 August 1914, and that when it was rung up again, the scene was very different. The 'war to end wars' and 'a land fit for heroes' were more than catch-phrases, and certainly had no cynical undertones in our family. There had been an enormous upheaval. Nothing would ever be the same again. That much was registered and recognised, because the pre-war fashions looked so outlandish. When visiting London I saw the ex-servicemen's bands playing in the streets and was distressed by their disfigurements. But the wider social implications of the war could not be understood by a child, and the one thing everyone apparently wanted was to get back to pre-war standards.

At Cothill the war seems to have made very little impression on the day-to-day life of the school, though in the very early days boys were allowed out of the classroom to watch an aeroplane fly over the school – a practice that soon stopped. However, 'There was great excitement when an Old Cothillian landed in a Sopwith plane on an adjacent field to pay his respects to the Head Master. On one memorable day Tomkinson appeared in a grey uniform with a red arm-band bearing the letters CDV and we were drilled by him on the cricket field using dummy wooden rifles, no doubt produced by Mr Short.

A. C. Phillips (left) *and Mr and Mrs Tomkinson and M. J. Dauglish* (centre) *of the* 1914 *group.*

Two young women cyclists on the Frilford Heath road stopped to watch us and burst into merry peals of laughter, which we found deeply offensive to our sense of patriotism.'

M.J.D. evidently took pains to keep the senior boys informed about the war; extracts from *The Times* were read out, and copies of the *Illustrated London News* and the *Sphere* were available. Pat Halsey says 'I still have a graph I made – with Phillips's encouragement – of U-boat sinkings in 1917. Graphs weren't really my line I'm sure, but this one is done in different-coloured inks and I must have spent hours and hours over it.' Hugh Stockwell remembers 'a large map of the battlefield, covered with coloured pins. Rations during the war were a bit tight, nevertheless it kept us healthy. Altogether a happy life.' Not everyone, however, appreciated M.J.D. or the school. Michael Stratton writes: 'My main recollection is that one was half-starved and almost perpetually hungry. Dauglish was about as bad as you could wish for. Tomkinson was even worse. By the time I left [1919] I think the numbers had sunk to 26 from 45 when I went [1915]. It was an appallingly bad school during that period.' In fact, numbers in 1915 were 28, and in 1919 were 49. Stratton's near-contemporary Michael Snow thought differently: 'I well remember how upset Dauglish was at having to announce that in future at tea we would be served with margarine instead of butter. . . . We were always well fed, even in the later war years. If it was not a luxurious school, it was certainly a well-ordered one and we were to some extent cosseted.' Kit Wilson corroborates this: 'The food was excellent in spite of the war being on. It was keenly supervised by Marie Tomkinson, and then when Raymond [Tomkinson] got married, by his wife Connie. One special dish was bubble-and-squeak, nicely browned and served with slices of meat. No doubt the smaller numbers were an advantage here. There was unlimited toast and dripping at tea.' Chocolates and sweets were strictly forbidden, and at least one boy recalls being beaten for going to the Fleur de Lys in search of the 'prohibited substance'. One popular wartime economy was when R.T. was told by Philip and Dick Kindersley's father 'that starched Eton collars were wasteful, so we were, to our great joy, thereafter clad in soft collars'. This can be seen in the annual school groups from 1917 onwards. The groups of the years 1915–18 were taken in the yard instead of on the front lawn, without the Head Masters or any members of staff.

Tony Farnell sums it up: 'Doggie was outstandingly good at keeping Cothill going during the Great War. We were in the depths of the country. Nobody had a car. There was not a car for miles around, during the whole time I was there. People only had bicycles, and perhaps bicycled into Abingdon on their free day. The laundry was taken in a cart. Farmers went around in dog-carts (pulled by a pony, but there was accommodation for your dog). . . . We boys were not allowed bicycles, in case – I think – we bicycled into the wrong social milieu. . . . In spite of this rural imprisonment in the depths of Berkshire, food-rationing and the awfulness of the Kaiser, we did pretty well at Cothill. Doggie maintained the academic staff, partly with the aid of lady teachers, such as Miss Phillips, who joined her brother. The drawing master continued to come out from Abingdon. Miss Spokes, the music teacher, bicycled out from Oxford. Mr Short went on carpentering our wooden bookshelves to take home with us. We played the usual cricket matches against Summer Fields and the Cathedral Choir School. . . . We never had to make our own beds, or wash up, or clean anything at all. Very bad for us, but a triumph for Doggie.'

The Peel brothers, Roger and Stephen, lived close by the school, at Upwood Park, Besselsleigh. Their sister, Catherine Eastwood, writes: 'When my elder brother Roger came to Cothill in 1916, my younger brother Stephen, aged between $7\frac{1}{2}$ and 8 and left behind with his two sisters in the care of the French governess, decided to run away – being lonely and aggrieved – but to run away to go to Cothill. Escaping between twelve and one o'clock when lessons were over he made his way through the woods – whether on foot or on junior bicycle I don't remember, and arrived at the school just when the boys were going in to lunch and was found by a junior master. He was taken in with the others and given a splendid lunch, while a messenger was sent hot-foot, or more probably hot-pedal, to tell my then anxious mother of his whereabouts – we having no telephone in those far-off days. My mother came to fetch him in our pony and cart.'

There was, however, even in such an enclosed community, the constant reminder of death. Jack Somers recalls: 'I vividly remember that on all too frequent occasions boys were sent for to be told their father or brother had been killed on active service.' M.J.D. kept a Roll of Honour, a finely bound book in which he pasted announcements in the press of all Old Cothillians who were killed or who received awards for gallantry. To these he added copies of letters, obituary notices, appreciations and poems. They make poignant reading. A letter to the then well-known writer Walter Sichel from the Company Commander of his elder son Geoffrey reads: 'I was your son's constant and close companion . . . he was shot dead through the temple as he was walking about, helping and joking with the men under a very heavy fire.' His younger brother Oliver was killed on 25 October 1918. Two other brothers, Charles and William Chapman, were killed within a week of each other in October 1917. Three of the four sons of Bishop Shaw of Buckingham were killed. Of these, Edward was at Cothill, as was the youngest, Robert, who joined the Navy and survived. He writes: 'To think that in under four years after leaving at the age of 12 I was at sea involved with the war.' It is he who has provided the photograph of his father having batted in his canonicals when Archdeacon of Buckingham. Of the three who died, 'J.B.' wrote:

'Falling they leave behind them as they fall
A nobler fame than that of bat and ball.
On English fields life's happiest years they spent,
Now, dead for England, lo! they lie content.'

Geoffrey Gilbey, MC, has a number of his own poems pasted in the book, including one from the magazine of the Eton Boys' Clubs, Hackney Wick, written in the trenches. Entitled 'The Best thing in the World', it starts: 'When I was three I used to think by far the greatest joy / Was going to the local shop and purchasing a toy'; and after listing all the chief pleasures as he grows up, ends: 'At twenty-six I tell you straight that life out here is grand. / I've found that work and happiness are always hand in hand. / So come, there's heaps of splendid work and happiness for you – / I've found the best thing in the world, so come and find it too.' Denys Morland's Military Cross, according to a letter from Driver Harry Barnes, RE, was well-deserved: 'It is not everyone who would go into a mine unarmed

Robert Shaw's father, as Archdeacon of Buckingham, having batted in his canonicals in a Fathers' Match, c.1911.

and capture 18 Germans with an empty revolver. . . . Mr Morland seems absolutely indifferent to danger, and one feels quite safe when out with him.'

Among those who were killed was Geoffrey, grandson of the Rev. H. C. Adams, who had owned Cothill House before it became a school. Geoffrey was an all-round athlete and classical scholar at Radley. The Warden, the Rev. E. G. Selwyn, wrote a Memoir of him after his death in 1916, in which he said: 'From the first to the last at Cothill he always displayed a spirit of keenness, both in work and games, and those who know the school will not need to be told that such a spirit was appreciated and encouraged with unfailing sympathy. . . . He came to Radley from Cothill with as good a training – moral, mental and athletic, as a prep school can give. . . . He owed a deep debt of gratitude to his masters for their unceasing care. . . . His happiest memories of Cothill life were that his keenest rivals were always his dearest friends.' It was of Geoffrey Adams that the Warden of Radley also wrote to *The Times*. He had received a letter from him containing what he called 'a spontaneous testimony of the Classics'. Geoffrey had written: 'A son of Science remarked to me the other day that he had never known a classical man out here who was not thoroughly happy on all occasions. In my own humble way I know the truth of this, even in the short time I have been out here.' He went on to say: 'I would give much for a game of rackets and an hour of Thucydides book VII.'

On 12 November 1918, M.J.D. stood at the high desk at the end of the Big Schoolroom and announced, 'At the eleventh hour of the eleventh day of the eleventh month of the fourth year of the war all fighting ceased.' Cakes and tinned fruit were provided for tea, the boys marched round the grounds waving flags, and Miss Hames draped bunting out of the dormitory windows. On the Sunday after Armistice Day, there was a special service in Dry Sandford Church, at the end of which a bugler blew 'The Last Post'. Guy Halsey, who was hearing this for the first time, writes: 'My appreciation and fascination apparently showed itself by my smiling, because I remember Doggie telling me that "The Last Post" was not an occasion for smiling, and that by doing so I showed disrespect.' To celebrate the signing of the Peace Treaty in 1919 the whole school was taken to see a mammoth firework display on Wittenham Clumps, though the proceedings were spoilt by torrential rain. In 1920 a War Memorial was completed. It was designed by G. E. Phillips, ARIBA, cost £400, and was paid for by subscriptions from Old Boys and parents. It occupies the north wall of the Dining Hall, and is a fine example of the period, with Bernard Partridge-like scrolls and flourishes. It contains the names of the 31 Old Cothillians, and underneath is the verse:

'They trod of old the fields we tread,
They played the games we play:
The part of them that is not dead
Belongs to us today.'

The names are given in *Appendix III*.

After the war M.J.D. continued as Head Master for another four years, though his health was declining. He was the object of an elaborate practical joke played on him by Pat Halsey and Philip Kindersley while they were at Eton. Guy Halsey describes it: 'They rang up Doggie, my brother pretending to be my mother – I suppose he was about 13 at the time and his voice had not broken – and told him that I was desperately unhappy and that he must send me home at once. I remember being summoned by Doggie in his study to talk about it, but he must have smelt a rat as he telephoned my parents to check. They, of course, were completely mystified by the whole thing. Patrick tells me that our father had to go down to Eton to sort it out and made him write a letter to Doggie apologising for the incident.' An extract from a letter Roger Peel wrote to his mother in October 1920 gives a boy's-eye view of M.J.D. and school life. 'Stir [Stephen] is still in bed and according to Hatter [Miss Hames] rather sorry for himself; Butler is in the same condition which is a pity as he will be a great loss to the XI on Wednesday. I have collected a

Figure of 8 moth and a Pink Barred Swallow, which is a very pretty little yellowy orange moth with pinky purple markings. J. and M.'s grandmothers and aunts etc. came over yesterday in a body but I never saw them, though they gave J. and M. some money. The 2nd dormy brought down on themselves the wrath of Doggie with a vengeance by breaking 2 water bottles. One evening when Dawson ma. was having a bath Roberts ma. put a brush and a comb in his bed and when he came back he threw the comb at Thomson and the brush at me; having missed me by 6 inches it proceeded to break a soap dish. Dawson had to pay. . . .'

M.J.D. kept up a correspondence with many of his Old Boys. In what must have been one of his last letters, he wrote to Pat Halsey at Eton on 6 March 1922. 'What a horrid bore for you about missing your Certificate owing to Mathematics. I so thoroughly sympathise with you, as I think they are most incomprehensible and soul-destroying abominations. I am glad you distinguished yourself so greatly in History. I suppose you had a whole holiday for Princess Mary's wedding. . . . The first three weeks of the term were spoilt by an epidemic of flu – everybody got it all at once, within 36 hours about 30 boys, Mr and Mrs Tomkinson, Miss Hames, Mr Phillips and most of the domestics. Fortunately it was a very mild type, so we managed to get through all right without any casualties. I haven't got quite enough money yet for the Eton Arms, but have been persuaded to order them in faith – as a matter of fact the balance has been guaranteed by the father of a boy who is due to leave in two or three years' time, so it will be all right in the long run. I hope they will be up in a week or two now.' This refers to one of several public-school arms painted on the Dining Hall walls. Doggie died on 30 April at the age of 54. The cricket pavilion was rebuilt and enlarged in his memory, and a memorial tablet erected by Cothill boys, their parents and other friends in Dry Sandford Church, where he had been Church Warden for 28 years.

After M.J.D.'s death R. Tomkinson became sole Head Master for another five years. According to Charles Close-Smith, 'it was a change for the worse. He overlooked nothing, appeared short in temper and in patience, and was loved by neither boys nor parents.' This is a minority view, for Oliver Barnett says he was well-liked by the boys. Of medium height, with a black moustache and melancholy eyes, he was in many ways a character. He would jump out of his classroom window to greet prospective parents, and should a pheasant stray near the football field he would rush for his gun with remarkable speed and invariably dispatch the bird. John Thomson describes Tomcat as lovable and a good teacher who kept the boys interested. One of his hobbies was to take the nests of crows at the top of tall trees which,

Four masters, R. V. Sessions, L. Williamson, A. C. Phillips and R. D. Busk, early 1920s. R.V.S. and R.D.B. still liked to be styled 'Captain'.

although he was in middle age, he climbed like a monkey. Elwes Duffield 'never knew what he did with the eggs'. According to Chris Barnett, he was famous for his outbursts: 'The words "As I said before" were often uttered with considerable menace. He seemed to rather thrive in a crisis. I can remember in 1926 [during the General Strike] his coming back from Oxford to tell us that armoured cars were out in the streets.' Gerald Hamilton remembers another occasion when 'we broke down on the way to a soccer match. I asked Mr Tomkinson if he had ever been a member of the AA or RAC. "Oh no", he replied. "One or other or both will be along shortly, keen as mustard to help me and to compete for my membership. I shall tip them but I shan't join either. I get better service this way." Those were the days.'

He kept a meticulously neat cash-book from 1911 to 1927. From this we know that in 1911 the fees were £30 per term, and that M.J.D. and R.T. both received £50 per term as salary. In 1922 each had £100 from the profits. After M.J.D. died, the fees were £45 per term. In 1924 there is an entry 'Closets and lavatories . . . £329.14*s*.1*d*'. In the same year land for the tennis courts and golf course was bought from a Mr Brewer at a total cost of £398.9*s*.9*d*. There is no mention in R.T.'s book of any salaries for the staff before 1922, presumably because M.J.D. paid them. Before she retired in 1925, Miss Hames's salary was £42 per term. In the same year A.C.P. received £90 per term, R.V. Sessions £66.13*s*.4*d* and L. Williamson £45.

These last two assistant masters are remembered especially. L.W., tall with a clipped moustache, had been, according to Fergus Higgins, 'a gallant artillery officer in the Great War and a good rugger player, although his skill was of no use in a soccer-playing school. I remember his mathematical problems often included sums involving Stock Exchange transactions and betting odds. I kept up with him until his death a few years ago and have shared his enthusiasm for the Stock Exchange and the Turf ever since Cothill days.' R.V.S. is described as a very genuine and pleasant man, and is remembered diving off a bridge during the Tomkinson farewell outing to Wittenham Clumps. John Stainer writes: 'We all had a great affection for "Sea-lion". He got that nickname as he was an excellent swimmer. He usually accompanied us to the swimming-pool on the road to Abingdon, where the water was of a green colour. . . . We were constantly trying to persuade Sea-lion to swim the length of the bath under water. When he eventually obliged he disappeared completely from view, but his progress could be observed by small bubbles rising to the surface. He was quite a good musician and played the organ in Dry Sandford Church. He had the reputation of not being much of a disciplinarian.'

In the early 1920s the country round Cothill had remained completely rural. Tony Farnell remembers the quiet after his home in Oxford. 'There was no bus, the largest moving object was a cow. . . . Across the level half-dozen miles of the Vale of the White Horse . . . you could see the long plume of white steam of the express train heading towards Bristol. . . . I could not take my eyes off it, for the cricket was boring and it was the only visible drama that Cothill provided.' He remembers another drama, not for the eyes but for the ears. Lying awake one hot, windless night in July 1919, he heard Old Tom 'striking his hundred and one strokes from Christ Church Cathedral. It sent me a message of comfort from my home, and I heard it. So it was at Cothill that I learnt really to gaze and really to listen. . . .

'The great glory of Cothill was the Ruskin Plot. This was a large area of wild woodland lying immediately beyond the football field. It had in some way been inaugurated or preserved by John Ruskin, perhaps to create an early version of a nature reserve. It was full of flowers, birds and ponds where in Winter we used to go skating. My parents and I loved it. When they bicycled over from Oxford, it was not really to see Doggie or Mr Phillips – it was to take their son to the Ruskin Plot. As far as I could see, nobody else ever went there. In April there was a mass of bluebells. You waded through them. Every flower came in its turn – snowdrops, celandines, primroses, dog-roses, spindlewort, yellow irises in the marshy parts, all appeared in due course. . . . Mr Phillips loved the places where the flowers grew, because he often used to take us there on a Sunday afternoon. We would choose a flowery place and sit down. Sunday afternoon is not a time to dash about and get muddy. We would relax in the warm sun and feel drowsy. One could listen to the bees. Some of the boys would potter about and pick flowers for Miss Hames, who could not often get there herself. Alone of all our activities, these Sunday afternoons were entirely unprogrammed, uncompetitive, undisturbed, full of good will.'

The Marsh, Summer 1981. A place where the flowers still grow.

Outside the Masters' Cottage, preparing for an outing in a char-à-banc *(a French Unic) and a Standard tourer, early* 1920s.

Cothill was still basically horse-orientated, although R.T. had a Morris and A.C.P., a motor cycle. John Thomson records that many of the boys came from 'what might be called country sporting families'. There was at least one lawn meet of the Old Berks at Cothill in the early 1920s, with the boys handing up stirrup cups, and John's father rode over the twelve miles from Woodperry, through the middle of Oxford, on his young horse which he then called 'Cothill'. When 'Cothill' won a point-to-point, the school was given an extra half-holiday to celebrate. John says it was the only time he was a popular boy.

The horse-drawn brakes in which boys were taken to and from Oxford Station and to away matches gradually gave way to *char-à-bancs* and two ancient Lanchester limousines. In other ways, too, modernisation came slowly. An Old Boy records: 'A very fashionable mother, Mrs Whitaker, came over from Paris to see her son. She is alleged to have asked a boy where the ladies' cloakroom was and she was directed to a very old-fashioned six-seater latrine, with no hand-washing facilities, in the field behind the squash court. Mrs Whitaker apparently complained to the Head Master and modern indoor lavatories were installed.' For many years afterwards the

A. C. Phillips with 'the last to go at Oxford Station', Spring 1925.

school prospectus contained the sentence, 'The drainage system is entirely modern, and is inspected regularly'. The school was lit by a petrol-gas plant beside the clock-tower. This was weight-driven and on one occasion the steel cable broke and the weight descended with a mighty bang.

To a new boy arriving on the London train, accompanied by A.C.P., the situation was not unlike that which confronted Mr Bultitude in Anstey's *Vice Versa*. One such, Hugh Barrett-Lennard, remembers, in 1926, a second-termer sitting down on one of the bus seats at Oxford and saying: 'This is the last comfortable seat I shall sit on for three months.' The only seats about the school were the benches in the Big Schoolroom and the Dining Hall chairs. The Head Master, though essentially a kind man, had a gloomy voice; Mrs Tomkinson (known as 'Ma Tomcat') seldom appeared in the school, as she was in poor health, and the care of the boys was mainly in the hands of the Matron, Miss Potter, and her assistant Miss Watson, known as 'Potty' and 'Watty'.

Hugh goes on: 'Getting up was somewhat of a ritual, because the dormitories were presided over by "Phillpots" [Phillips], and it followed a very strict routine. We were called at 7.15 [tepid water into china basins] and we washed and dressed, but a whistle went at half-past seven – a ritual called "all pyjama trousers off". That meant we had to have reached a stage of dressing where we'd changed from pyjama trousers into our ordinary knickerbockers. He used to come storming in to see if he could catch anybody who hadn't got his knickerbockers on by 7.30. At 7.34 a whistle went and we all had to get down on our knees and say our prayers. Another whistle went, and there was one minute for what was called "hair-brushing" that had to be done in silence, and then we went in single file down to the Big Schoolroom for prayers. We would say the psalm of the day, and Mr Tomkinson's intonations were sometimes a little depressing, and he would rather attack the psalms as if he were really angry with them: "Moab is my washpot; over Edom will I cast out my shoe".'

Breakfast normally consisted of porridge, bread and a small piece of butter. On Thursdays and Sundays there were sausages and marmalade. At lunch there was usually a choice of meat and boys were served by maids. 'Weekly fruit' was provided – apples, oranges and bananas – and twice a week each boy was given ten toffees. 'The curriculum was simple. Four periods: one hour Latin; three-quarters of an hour Modern; three-quarters of an hour French, after the 15-minute break; and one hour's Mathematics.' History, Geography and Scripture were taught in the afternoons, and there was a Greek set of half-a-dozen boys.

The usual games were played, but under R.T. they do not seem to have been taken very seriously. A great feature of the outdoor life of the school was the Marsh, of which the Ruskin Plot (or Reserve), already referred to, formed a part. Here A.C.P. inspired boys in the Summer to collect the eggs of puss moths, poplar hawks, etc., which were then hatched out in little wooden boxes, glass-fronted. Walter Somers writes: 'The replenishments of leaves and watching the caterpillar change skin is something I have never forgotten. We all had a lot of fun and I don't think we depleted the wild life too much. Now, of course, it is a Nature Reserve and no one is allowed in.' In the Winter, during the periods of icy weather which appear to have been more frequent than nowadays, A.C.P. would assume the rôle of o/c skating. When he had satisfied himself that the ice was thick enough ('ooh sir, is it safe?'),

A. C. Phillips skating on the Marsh pond, early 1920s.

A slide, Winter 1902. Three decades later, a slide was covered at the record 'alarming pace of 18 miles an hour (2 secs)'.

skates would be fitted to boys' boots, and the frozen rushes in the Marsh pond would be shaved off with spades, to enlarge the skating area. Chris Barnett asks: 'Who could be better equipped than old Phillips for stimulating an interest in winter sports? – "The benefits of a continental education" [as he used to say]. When I left I knew well enough how to skate at Eton and was able to enjoy that Arctic Winter of 1929... also skating at Cliveden... Nancy Astor a dream of fur-trimmed elegance in a black trouser-suit. But I must not detract from that earlier vision of Harris tweed plus-fours in full flight – Phillips of course giving a superb performance of the spreadeagle.' For the non-skaters one of the most popular and exciting of Cothill sporting activities of those days is describes by Michael Snow. 'Running parallel with the squash court and ending at the carpenter's shop were two "slides" of concrete, laid side by side about 30 feet long and 2 feet wide, surrounded by a shallow lip, so that in freezing weather hot water could be poured on to them, quickly turning them into two sheets of solid smooth ice. Quite high speeds could be attained on these slides, particularly by those wearing steel-studded boots or shoes. As I remember it, two mattresses were propped against the carpenter's shop wall to lessen the impact for the more courageous or impulsive sliders.'

Entertainments in the evenings were few, but as Hugh Barrett-Lennard recalls, 'occasionally there were lantern lectures, and people used to come down and there was a most extraordinary lantern. It always looked as though it would blow up at any time and very often filled the Big Schoolroom with smoke. Lecturers armed with a clicker, for changing slides, used to give us lectures and we always rather looked forward to them, on Saturday nights, and especially, as most generally happened, so many of the slides went in upside-down.' In 1924 three tennis courts were created behind the cricket pavilion, and beyond it, towards the Marsh, a nine-hole golf course was laid out. Senior boys were made responsible for the upkeep of the bunkers and greens. Cothill was one of the few prep schools at the time to have its own course, the holes varying in length from 90 to 150 yards. Boys were encouraged to play golf and tennis in their spare time, and members of the staff played with them, thus providing a link between school and holiday sporting activities. Bill Waller recalls 'somewhere about 1925 the butler – a Mr Argent – making a crystal set. Some of us with Mr Tomkinson were allowed to put on headphones and listen to this marvel of wireless.' Evelyn Hulbert-Powell remembers seeing Lord Oxford and Asquith, the former Prime Minister, passing beside the cricket field in his open Rolls Royce. Another phenomenon recalled by him was a fine display of the aurora borealis, very rare so far south, which caused great interest.

Lawn tennis courts, against a background of elms, c.1924.

The school remained comparatively small. The numbers of boys, which had averaged 38 from 1900 to 1910, fell to 27 in 1911 and remained about 30 until 1917. In 1920 they rose to 50; these numbers were maintained and in 1927 there were 47 boys in the school. But Mrs Tomkinson's health had been declining for some time; and so R.T. decided, at the age of 47, to sell the school to my father, Major S. A. Pike. He announced his intention to the boys one morning at prayers. Hugh Barrett-Lennard describes the scene. 'In the middle of the psalms, he suddenly collapsed over the desk, gave a loud "Croop" and burst into tears. We waited to find out what had happened. Some of us thought he had had a fit. But at the end, in his usual way, he said "Siddown", and he then broke to us the news that he was having to sell up the school, his wife was ill, and that he would be leaving at the end of term. He told us that a man called Pike had bought the school, and added that "if any of your parents want to take you away, of course they are perfectly free to do so". I remember the effect of all this emotion was rather electric, and small boys are very sympathetic, and very soon the entire school was in tears. I was quite young and I stared round at this rather amazing sight of the Head Master and the entire school blubbing away, and I was only brought to my senses when I received a severe kick on the ankle from the boy next to me, who hissed into my ear, "Swine, you're not blubbing".'

In the Summer term of 1927 there was a farewell outing and picnic to mark the departure of the Tomkinsons. Chris Barnett remembers it: 'Some boys had got through a hedge into a hayfield ready for harvesting. All of a sudden an extremely red-faced and infuriated farmer roared up on a motor bike across all the picnic stuff laid out, and started swearing at Tomcat with some very Anglo-Saxon oaths. Our dear Head Master remained utterly calm, and with the politest of gestures completely deflated the poor man with the offer of a ripe banana.'

4
THE ARRIVAL OF THE PIKES

It was with some sense of expectation that the boys returned in the Autumn term of 1927. What would the new Head Master be like? By any standards my parents, Sam and Dorothy, were a remarkable couple, combining unusually good looks with tremendous energy and enthusiasm. He was 39, she 37. They had three children, of whom I was the eldest, with two younger sisters, Diana and Audrey. We had lived in London, for my father had been in the family hop business in the City. But, as he wrote in the 1970 Centenary *Magazine*, 'having decided in 1926 that what I really wanted to do was to have a boys' preparatory school, my first job was to persuade Dorothy to feel likewise and in this I succeeded. We inspected several schools [among them Evelyns, where, as already mentioned, M. J. Dauglish had taught] and when we saw Cothill in the Summer of 1927 we both fell for it in a big way, with its lovely grounds and inspiring views of the Berkshire Downs as seen from the cricket field.'

My father had had no experience of teaching and was quite outside the prep-school world, having felt the lack of a prep-school education when he had gone to Charterhouse from a dame school in Reading. He used to describe how he and his great friend J. F. Roxburgh had planned as schoolboys to run a prep school and a public school respectively. By 1927 J.F. had already been the first Head Master of Stowe for four years, and he gave invaluable advice and encouragement to my parents in their determination to create their special type of school at Cothill.

Some who remember the arrival of the Pike family have described it as a breath of fresh air that blew through the hitherto rather Spartan corridors. Brown paint was replaced by bright colours, there was Morris wallpaper in the front hall, flowers on the Dining Hall tables, together with excellent food. 'The whole atmosphere changed, it became a very happy place.' A new boy that term, David Gardiner-Hill, describes how S.A.P. 'gathered the whole school together on the morning of his first "Blub Sunday" and officially silenced it for ever'. This refers to the last Sunday of term, when traditionally old scores were settled and new boys in particular lived in dread of what might happen to them. Forty years later it still lurked, transferred to the first

With my parents, grandmother and two sisters, 1935. 'The Pike family was Cothill and Cothill was the Pike family.'

Sunday of term 'when new boys were told they could expect to be bashed up all day'. But Hugh Barrett-Lennard says that Blub Sunday 'was not as terrible as it sounded, because it really was a form of bravado and nobody ever seemed to blub'.

Tim Bailey remembers S.A.P. as 'an imposing figure, upright and of military bearing, enhanced by a short black moustache. He was invariably smartly dressed . . . in double-breasted suits and club ties.' Others have remembered his 'co-respondent' black-and-white shoes; 'eyes piercing under bushy black brows; if you were contemplating telling him a lie you tried to avoid eye-to-eye confrontation'. One of my father's early pupils, Richard Symonds, has written that he never could quite understand why Sam Pike had acquired a preparatory school: 'He did not seem particularly interested in teaching, though I suppose he liked the idea of formation of character.' This was indeed to my father the object of the exercise, and he himself wrote later, at the time of the Centenary: 'Our job was to train Cothill boys to be the future leaders of Britain, men of integrity; wise, tolerant, kind men of vision and Christian ideals.'

I remember how excited we all were at the thought of moving into a school in the country. I had been sent to King's Mead, Seaford, in 1926, and was happily established there. To a certain extent, therefore, I knew what to expect when we piled into our Fiat and rattled noisily along the Great West Road, through Slough and Henley, ending up at the Mitre Hotel, Oxford, for an exploratory visit to Cothill. The builders, Hinkins & Frewin, had been given less than two months to extend the front of the house to provide a drawing-room, bedroom, dressing-room and bathroom, and this addition was carried out from plans made by my grandfather, Joseph Armstrong Stenhouse, a distinguished architect who had been very successful in New York designing houses for millionaires Otto Kahn, Leo Blumenthal and others. He had recently retired and now produced the first major alterations to the house since 1879; it made possible the provision of a Common Room for the boys, something which was greatly appreciated. There were comfortable chairs, table tennis, a pleasant room to which they could go on Winter evenings. That was the first of the many building improvements that my parents introduced for the boys.

My father was in his element running the games. He had been a Corinthian footballer, a Crusader cricketer at Cambridge, a four-handicap golfer and excellent real-tennis player. His skill and enthusiasm as a coach soon transformed the standard. Ken Tomkinson, a nephew of R.T.'s and a new boy in 1927, gives an impression of the new management: 'My first recollection of Major Pike was in a game of internal school football [probably the youngest game]. He gave us a lesson in the art of dribbling and very well he did it; while encouraging us to get the ball off him, he passed us, all in a very skilful demonstration.' S.A.P. found the 1st football game playing in caps –

Football, 1912. My father outlawed the caps in 1927.

Putting green, 9th hole, c.1930.

'how on earth they thought they could have headed the ball' – and going indoors as soon as it started to rain. Cothill used to play the 2nd XI of such schools as the Dragon, Summer Fields and Horris Hill, but this was quickly changed, even though it resulted in heavy defeats at first. The golf course at Frilford Heath was an added attraction to S.A.P., and he quickly engaged the head green-keeper, Prickett, to come over and advise on the greens of the nine-hole school course. Tim Bailey appreciates how S.A.P. encouraged the more individual sports at a time when the accent was much more on team games. 'He will never know how much this enlightened policy helped us older ones to enjoy our mid and later years on the golf course and tennis courts.'

My father found a kindred spirit in the groundsman, George Leader Fairbrother, known as 'Fairbro''. He had lost both legs at the battle of the Somme, and as his grandmother had been a sewing maid at the school from 1879, he had been offered a job in 1917 looking after the horses. He graduated to groundsman, and was to remain in that post for fifty years. Tony Findlay's description of him will bring back memories to generations of Cothillians. 'Fairbrother, the groundsman, shoe-cleaner, boot-stud repairer, general handyman and the gruff, unsmiling friend of all the boys was universally liked because he seemed to us to do his variety of jobs so well despite two tin legs. He carried baskets of shoes across the yard to his "shop" and back again, he hand-weeded the tennis courts with painstaking care and the cricket pitches. His old hand-cart was constantly in use repairing goal mouths, putting stakes and ropes up for the firework display, taking chairs out to or back from the cricket grounds or school play area beyond the 1st XI football pitch. A stalwart figure with cloth cap, full black moustache and an enormous watch chain.' Franko Seymour remembers that Fairbro' taught him how to trap moles, and how, 'with the tactlessness of youth one November 11th I asked him why he was not wearing his poppy. Whereupon he pulled up his trousers and tapped his false legs with his walking stick and said, "I wear my poppies every day". I was suitably abashed.'

As my father had no experience of schoolmastering, it is doubtful if the change-over would ever have got off the ground without the help of A. C. Phillips. He knew all about the running of the school down to the smallest detail. Everything that had happened for the past twenty-five years had been recorded, charted and filed. My father gave him his head, and relied on him as a source of information. He quickly endeared himself to us children by his exaggerated stories, his splendid phraseology, with expressions like 'Rich beyond the dreams of avarice' apropos a certain Cothill family, his peculiarly rasping voice, and the machine with which he rolled his cigarettes. He seemed to enjoy our childish jokes and his return to school a few days before

Outdoor staff, 1930s. From left: *Leader Fairbrother (Fairbro'), Charlie Denton, Nelson Battell ('Batty'), Leader's father (known as 'Moses'); Tweedledum or Tweedledee between the shafts.*

the beginning of term was always welcomed. He opened up a new world to the Pike family, providing a link with the early days of the century, telling us stories of M. J. Dauglish to whom he had been devoted and after whose death in 1922 his life had been greatly diminished. Now, with an appreciative audience, he blossomed again.

Another who helped greatly in the transfer from London to Cothill was J. C. Banks. He had come, at the age of 20, to be my tutor in 1925, when my departure to prep school had been postponed through ill-health. Fresh-faced, thick-set, with a booming voice and an infectious laugh, he became a great friend of the family, travelled abroad with us, and acquired the nickname 'Bonko'. He writes: 'This was an exceptionally happy household with rarely a dull moment and all enjoying life to the full. . . . I never guessed it but Sam had intended for some time to run a prep school. We went to many race meetings and I remember well playing many a family game of poker. Sad to relate Sam never played poker again once he became Head Master. . . . We had terrific duels at table tennis, wearing dinner jackets and ruining our stiff shirts.' He came with us to Cothill, announcing to his colleagues in the Masters' Cottage: 'I'm not an ordinary master, I'm a friend of the Pikes.' J.C.B.'s loyalty and enthusiasm were invaluable to my parents in those early days, when they were suddenly faced with so many new problems and responsibilities.

A major hazard of boarding-school life was serious illness. Bill Lanyon describes how he developed double pneumonia his first term in 1927: 'I was a sickly child. Your parents coped very well, putting me in their spare room and arranging oxygen and 24-hour nursing. I give them full marks for that, only blotted a bit by your mother passing on chicken-pox to me before I had fully recovered from pneumonia.' My sister Diana has 'a vivid memory of the fairly frequent drama of boys being desperately ill. Pneumonia and mastoids with no antibiotics; the place was invaded with extra nurses; hush-hush areas and very great anxieties.' Luckily there was an outstanding school doctor, F. G. Hobson, FRCP, consultant physician at the Radcliffe Infirmary in Oxford. He was a brilliant diagnostician, and now began a long friendship with my parents. He and S.A.P. spoke the same language and looked very much alike. Fred Hobson had enlisted in 1914, in what he referred to as 'our war', as a despatch rider before being commissioned and winning the DSO. He conducted regular sick parades in true military fashion, and wrote a termly, individual report on every boy. Thus, 'Summer term 1929. C. R. C. Weld Forester. Had had measles during past term. Is now quite fit.' For the next thirty years he would make a point of visiting the school on Thursday afternoons, when he said he could be sure of cream cakes for tea with my parents.

Teaching staff, Spring 1931. Standing: *E. H. Butler, V. K. D. Waite, J. C. Banks;* sitting: *H. A. G. Phillimore, S. A. Pike, A. C. Phillips.*

S.A.P. soon appointed three new masters who were to serve for many years on the staff and make their own invaluable contribution to the life of the school. First was H. A. G. ('Dust') Phillimore. Though he was much ragged at first and much imitated always, his total devotion to the school and his qualities as a man and teacher of the Classics were such that my father made all sorts of special allowances for his eccentricities. Hugh Barrett-Lennard remembers his first days: 'He had a certain amount of difficulty in establishing discipline. He used to utter threats: "If I hear another sound, preparation will be prolonged by two minutes". Then the whole school would yell out a tremendous "Ooh, sir".' Soon he was not required to undertake any supervisory duties. Tim Bailey remembers him at this time when he was about thirty: 'He dressed in grey flannels and a coat which fitted very tight over his thick chest. He always wore steel-rimmed glasses and if standing in contemplation he would cock his head sideways like a bird, often bringing a pencil up to his mouth, presumably to help concentration.... It was rumoured that he had been gassed or shell-shocked in the war. [He certainly always absented himself on Guy Fawkes's Night.] He was agonisingly shy, squirming and shifting his weight, and finally darting off with a little hop and a skip.' Small wonder that every boy imitated him, but from the first his teaching was appreciated by the seniors: 'His academic knowledge was prodigious, . . . he would relate events in the Greek and Roman wars with a wealth of detail and names and such fascinating word pictures as to make them come alive and silence the sniggering of even his most sadistic tormentor.' H.A.G.P. was a man of considerable means, from a distinguished family, and shared a flat in Cadogan Gardens with his sister Hester. There he would entertain boys: 'As one left, after a theatre and lavish tea, one wondered why in term-time one was so unkind and mocking to and about this kindest of men. . . . '

E. H. Butler, the second master to be appointed, was altogether different. 'Short, balding, with a small Hitler moustache', he had lost his left arm in the war. He and my parents had much in common, and he soon made himself invaluable as a counterbalance to A.C.P., acting as S.A.P.'s 'adjutant' in a number of ways and sharing my mother (D.E.P.)'s enthusiasm for gardening. He has been described as a good and patient teacher, particularly of History, and he organised general knowledge papers for the whole school at the end of term. E.H.B. took junior games, and played one-armed tennis and golf and could even tie a bow-tie. The boys respected him for his unfailing good humour and common-sense discipline, while they and his colleagues on the staff were 'amazed by the courage and determination he showed in overcoming his daunting physical disability'. Michael Knutsford (as Holland-Hibbert) remembers that he 'used to get into a tizzy when his armless sleeve would come out of the pocket it should have been tucked into'. According to John Cartwright, 'his nickname was "Butterballs" – from table butter, I think – nothing physiological', or 'Preut-à-beurre', meant to be his French for pass or take the butter.

The third member of the triumvirate was V. K. D. Waite. He had given his age as 21, but in fact he was 19. He had recently been living in France and spoke French perfectly. He was half French and he retained a faintly Continental look, with his black hair, moustache and sensitive face, and he had the mouth of a mimic. Tony Findlay recalls how 'chalk flew around his classroom aimed at the inattentive, the idle or the fatuous' and Jonathan Janson 'was always in fear of Mr Waite who taught French, probably due to my dislike of the language'. By contrast, an early pupil, Kemmis Buckley, considered him 'highly cultured. He brought us almost with pleasure through a potted version of *Les Trois Mousquetaires*.' For the next 17 years he proved himself, in S.A.P.'s words, 'an unusually good and stimulating teacher, musician and play producer . . . with a versatile and creative mind, combined with nervous energy which got things done. . . . A great preparatory schoolmaster and a most talented and likeable man.' In the early 1930s, with a school numbering only 64 or so, he had less than 40 boys over the age of 10 from which to cast his plays. Francis Pym (ex-Foreign Secretary and a life peer) was cast in the role of Bardolph when only nine or ten 'and somehow he got me into the way of the part even though I did not understand the meaning of the lines'.

Vincent was a gifted musician with a beautiful touch on the piano, which he played for evening prayers. He recalls his first interview with S.A.P.: 'One of the requirements of my appointment to the staff was that I was to play the organ at the village church on Sundays during term-time when the school attended matins. I was a keen organist and in my youthful enthusiasm imagined everybody knew all about the King of Instruments. "Has the organ two manuals?" I innocently asked S.A.P. He looked completely bewildered, but with the ignorance of youth I continued "Has it got pedals?" When he murmured something about "loud" and "soft" I realised that I would have to examine the instrument myself.' V.K.D.W. was to take on more and more, but even in the early days he established a close relationship with S.A.P., who appreciated his cheerful enthusiasm and wonderful sense of humour. He seemed to us children to be always laughing, and all three children became devoted friends of his. I was later to spend a hilarious Spring holiday with him in France and Catalonia in 1933, learning a lot about life in general and about Cothill gossip in particular.

Of the early Pike days, Walter Somers writes: 'I had a lovely time recuperating after pneumonia, going out in the pony and trap with your sisters plus governess.' This must have been in 1927/8, and the governess was Muriel Wright. Shortly afterwards she began to teach the bottom class and continued to do so for the next 26 years. A short, dumpy woman, nicknamed

Muriel Wright, 1938. She taught 'the babies'.

'Waggle bum', she is remembered by one of her earliest pupils as 'pleasant and good at dealing with the "babies", ... gave us a good grounding, ... general peace and harmony'. She had the sense of humour without which her job would have been intolerable, and she used to regale the Head Master with the latest boy 'mot'. I have a leather-bound book, with gold blocking 'Cothill House, M.W., Her Book', given to her by my grandmother, which contains various jottings. One of them reads: 'When he was going to bed I asked one boy who had had a "bad" day to be good in the morning. He replied "Please remind me in the morning" – no rash promises.' She notes the charm, naturalness and friendliness of boys, that the most difficult often proved the most interesting; 'Each boy is like a bud. You can never tell what he will be like when he opens out. ...' She is on record as saying: 'The babies use their pens like pepper-pots.'

From the first my parents were strengthened and refreshed by the beauty of the place. I remember being amazed by the size of the elms, which grew on either side of the cricket pavilion and down to the Marsh and dominated the landscape. In 1927 there was no aerodrome to disturb the quiet and very little traffic on the road. It was an ideal spot for an 11-year-old boy. The clock-tower, with two classrooms on either side, was at that time still not attached to the main building and there were days before the boys came back when I had the place to myself and could bicycle in an uninterrupted circuit of hardstanding, or go further afield into the Marsh, following the path opposite the Fleur de Lys, into a magical world of morning sunlight slanting through the trees and what sounded like all the birds in Berkshire.

When the boys came back I was fascinated by the game of Snob. My original introduction to the game occurred when my term began later than Cothill's. Many of my contemporaries, Angus Bruton, Hugh Barrett-Lennard, Walter and Chris Somers, all remained good friends. Hugh remembers: 'On that first day of that Autumn term 1927 there was a boy called George, wearing the blue cap of King's Mead, and he turned out to be Sam Pike's son. Before he went back to his own school he was able to spend a couple of days with us, and I doubt if we should have thought of him then as a future Head Master.' John Saunder describes 'a lad coming into the Big Schoolroom and swinging from desk to desk on the lights. He claimed to be the Head Master's son.'

My mother has been described as 'the power behind the throne' and from the start her influence was felt. To her must go the credit of providing a more civilised and homely atmosphere, which the boys noticed immediately. 'There was soon a smarter look to the school. We came back ... to find the rather drab dormitories beautifully painted and decorated, each in a distinctive way.' Ken Tomkinson gives an impression of her: 'Mrs Pike seemed to enjoy her part in running the school. If she had something to say, the school shut up and listened until she had said it. She was a very charming and able lady.' She presided over a considerable number of domestic servants. The indoor staff was headed by Newton, the butler, who lived with his family in no.12 Cothill, which at that time had no running water and was lit by oil lamps. My parents had brought with them from London our parlourmaid, Lena, a great character, though inclined to suffer from BO. In addition, there were maids to serve in the Dining Hall, wearing frilly caps and aprons, housemaids for the private side and others to clean the dormitories, empty the chamber pots and make the beds. The cook, Mrs Bartlett, with her husband, had been employed for some years by my mother's parents. He became the gardener, and they lived in the Sanatorium where an adjoining water-wheel provided well-water for the school. Every day Bartlett brought in fresh vegetables from the garden to the kitchen, which was then the present sitting-room and was approached through a door from the 'lamp-room'. The Bartletts left after two years, and were succeeded by their daughter Violet and her husband Charlie Denton. Violet was large and friendly, but of uncertain temper; Charlie was a good-looking charmer. She was an excellent school cook, while he maintained the vegetable and flower gardens until the war. Meals in the Servants' Hall were presided over by the butler and cook. My mother supervised every detail of the domestic side of the school, ensuring a high standard of food and hygiene. D.E.P. never cooked nor did any housework herself, depending all her life on having servants, who gave long and loyal service. She took in her stride the many new experiences, duties and responsibilities.

My parents often described how, before the arrival of their first prospective parents, they hid in the rose garden, peeping round a bush, to see what the visitors looked like, and then summoning up courage to greet them outside the front door. They both then showed the young couple round the school, hoping that they did not contradict what each had just said. Only months before they had themselves been shown round by R. Tomkinson. During the course of the tour of inspection he had intrigued them by taking a banana out of his pocket, peeling and eating it; then taking out a bar of chocolate, which he also ate – 'but he never offered us any!'.

From the first both had breakfast and lunch with the school, together with all members of the teaching and matrons' staff. Lunch was a formal occasion, a commanding officer's parade, with the boys lining up in the passage to have their hair and hands inspected, then walking in single file and in silence to their places. Grace was said, the level of noise would be controlled, table manners strictly supervised. Franko Seymour 'can seldom eat peas without thinking of Mr Banks's instructions to some boy sitting half-way down his table who was spearing each pea individually. At the top of his voice (and he had a powerful voice), "Crush them against your fork, boy".' My parents kept an eagle eye on everything, and would correct any faults in a tactful way afterwards. I remember my mother telling me how in the early days she had asked my father to speak to one of the matrons who had slipped up in some way: 'Oh no, that's your department; you must speak to her yourself.' She gained confidence and became, in my father's words, 'my best duty master'. We used to imitate her 'Less noisse boysse', and 'Sam, Sam what are those boys doing over there?'. D.E.P. was greatly helped by her old friend, my godmother, Vera McMillan, who is remembered by Kemmis Buckley as being 'competent and agreeable, . . . packing and unpacking large trunks, dealing with piles of linen ("Always take a clean handkerchief from the bottom of the pile"), and reading to the younger boys the A. A. Milne books and *The Wind in the Willows*.' She remained the perfect assistant matron from 1927 to 1936. For much of this period the Matron was Sister Hedges. She had nursed my sister Diana in London after peritonitis, and was a great support to my parents.

Nowadays it is extraordinary to think of a married couple in their thirties acquiring a school (which, as Richard Symonds points out, 'in those days could be bought like a farm, with goodwill and all stock included') with full confidence that they could make it pay sufficiently well to be able to educate three children and maintain a standard of life that was, to say the least, unusually civilised. My mother had some money of her own, and her parents undoubtedly helped finance the start. As my father wrote for the Centenary *Magazine*, 'What an adventure it all was! 37 [47] youngsters in our care and neither of us with any previous experience. Army life helped, otherwise we could only rely on our affection for the young male, our ideals and our desire to be of real help to the parents and to turn out first-class Christian leaders of a country we loved. . . . We felt, I think, that what was even more important than work standard was to aim at specially all-round high standards of conduct, i.e. character training. . . . In our early days at Cothill we still had the world's largest empire, and to aim at turning out British Empire builders . . . made every geography lesson and every day of our job a challenge and a wonderful adventure.'

I remember one Summer evening at my prep school talking to one of the assistant masters called Mayall as he was digging his garden. I don't think he knew S.A.P. very well, but he suddenly said: 'Where your father was so

An early Pike group, Summer 1929. Standing: *J. C. Banks, E. H. Butler, Miss Spokes, A. C. Phillips behind my parents, V. K. D. Waite, H. A. G. Phillimore;* sitting: *Vera McMillan (with Darkie), Sister Hedges.*

sensible was that he didn't think he knew all the answers and so he asked the Boss to give him some good tips.' As King's Mead was a happy school the advice he got paid dividends, for happiness was to become the main characteristic of Cothill in the years to come. Another King's Mead master, W. E. P. Estridge, was related to the Morland family in Abingdon, and I remember a leisurely motor journey in an open Clyno from Seaford at the end of the Summer term of 1928 when Estridge took me home. This was an adventure in those days, as normally we boys travelled by train to Victoria, then went across London to Paddington to catch an Oxford train. On this occasion I had the comfortable feeling that the family had joined a headmasters' club, and that I was being given special treatment.

STATIONS:
ABINGDON, 3 MILES.
OXFORD, 6 MILES.

TELEGRAMS: COTHILL.
TELEPHONE: ABINGDON 24.

COTHILL HOUSE, near ABINGDON,
BERKSHIRE.

Major S. A. PIKE, M.C., M.A.,
Trinity College, Cambridge,

assisted by graduates of Oxford and Cambridge, prepares boys between the ages of 8 and 14 for the Public Schools and the Royal Naval College, Dartmouth.

The situation of the School was chosen with special regard to the health of the boys. The house, which stands on a deep bed of sand, is 260 feet above the sea-level, and faces the Berkshire Downs, some 12 miles distant. It is, therefore, very dry, and has the advantage of remarkably pure and bracing air. The buildings, for the most part, were designed expressly for School purposes.

The drainage system is entirely modern, and is inspected regularly.

The water supply is excellent.

The ordinary course of instruction includes Scripture, Latin, Greek, French, English, Mathematics, History, and Geography.

In addition to the Class-rooms and other usual buildings there are good grounds for Cricket and Football, and two Racket Courts, one of which is covered. The bathing place belonging to the School is close by, and every boy is taught to swim. The School has also its own 9-hole Golf Course, and Tennis Courts.

A short distance from the School is the Sanatorium for any case of infectious illness.

The household arrangements are under the control of Mrs. PIKE, assisted by a Matron and an Assistant-Matron.

—:—

TERMS:

£45 a Term, payable in advance.

The only necessary extras, except purely personal expenses, are Laundry £1 1s. a term, and Stationery 5s. a Term.

EXTRAS (Optional):

Piano	£3 3s. 0d.	a Term.
Violin or Violoncello ...	£4 4s. 0d.	,,
Dancing	£2 2s. 0d.	,,
Carpentering	10s. 6d.	,,
Drawing	10s. 6d.	,,

The Dancing and Carpentering Classes are held during the Winter terms only.

Physical Drill and Class Singing are included in the ordinary course.

A term's notice is required before the removal of a boy from the School, or, in lieu thereof, a term's fees.

There are three terms in the School year, and the holidays are about seven weeks at Midsummer, five weeks at Christmas, and four weeks at Easter.

REFERENCES.

THE REV. H. E. D. BLAKISTON, President of Trinity College, Oxford.

C. W. CARRINGTON, Esq., D.S.O., The Copse, Harrow-on-the-Hill.

THE EARL OF CASTLESTEWART, Old Lodge, Nutley.

THE RT. REV. THE LORD BISHOP OF OXFORD.

SIR HERBERT WARREN, K.C.V.O., President of Magdalen College, Oxford.

THE RT. REV. J. E. C. WELLDON, Dean of Durham.

THE LOWER MASTER of Eton College.

THE HEADMASTER of Stowe.

THE HEADMASTER OF CHARTERHOUSE.

THE WARDEN of Radley College.

GENERAL MACKENZIE KENNEDY, C.B., Eastbourne.

And to the following Parents of past or present boys:

THE RT. HON. LORD BRADBURY, G.C.B., Millbrook House, Shepperton.

HIS EXCELLENCY LORD CHELMSFORD, Government House, Calcutta.

G. C. DAY, Esq., Quenington Court, Fairford, Glos.

W. J. HALSEY, Esq., Westfield, Hatfield.

D. G. HOGARTH, Esq., D.Litt., Keeper of the Ashmolean Museum, Oxford.

SIR EVELYN MURRAY, K.C.B., 19, Manchester Square, W. 1.

REV. E. MARLING ROBERTS, The Vicarage, Kensington, W. 8.

THE RT. REV. E. D. SHAW, Canon of Christ Church, Oxford.

CAPTAIN SIR GEORGE WICKHAM LEGG, K.B.E., M.V.O., 14, Pembroke Gardens, Kensington, W. 8.

First Pike prospectus, c.1927. *In content it is little different from those of past decades: the 'pure and bracing air', 'entirely modern' drainage, the curriculum, the fees. The golf course and tennis courts are now mentioned, 'Drawing' becomes an extra at 10s. 6d a term, the referees have been augmented and now include, predictably, the Head Masters of Stowe and Charterhouse.*

5
THE THIRTIES

Franko Seymour, who came in 1931, when asked in the 1970s 'What person, other than your parents, do you consider has had the most effect on your life?', unhesitatingly replied 'Major Pike'. 'It was the example he set us. He had such gusto for life and instinctively seemed to know what appealed to us boys. He knew how to channel our energies with his enthusiasm, so we tried to fulfil his expectations. . . . I can never recall his ever being, or appearing to be, put out. That some sort of crisis must have occurred from time to time was inevitable, but we boys never knew of it.' One early crisis occurred, however, when two boys ran away. Francis Pym records 'the shock horror event that rocked the whole school. . . . The scale and enormity of this breach of every known rule was hard to grasp. It was a total sensation. S.A.P. was extremely angry but remained as rational and authoritative as ever. He told us at once what he knew and then kept us all informed as the story unfolded. In this way he retained our confidence. . . . On S.A.P.'s part it was a virtuoso example of crisis management.'

It was the family atmosphere which is recalled by so many. S.A.P. 'towered over the school in every sense'. His immaculate clothes: Franko 'always admired his shoes. I used to think that when I grew up I would have shoes like his. Of course I never have, more's the pity.' An aroma of Turkish cigarettes and 'Aleima' hair lotion contrasted with the smell of gaspers which pervaded the Masters' Common Room. To David Heaton, D.E.P. was 'radiant, motherly, concerned, relaxed, generous in feeding us as in everything else. . . . The Pike family was Cothill and Cothill was the Pike family.'

On 6 and 7 February 1930, the school was inspected for the first time. His Majesty's Inspectors found that the staff discharged their duties 'in a workmanlike and effective way', but were considered 'not distinguished academically', a judgement open to question, especially with regard to H.A.G.P. and V.K.D.W. In Latin the Inspectors found that good results were achieved on traditional lines, but because the boys read no consecutive matter, 'a vast deal of accumulated mental stock lies unrelated to anything but paradigms'.

Masters were advised to be more severe with themselves over the 'restored' pronunciation, 'so that they can with good conscience insist on the boys using properly the guides to quantity and pronunciation provided in their tests'. It was clearly felt that rather too much of the curriculum was devoted to Latin, and it was suggested that the first year should be spent on a 'Modern' or English course, teaching boys the grammar 'common to the languages they are likely to learn, with plenty of prose and verse memorising... and a little intensive drill in clear articulation'. If another language was thought necessary in the first year, 'a little French, taught conversationally with wall pictures and a minimum of grammar, should be enough'. It was thought most undesirable to begin Latin and French in the same year.

For the teaching of History, two periods a week was considered a meagre allowance. The teaching seen was incisive and thorough with regard to facts and dates, but some picturesque and personal history of a general type, read in well-illustrated books, would be a valuable stimulus. 'It is desirable that the basis of study should be a book read; how to read History books can be learnt only by practice.' No Geography teaching could be heard during the inspection, but the study of the local geography and of Ordnance maps was recommended. The standard in Mathematics was judged 'moderate', and frequent oral drills were recommended for the lower forms as a preparation for Common Entrance work. 'The value of such training in the mechanical habit which produces accurate and rapid answers can hardly be overestimated.' It was noted that no Science was taught, but 'one of the masters [A.C.P.] is a keen naturalist and boys are encouraged to follow some outside hobby in the Summer months'.

The general conclusions were: 'The school gives a most favourable impression both in and outside the classroom. The general atmosphere is one of happiness combined with keenness for work. Not only is the general welfare of the boys cared for, but there is a genuine desire among all those concerned to strive after the best form of training at this stage of a boy's career.'

An event of great importance was the starting by S.A.P. of the *Cothill House Magazine* in April 1929. He stressed that 'the *Magazine* is intended to be a bare record of the chief events of each term; in fact a sort of glorified diary'. At the time of writing, Volume I is missing, but Volume II mentions the building of the gymnasium next to the squash court. It was lavishly equipped and included a badminton court. Next came the new Library and changing rooms, with dormitories above. The Library was opened on 14 December 1929 by Roxburgh of Stowe. The *Magazine* describes him as

New Library, December 1929. Most of the books are behind the camera.

giving an excellent address on 'Reading and the use of libraries'. It was better to read anything than nothing at all. Cultivate the habit of careful, intelligent reading, and so learn to better one's tastes so that one could appreciate the classical authors in due course. His motto for an ideal library was 'Peace and Plenty'. The Library itself is described by an Old Boy as 'perfect; in any house it would have been a gem'.

The 'Library Book', leather-bound and meticulously kept by A.C.P., shows that Conan Doyle's *Tragedy of the Korosko* was the first book taken out. The most popular authors were Kipling, Ryder Haggard, 'Sapper' and Buchan. There was a wide range of books and the room was greatly appreciated, as it was comfortable, with a fire in Winter, and it was quiet until the New Hall was built in 1933, when it became something of a passage.

The *Magazine* records that in 1930 the golf course was in constant use and that Sergeant Eyres taught gymnastics and boxing. Several Old Boys have described him: 'Very impressive, barrel-chested yet light on his feet. Typical old-world RSM, waxed moustache and all. Rough barracks humour ("You, with the red cap on" – we all had red caps on) endeared him and terrified us.' 'Nicknamed "Sergeant Stand Still".... I have memories of vaulting the horse while his arm which appeared to be made of steel caught you.' 'He taught me how to box – something I found useful in later life.'

One of S.A.P.'s earliest editorials describes 1930 as 'a most worrying and perplexing year for Great Britain', singling out unemployment and the future of India. He concluded: 'Let us all go to our work and be strong, halting not in our ways.' (This was, of course, during the time of the 'Slump' and the collapse of the stock market.) From the same volume we learn that 81 lb of blackberries had been picked on 23 September. It was a yearly custom for the whole school to go blackberrying in the Marsh at the beginning of the Autumn term, before the games clothes had been unpacked. In those days the Summer holidays began and ended much later than nowadays. John Cartwright recalls that 'about mid-October [not 'Stir-up Sunday'?] an enormous round pot filled with Christmas-pudding mix was placed on a stand in the passage outside the Dining Hall and everyone had to have a stir at it and a wish'. Not surprisingly S.A.P. recorded football matches at length, for he was improving the standard, and was delighted that both Summer Fields and Horris Hill had been beaten at home. There was a 'Review of the Season' and reports on individual members of the 1st XI.

A *Magazine* feature of the early 1930s was 'Lectures and Entertainments'. This particular term produced 'Gordon and the Sudan', 'Round the World in a Sailing Ship', 'On the Trail of the Cowboy', and an entertainment by Mr Frank Chester, which included West Country dialects (well-known to 'listeners-in'). 'The Pedagogues' gave a performance of a farce entitled 'The Iron Anne'. V.K.D.W.'s performance as the robot domestic was much praised ('hilarious'), as was H.A.G.P.'s as Aunt Amy Habbijams. It was all adjudged 'a howling success'. The Christmas entertainment consisted of a concert and play ('A Mistake at the Manor'). Two performances were given, the first to the village and the domestic staff, after which there was a tea at which senior boys and the masters were waiters and general all-round helpers.

The Summer of 1931 was recorded by A.C.P. as the wettest for 25 years. Four awards were won: scholarships for Mike Palmer, Barry Kemball-Cook and Richard Saunders to Shrewsbury, St Paul's and Marlborough, respectively; a Radley exhibition for Keith Rumbo. This was a school record at that time and in the *Magazine* S.A.P. congratulated H.A.G.P. and the other masters. The scholars attended the first day of the Henley Regatta. Not until 1984 were four awards again won in the same year. There was also a notable victory by the 1st XI over Horris Hill, who were all out for 43 (Pawson 16, the last 8 wickets falling for 6 runs). There follows a gap in the *Magazine* records until the Summer of 1932, with accounts of a particularly successful cricket season of 11 victories by the 1st and 2nd XIs in 15 matches. Promising cricketers of this year were Jimmy Prioleau, Charles Weld Forester, Alan and Micky de Piro and Tim Bailey, all of whom did well at their public schools.

Fathers v. Sons cricket group, 1912.

The annual Fathers *v.* Sons cricket match had long been the great social event of the Summer term. Oliver Braybrooke remembers the fathers just after the Great War (and perhaps some of the mothers) coming out from either the Randolph or the Mitre Hotels in Oxford by horse-drawn brake: 'We boys decided that the wealthier parents stayed at the Randolph.' Gully Nickalls describes, in his book, the mid-morning arrival of parents as 'a moment of tremendous excitement. They seldom looked their best on arrival. The six-mile journey had been both leisurely and dusty.'

Tim Bailey recalls this occasion: 'Parents' day was very special, and all the boys put on their best clothes. Lunch was rushed through because around 2 o'clock the cars began driving up. The worried anticipation of one's own parents' arrival was lessened by comments on the cars ("Gosh, look at Bickmore's Peugeot") and eventually the family Clyno arrived. At this moment sentiment was muddled – pleasure at seeing one's father and mother and the safe back-to-the-womb feeling was often overshadowed by the worry as to whether they would be properly dressed. One's father was not much of a bother – he'd be in his regimental blazer and white flannels, with a hold-all containing his cricket boots and a suit to wear later. The agony was over

Conversation piece at Fathers' Match, 1904.

Tea after Fathers' Match in what was to become the rose garden, Summer 1925.

one's mother. Would she be smart enough? Might she have a new hat? If so, would it be as chic as Mrs Pike's (unlikely!)? There was a kind of parade from the rose garden to near the cricket pavilion, where deck chairs were lined up for the visitors – to us as important as the parade round the enclosure at Ascot became later – when one felt one's parents were under close scrutiny by their opposite numbers. Discipline was tried to the limit when one's mother greeted another whose progeny was a particular *bête noire*. The Fathers' Match got under way – of course the sun was always shining from a cloudless sky and there was only a mild breeze – and the only minor trauma was how one's father would perform. You didn't expect him to make as many runs as Weld Forester's, displaying an IZ belt. You prayed he would not miss a catch, and that his inadequate bowling would not be required. Soon the preparatory noises of tea made your attention stray from the cricket. Trestle tables were set up under the trees by the rose garden, and enormous gleaming metal urns shone on white tablecloths. There were strawberries and cream and cakes and every kind of high-cholesterol pass-keys to a boy's heart.'

Tim goes on: 'There was not at that time a theatre/concert-hall, so the theatrical entertainment in the evening was *al fresco*. *A Midsummer Night's Dream* [by V.K.D.W. in 1932] is the production I remember, particularly for being cast as Titania, a role engendering knowing smirks in one's school-mates. Scenery was improvised on the west side of the football pitch under the trees, and there were curtains behind which actors waiting to appear and

A Midsummer Night's Dream, *Summer 1932. Bottom and the fairies.*

the producer followed the action. The youngest boys were, of course, the fairies ['3rd Fairy . . . F. L. Pym'], the head or a very senior boy [Pat Cook] Oberon, the school clown [Richard Symonds] Bottom. I think we played barefoot, and I remember that a small sloping mound had been built for Titania so that she was in full view of the audience. Attended by her courtiers, "she" half lay on this mound waiting for the big scene with Bottom. A *papier mâché* wall was built for Pyramus and Thisbe, "to blink through with mine eyne". This well-intentioned rape of Shakespeare ended about the time darkness fell, and one said goodbye to one's parents still in drag and make-up.'

A parent is quoted in the *Magazine*: 'I was charmed and spellbound from the first note of music to the end of Puck [John Moon]'s beautifully spoken epilogue, and was sorry to come back to earth again, and to realise how busy the midges had been with us all. And so to supper – and what a supper! Who but Mrs Pike would have thought of such a perfect finish to the day as hot sausages and mash? What fun it all was! Fathers imbibing spirituous liquor, sons rushing round for second helpings of sausages, everyone talking at once and congratulating everyone else. Altogether one of the loveliest parties I have been to.'

Parental visits have always been occasions for car snobbery. The earliest mention is by Gully Nickalls. The parents of a boy called Hull 'were more affluent than the majority. They arrived in their own majestic Daimler. If memory serves me right their particular model was known as "The Silent Knight". Many boys were so overcome that they removed their caps in its presence.' When cars became more common, many boys were very self-conscious of their vehicle as it arrived in the yard. Roger Leigh's old Morris Oxford had 'cracked talc windows, and most other parents' cars [in the mid-1930] had glass ones. One would be very proud of it now.' Tim Bailey was relaxed about the family Clyno, but in the early 1950s Jonathan Stedall suffered when, 'amid the grand and shining chariots, there suddenly appeared my mother's scruffy little Austin Seven. The whole school, it seemed to me then, began to laugh.' Twenty years later, Tom Harley was 'embarrassed by our incredibly battered old Renault 4, parked conspicuously by an assembly line of gleaming BMWs and Mercedes's'.

Tim Bailey was also an exceptional golfer ('pretty certain to become a scratch player') and was largely responsible for the golf team's successes against Summer Fields and a team of 'Newbury Ladies' in the Summer of

My father and other skaters in the Marsh, December 1933.

1932. 'Nature notes' mention that many more boys were becoming keen naturalists. For this the school had to be grateful for the uncommon alkaline fen, which enabled Charles Weld Forester to find a perfect specimen of a leopard moth. A.C.P. was delighted, declaring that in all his 30 years at Cothill he had only once seen such a moth in the neighbourhood.

The Autumn term saw an outstandingly good football XI, with only one defeat by Horris Hill and 34 goals scored, with only 4 against. The Summer Fields *Magazine* correspondent wrote: 'It is right to say they were an excellent side – the best we have seen at any school for some years.' A debate on a Channel Tunnel was reported at great length. S.A.P. was in the chair and there were excellent speeches by some of the boys, including Alan de Piro (now a judge) and Pat Cook (later an ombudsman). Alan won an exhibition to Repton, and both got awards to Cambridge in 1938. The motion in favour of a tunnel was defeated by 13 votes to 6.

January and February 1933 produced 'good wintry weather' and many days of skating in the Marsh. 'We daily cleared more ground of reeds and soon had a rink as fascinating and varied as in 1929.' The slides, too, were in excellent condition and some very fast times recorded: 'On February 24 two most important records were broken – Sir Malcolm Campbell did 272 miles per hour on Daytona Beach, and the Cothill slide was covered in the equally alarming pace of 18 miles an hour (2 secs).' The Hon. Mrs Victor Bruce got rave notices for her lecture 'Flying Alone Round the World', especially for her 'femininity and guts with humour'.

The RAF Station at Abingdon had opened in 1932 and many boys immediately became involved. John Cartwright confesses, 'I'm afraid I was more interested in watching the Avro and Hawker "stringbag" planes taking off than in the soccer and hence, I think, Banky Boy [J. C. Banks]'s antipathy towards me'. Empire Day produced an air display which, according to Mike Atkin-Berry, 'distracted us during a cricket match. Hawker Hawks and Furies... thrilled small boys with their aerobatic displays.' Anthony Gill's father had known the Station Commander since the war: 'One great day he sent a staff car to collect Patrick and me, and we drove to the aerodrome and each went for a flight in an Avro, the Wingco flying it in the rear cockpit.'

A landmark in the development of the school came when work began on the New Hall, with dormitories above, in July 1933. Numbers were by now between 70 and 80, and this was considered ideal, but as S.A.P.'s editorial in the Autumn *Magazine* put it: 'We do not want to rest on our oars or get into any cut and dried routine. We wish to be constantly on the look out for any necessary changes or fresh ideas that may in any way improve the general standard: a school either goes forward or backward, hence these additions.'

A hard Winter in 1979, with the New Hall and dormitories above, which were built in 1933.

He writes that at Cothill 'real teamwork does exist and flourishes, and seldom can a school have had such a loyal, conscientious and efficient staff'.

It was, of course, the S.A.P./D.E.P. leadership which had been chiefly responsible for the increased numbers. They had been greatly helped, however, by good local friends such as Charles and Kathleen Gore, who had 'spread the word'. Another to do so was our family solicitor and friend, J. B. Rosher, who had negotiated the purchase of the school for just under £10,000. My parents were very excited by the new addition, as were the boys. The architect was an old boy-friend of my mother's, Gordon Hake, and of course there were family jokes that 'she had exchanged a Hake for a Pike'. The end result gave aesthetic pleasure as well as transforming much of the life of the school. Morning and evening prayers no longer had to take place in the Big Schoolroom. Thanks to the generosity of many parents (though there were some grumbles), the Hall was furnished with 80 specially-made wheelback chairs, each with the school crest and motto, '*Dum spiro spero*', on the back. There was a parquet floor for dancing and a raised stage which also served as a classroom when partitioned off. The stage curtains and the long window curtains were of green, lined silk, which were to last for 30 years. The Crittal french windows facing north and west opened on to the football field and the garden.

Nico Craven recalls: 'One particular memory is of S.A.P. crunching his way along the terrace outside the fine assembly hall before coming in through the french windows to take morning prayers.' No other member of the staff ever attended, there was no hymn, only a psalm for the day said alternately, a reading from the Bible by one of the prefects and prayers from *The Book of Common Prayer*. Francis Pym is among several contemporaries who have expressed gratitude for being made familiar with the words of the General Thanksgiving, read from the large, well-bound copy of the prayer book dated 1845. It mentions 'Adelaide the Queen Dowager' in the prayers for the Royal Family and includes the thanksgiving services for Charles, Martyr, and Gunpowder Treason. S.A.P.'s religious faith was simple and sincere, the result of his Nonconformist background.

From now on this Hall was to be the nearest thing to a chapel that the school has had. There has been an unbroken tradition of worship on Sundays at Dry Sandford Church. Since 1879 the boys have walked to church, where they have provided the choir and most of the congregation for matins, originally according to *The Book of Common Prayer*. This school service was, however, considerably modified, first after the publication of *The Alternative Service Book* and now has a distinctly ecumenical flavour, with little reference to either prayer book.

The Vicar of Dry Sandford with Shippon was, from 1911 to 1934, the Rev.

J.H. Kirkby, a short, rosy-faced figure. Hugh Barrett-Lennard says: 'I remember once, when Phillpots was very ill, he was asked if he would like to see Mr Kirkby, and he said "God save me from that". But actually the Vicar was a very mild person and had a funny pronunciation. I remember his saying one Ascension Day, "Today we'll have Aa-nte Communion", and I'm afraid, in my ignorance, I thought "Auntie Communion" was a person. The church had a very unreliable organ, for which a boy – we always liked getting the job – pumped from behind in the vestry. There'd be times when the thing would suddenly cipher, and there would be a long period of cipher interrupting the service – the sort of thing that every small boy enjoys. On one occasion an owl got into the little church and flew round during matins and ended up googling down from the lectern. It was a very great moment.' Another clergyman who is remembered from this time is the Rev. H.E. Salter. John Thomson describes him as 'the eminent Oxford historian', who helped the Vicar with the church services from the early 1920s, and adds: 'He became a great friend of mine in my undergraduate days as he struggled in his clerical suit through the mud with the New College and Magdalen Beagles in the Old Berkshire Vale. His daughter, Tiny Salter, "walked a puppy" for us.'

Above the New Hall was a second bathroom with four baths, a clothes room with lockers, where the clothes matron sewed and mended, and two dormitories, the larger of which contained 11 beds and became known as the

Senior Dormitory, 1933.

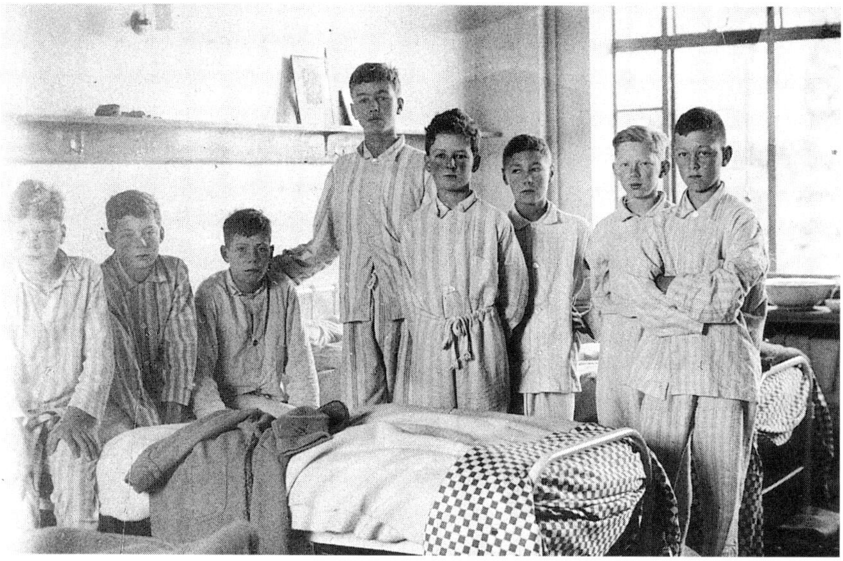

Senior Dormitory. Here the boys kept bound leather journals known as the 'Senior Dormitory Magazines', inspired by A.C.P., in which neatly-written accounts of school matches, lectures, entertainments and outings provide an additional record of the life of the school of over 50 years ago. The volume for 1933–37 survives. Micky de Piro, one of the school's legendary all-rounders, describes the opening of the New Hall on 9 December 1933: 'Mr Roxburgh made a very interesting and amusing speech to some two hundred people, who were then given a splendid tea and an entertainment, the first on the new stage.' A fortnight previously Dr Raymond Greene had lectured on the 1933 Everest Expedition. Neil Mackenzie ends his account of this: 'They found Malory's or Irvine's axe, which showed that one had slipped and dragged the other after him.'

In that Autumn term of 1933 the school had a piece of good fortune when S.A.P. persuaded Archer Vassall to give the senior boys Natural Science lectures on Monday evenings. A.V. was then a retired Harrow housemaster living in Oxford. As a young man he had been on the staff of the Dragon School, and in 1898 he had written an article entitled 'Natural Science in Preparatory Schools' in the *Preparatory Schools Review*. He had made a plea for 'letting the imagination and observation of a boy be devoted to the study of nature under the direction of the fact-holder in the person of the master'. No laboratory was necessary. For one hour a week 'the cricket ground, the sky and the kitchen will afford ample material for five years' work.... Why is such a flower coloured, another not? Why is a chestnut prickly? Why do the clouds go in such a direction? Why does such an animal live in one place, another elsewhere? What effects does heat have on matter?... Boys will come armed with the most appalling questions. Insist on their attempting an explanation, giving reasons clearly and lucidly.... An assistant master will find at the end of a term of such an hour every week that he knows a great deal more than at the beginning, and that most books of reference are expensive and bad.'

Now, 35 years later, according to John Cartwright, 'we were treated to a series of fascinating lectures on elementary natural history and chemistry. ...There were illustrative practical experiments/demonstrations which changed my life by getting my feet on the Science "ladder" when it came to specialising at Winchester....I always remember H_2SO_4 + sugar bubbling up in a sort of black sludge and overflowing on to the demonstration desk.' Dick de la Hey remembers how 'Mr Vassall had such apoplectic fits of coughing that one feared for his life'; a third describes the lectures as one of the 'reliefs from the curriculum'. This would have delighted A.V., who maintained that the ideal education and the ideal curriculum did not coincide; 'the former would only benefit the boy, whereas the latter brings in the shekels'. The boys were very appreciative and wrote up weekly accounts of these lectures in considerable detail, with some neat diagrams, in the 'Senior Dormitory Magazine'. The subjects covered over the next seven years included: Pasteur, bacteria, vaccination, inoculation and anti-toxin (none for smallpox at the time), leeches, anthropods, colour and colouration, silkworms, molluscs, solids and fluids, the four main substances (nitrogen, carbon, hydrogen, oxygen), pollination, the human body (blood, spleen, stomach, liver, glands, veins, etc.).

According to the Autumn *Magazine*, apart from a good cricket XI, captained by Micky de Piro, the Summer term had seen a scholarship trip on the river, during which 'the boy Figg fell in and had to have tea dressed like Gandhi'. A short Empire Day service prompted S.A.P. to write: 'It seems to us that it is of vital importance . . . to instil into the rising generation some idea of the duties and ideals of the great British Empire, trying to help the rest of the world and to give them a friendly lead towards general goodwill and peaceful prosperity.' The patriotic theme was continued in the next volume, taking up King George V's Christmas broadcast, in which he spoke of 'the unshakeable sanity, invincible patience and tireless goodwill of all my peoples': 'Let us pray', writes S.A.P., 'that boys . . . may be wisely guided by all here towards gaining the necessary strength and nobility of character which is so essential these days in the future leaders of our race.' He was at this time much impressed by General Seeley's *Fear and be Slain* – recently described by one who remembers it 50 years later as 'a singularly reactionary book of reminiscences which does not bear re-reading: I tried the other day'.

S.A.P.'s enthusiasm for games and the Empire is encapsulated in a memory of Richard Symonds's: 'Games seemed the main interest of the Head Master, particularly soccer. When we lost a match against another school, I remember him coming into the Dining Hall at our tea time and saying: "You will notice that there is no jam for tea. That is because the 1st XI has let down the school, has let down the country and has let down the Empire".' Richard also quotes a song which he says was sung at one of the Winter entertainments. The chorus ran:

> 'We're all anti-red and we're proud of it,
> We're Britons and we sing aloud of it;
> If the Red, White and Blue
> Isn't good enough for you,
> If you don't like our Empire, then clear out of it.'

Both stories are probably apocryphal, but 'no jam for tea' was certainly part of local prep-school mythology when I joined the staff in 1947.

An undefeated football 1st XI in 1933 was commented on in the Summer Fields *Magazine*: 'Cothill have once again turned out a really good side, and we congratulate them on a remarkable season. ... They scored 61 goals and had but 4 scored against them in 10 matches.' Geoffrey Bolton and two other SF masters came over to watch the Horris Hill match, which Cothill won 2–0. April 1934 saw the retirement of Mr Kirkby; £50 was raised by the school and the village, and the Vicar was heard murmuring, 'My last Arsh Wednesday, my last Arsh Wednesday'. The Summer was unusually hot and dry, with temperatures of 80°+ on 11 days. The spring failed to fill the bathing-pool, so that there was no swimming in the exceptionally hot weather. The 1st and 2nd cricket XIs lost only one match apiece, Micky de Piro being an inspiring 1st XI captain. The 'Under-10' beat the Dragon 121–75. Two or three privet-hawk eggs and caterpillars were seen for the first time in living memory, crowning three years' efforts to introduce the species. V.K.D.W. produced *Henry IV, Part I* in the open air. The *Magazine* reported that 'during the term chest expansion improved steadily, and very few boys failed to pass the standard 4 inches; John Matthew did 5¾ inches – the best for over ten years'. A.C.P. was in his element with these statistics.

W.T.C. (Waltsham) Maynard, subsequently Head Master of St Andrew's, Woking, was on the Cothill staff from September 1934 to April 1935. His memories and extracts from his diary give a young master's-eye-view: 'I found the staff included five other bachelor assistant masters. ... Four of us lived in the cottage, just across the road, which had an outside loo and no electric light. Waite and Butler were generally sociable, but all of us were highly individual and went our own ways.'

Food figures prominently in his diary. 'Our first meal, taken with the Pikes, included cocktails, claret and grouse. A butler, Newton, ministered to our wants.' Later in the term, on 28 November, 'a special staff dinner included caviare, sole with mushrooms, pheasant, ice cream with hot chocolate sauce, and dessert, and was accompanied by sherry, champagne and liqueurs.' After dinner there were staff games and competitions: 'I won first prize of 100 Turkish cigarettes. As a non-smoker I prudently exchanged them later at a shop for two pipes, 50 Virginia cigarettes and five ounces of tobacco, to be distributed as presents. I then found out that the original prize had a value of 12/6*d*.' W.T.C.M. noted the prices of everything: 'Half a bottle of burgundy cost 2/6*s* and a pub lunch at Wantage of cheese sandwiches and ginger ale cost me 1/3*d*. . . . A topic of recurring mention in the diary was the staff car, called by Phillimore "Jeremy Bolton". . . . "Jan. 25: The new staff car . . . a beast to start and to reverse. Jan. 26: The car never budged from the garage all day, no one being able to start it. . . . Feb. 11: I was asked by Butler to take him to Abingdon and Marcham. . . . I spent half an hour at the car in vain." . . . Perhaps this explains why, three days later, Phillimore elected to walk into Abingdon to see the film *Queen Christina*.' W.T.C.M. added that it was fair to say that J.B. did move at times, and that his bill for 253 miles came to 10/8*d*, or ½*d* a mile.

There was one particular staff anxiety: 'The supervision of 59 boys through 9 lavatories in 15 minutes. The Head Master seemed totally unaware of the stress this exercise caused to all concerned.' It was carried out by the Duty Master, and W.T.C.M. writes: 'Masters went on duty for a whole week at a time. . . . This long spell caused a good deal of strain and is not recommended.' Another criticism was the 'unusual feature of the division of the whole school into sets for each subject. . . . It sounds ideal for the boys, but does not breed contentment among the masters. . . . A parallel scheme was for masters to set exams for boys in sets taken by others. This also caused considerable friction at times, although in theory it may have appeared excellent, and corresponding to a neutral referee for school matches.'

How did the Head Master appear to the boys? Francis Pym was one who appreciated S.A.P.'s intensely human side: 'He played with us as well as taught us. His Sunday evening sessions in his study with the gramophone were always enjoyed. They were a lively mixture of music and humour, Cicely Courtneidge songs, Albert and the Lion, and so on. He also used to spring the most lovely surprises: an unexpected whole holiday; a trip in a Thames launch for the whole school; or concluding Guy Fawkes's Night by allowing us to let off fireworks in the squash court – until the smoke was too thick. He enjoyed all this as much as we did. These and other activities provided excitement and enthusiasm and enjoyment, and gave us a rounded approach to life.' Franko Seymour 'can still see him to this day, running full speed at the slides on a frosty morning and enjoying it as much as we were'.

Ten years later it was much the same story. Dan Massey remembers how, in 1946, 'Sam appeared, as was his wont, to bid us all good night, a word here and there, a little joke, at which we all laughed, and then he suddenly shot out his hand, bounded over to me and said, "You can have your colours!", with which the whole dorm dissolved into cheers. I slept that night in a shower of

'A trip in a Thames launch for the whole school', Summer 1934. My sisters and a friend in the foreground.

My parents relaxing with prefects on a Henley excursion, Summer 1934. My father is wearing his 'co-respondent' shoes.

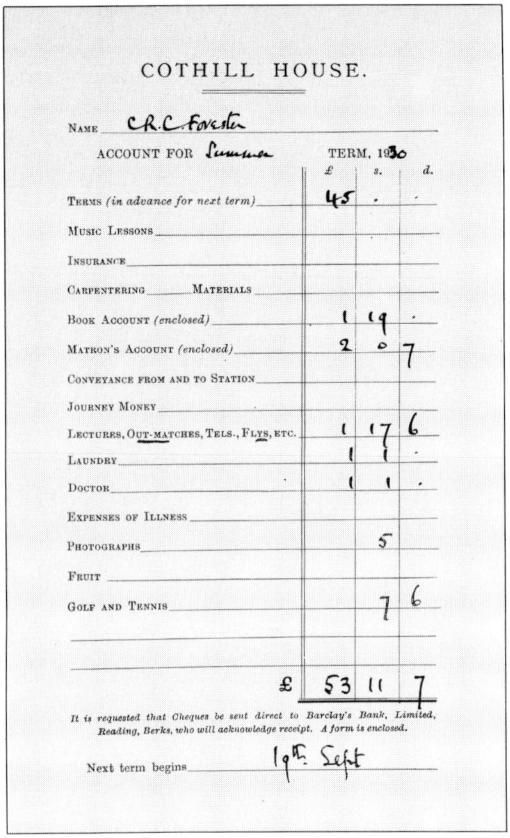

COTHILL HOUSE.

NAME C.R.C. Forester

ACCOUNT FOR Summer TERM, 1930

	£	s.	d.
TERMS (in advance for next term)	45	.	.
MUSIC LESSONS			
INSURANCE			
CARPENTERING MATERIALS			
BOOK ACCOUNT (enclosed)	1	19	.
MATRON'S ACCOUNT (enclosed)	2	0	7
CONVEYANCE FROM AND TO STATION			
JOURNEY MONEY			
LECTURES, OUT-MATCHES, TELS., FLYS, ETC.	1	17	6
LAUNDRY	1	1	.
DOCTOR	1	1	.
EXPENSES OF ILLNESS			
PHOTOGRAPHS		5	
FRUIT			
GOLF AND TENNIS		7	6
£	53	11	7

It is requested that Cheques be sent direct to Barclay's Bank, Limited, Reading, Berks, who will acknowledge receipt. A form is enclosed.

Next term begins 19th Sept

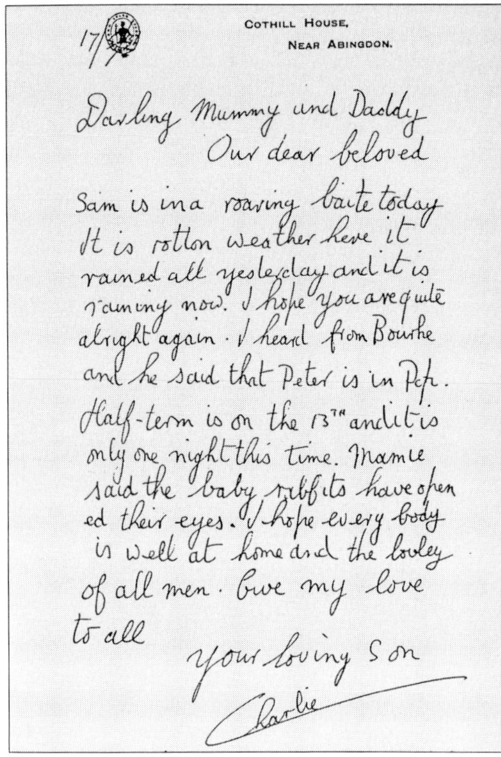

COTHILL HOUSE,
NEAR ABINGDON.

17/5

Darling Mummy and Daddy
Our dear beloved

Sam is in a roaring baite today
It is rotton weather here it
rained all yesterday and it is
raining now. I hope you are quite
alright again. I heard from Bourke
and he said that Peter is in Pop.
Half-term is on the 13th and it is
only one night this time. Mamie
said the baby rabbits have open
ed their eyes. I hope every body
is well at home and the lovley
of all men. Give my love
to all

your loving Son

Charlie

LEFT *Account, Summer 1930. It is in my father's handwriting.*
RIGHT *Letter home, 17 May 1931.*

stars.' He was a painstaking and successful coach of all games, golf and lawn tennis included, until he was well into his sixties. Another recalls: 'He would instruct us in the business of keeping the ball down when shooting. We had a suspicion that his smart black brogues with pointed toes were more suitable for this than our stubby-toed boots, but he certainly could rifle shots into the corners of the net with considerable force.' Five years later, Roger Carrington was struck by his energy and enthusiasm: 'His long stints at the nets of crafty off-breaks, his speed as a referee on the soccer field were prodigious.' His boyishness and sense of fun never left him. Roger Leigh remembers him enjoying 'being trundled fast down the dormitory corridor squashed into a laundry basket on wheels'. He needed excitement, and this he found in his great hobby, racing on the flat. Bev Stanier was one of many boys who appreciated this (though some parents found it very inconvenient): 'The Summer term always ended in time for Goodwood. . . . Major Pike was often away on a Saturday afternoon.'

His study was a friendly place, even to some defaulters. One of these was Johnny Manningham-Buller, who had been doing no work. 'I thought that this time I really had to give him a fright', S.A.P. told us afterwards, 'so I pitched in pretty strong. After I had finished, there was a long pause. "Sir, do you know my rabbit has just had babies?"' Humphrey Stone, although he recalls 'the nerve-racking wait outside', played, as a homesick seven-year-old with Dinky toys inside. There would be a constant crowd of boys buying something from S.A.P.'s 'shop', mostly batteries, wire and bulbs for desk displays; or in the Summer, cricket bats, balls, pads, gloves and pocket scoring books. Here he wrote all his letters by hand with a 'squeezer' or a 'J' nib in a long pen-holder, dipped into a large square glass ink-well. (Julia Budworth recalls being told that at the beginning of the war S.A.P. would not allow fountain-pens in the school, thinking them 'foul things'.) In the early days he made out by hand each boy's account. Thus, in the Summer term 1930, Charles Weld Forester's account with extras came to £53.11*s*.7*d*; the extras included 'Text books and Protractor' 2/9*d*, 'Sing-Song Book' 6*d*, 'Squash Racquet' 16/6*d*. It was Charles who began a letter home: 'Our dear beloved Sam is in a roaring baite today.' Michael Knutsford remembers 'knocking on his study – "come in" – smile on his face – always put one at ease. I was told the facts of life and not to mix with solicitous older boys at Eton – very embarrassing for me.' To another, S.A.P. was less specific. 'Now, John, you may not know about the birds and the bees, but – er – don't worry, old chap.' This was all that Johnny Peel can recall of a session which lasted 'slightly less than two minutes'. The schoolboy howler 'A wedge is something you put in widows to keep them quiet on windy nights' was quoted by S.A.P. in his opening remarks in one number of the *Magazine*. As Alastair Aberdeen has remarked: 'I was never quite sure where your father stood, morally speaking.'

In 1934, for the first time, S.A.P. encouraged *Magazine* contributions from the boys, such as a poem or a description of a 'locker show'. These were a feature of the time in the six-locker desks of the Big Schoolroom. Tableaux such as 'African Jungle by Moonlight', 'Sea Scene', 'Loch Ness Monster', were constructed out of various materials, illuminated by bulbs and batteries bought from S.A.P. and viewed through spy-holes for two drawing-pins a peep. Anthony Gill recalls the king of shows in his time was the jungle show. 'It consisted of a large mass of miscellaneous plants and leaves, placed in a jungle form and illuminated with bulbs hidden in the undergrowth. Model animals were placed in various strategic locations.... One year somebody had a series of groups of lights which were connected in turn, while a commentary was given on the events in each set piece. . . . After a few weeks the vegetation used to begin to rot – a putrid smell.' In other lockers there began to appear 'roller-pill tracks'. These were plasticine roads, bridges and tunnels on the sloping backs of open locker lids, with ball-bearings to run down them. Described as 'an extremely good form of wet-weather amusement', they were to remain a feature of school life until the alteration of the Schoolroom and the disappearance of the old six-locker desks in 1980. In another variation, John Rucker and Tim Freeman 'got two adjacent lockers and bored a connecting hole between them. Inside the two lockers we constructed a miniature golf course with tees and greens, bunkers and other hazards. The balls were small ball-bearings and the clubs shafted with matchsticks. It was a great success and earned us a lot of drawing-pins, and although it must have made an awful mess of the two desks, your father was very tolerant and played several "rounds" himself.'

The 1st football XI was taken to see Arsenal *v.* Oxford University in the Autumn of 1934. This sort of fixture is inconceivable nowadays. After the match S.A.P. wrote that 'it showed the differences in style and pace between the present-day amateurs and professionals. The latter were quicker on the ball and more dangerous near goal.' The 1st XI contained only one boy from the previous year's victorious XI, and after beating Summer Fields 5–1, were beaten by Horris Hill 0–12 – luckily S.A.P. was unable to watch this match.

In the Spring term of 1935 various golf matches were played, with two defeats by Summer Fields and the loss of an unbeaten record on the home course. Against the masters the boys' play was 'very sound', but their opponents 'gave a rather lifeless display'. A squash match was played against Major Horsfall's team in his own court, a fixture which was much appreciated, as it entailed the whole day away from school. In the Summer the Silver Jubilee of the King and Queen was celebrated; tea parties were given for the children of Cothill village and for the old-age-pensioners. Almost the entire village was taken to London in 'two *char-à-bancs*' to see the decorations, ages five to 80, many of whom had never been to London before. The leaving boys were taken to the Naval Review at Spithead as the guests of Mr and Mrs Gemmell on their yacht *Romany Rye*. An hour's cruise by motor launch, lunch and supper, fireworks, and a 4 a.m. return made an unforgettable expedition.

The prefects had weekly talks, plus cakes and lemonade, with S.A.P. This was said to be 'a helpful innovation to all concerned'. The January 1936 editorial concludes: 'Away with all dullness, moodiness, pottering and aimless dreaming; whenever this condition is seen to be attacking anyone,

On board the Romany Rye *for the Silver Jubilee Naval Review.*

approach the victim quietly, tap him on the back (don't shove him over) and say "Hi! You can't do that there 'ere!"' (a current catch-phrase from the music hall). V.K.D.W. produced Sheridan's *St Patrick's Day*. General verdict – best ever – was endorsed by some 70 from the village. A debate motion that 'Lectures in our schooldays give greater pleasure than Entertainments' was carried 26 to 7.

Entertainments and lectures were a feature of school life in pre-television years. A flavour of their quality can be caught from the pages of the 'Senior Dormitory Magazine' for the Autumn term 1933. The first entertainer was a Mr Sydney. His best items were sketches entitled 'The Barber's Chair', 'The Village Council' and 'The Marriage Breakfast'. He also sang sea shanties and a chorus 'Round the Next Bend'. The customary three cheers given at the end were apparently well-deserved. A month later it was the turn of Mr Hubert Leslie. Drawings and balancing tricks were considered especially clever by the reviewer. A sketch on the blackboard of things Robinson Crusoe collected, when turned upside down, became 'a fashionable lady walking down

Bond Street'. He balanced a glass of water at the end of a long thin stick on his nose and played the mouth organ at the same time. While cutting out a silhouette of a girl he told a story of 500 words, each beginning with the letter 'S'. On another occasion a Mr Playfair gave a conjuring display which was considered first class. Mr Vernon Lee was 'frightfully funny' when entertaining boys and parents after the opening of the New Hall. Examples of his humour were: 'Take your pick' while offering rock cakes, and a competition for making funny faces which was won by an old lady who said she was not playing.

Lectures during that term included such titles as 'Lawrence of Arabia and King Feisal', 'A Week in a Deep-sea Trawler', 'Dr Barnado's Homes'. Other favourites were Captain Knight's 'Golden Eagle', Mr Ramshaw, and Chief Os-ke-non-ton, in full feather. The latter had changed in one of the sick-rooms, where he detected an unpleasant smell: 'It's a morgue', he complained. He then proceeded to make a fire on stage in thirty seconds, 'using only the traditional friction stick and mouse-nest tinder'. Malcolm Campbell, Captain Evans of Scott's Expedition and Amy Johnson came to tell of their adventures; P. G. H. Fender and E. W. Swanton to talk about cricket. In 1936 the school was presented with a Bell & Howell cinema camera and a projector. From now on the school enjoyed weekly silent films, and in an era that produced some of the best talking films the boys were more than happy to watch silent 'home movies' taken by S.A.P. of school life and a Hellenic cruise; Wild West dramas, Charlie Chaplin, Buster Keaton and Laurel & Hardy; cartoons like 'Felix the Cat' and 'Out of the Inkwell'. The worst punishment was to miss films.

On 21 January 1936 King George V died. The top three Latin classes were taken to London to see the Royal Funeral. S.A.P. wrote in the *Magazine* a long editorial on the nation's great sorrow and of confidence in the new King: 'He has already given proof of some of his father's great qualities.' He ended: 'Long may King Edward VIII reign over us.' When later in the same year, the King abdicated and became the Duke of Windsor, there was no mention in the *Magazine*. In that Spring term an Appeal was made for the restoration of Dry Sandford Church organ. Only 100 guineas were needed to restore it to pristine condition. The same term the Group system was started: the school was divided into Carthaginians, Gauls, Greeks, Parthians, Romans and Trojans. Each Group had its leader, and competed with the others by means of Good and Bad Marks. A wall ladder was constructed in the Big Schoolroom, up which climbed six wooden figures in distinctive armour and head-dress. In those early days, a Good Mark was really worth something, and a Bad

Mark was a disgrace. Years later, with inflation of Good and Bad Marks, the ladder was replaced by the present system of running totals.

H. R. Bryant joined the staff and was immediately nicknamed 'Brymay' by the boys. Tall, balding, with a short moustache, he invariably wore loud check plus-fours. I remember driving him in the new family Studebaker at 90 m.p.h. along the recently opened three-lane stretch of road between Hinksey and Botley. Now it is part of the dual-carriageway ring road, but then it was almost always empty of traffic and an ideal race track. Humphrey declared himself 'frightened to death', but as always was tolerant of the excesses of the young. According to Bev Stanier, he was 'a great schoolmaster, everybody liked him. He kept order well, taught well [top Maths and second Latin], and his interests were innumerable.' High among these was county cricket, and many will recall his announcing the scores as he presided over the large round table in the Dining Hall.

The yard, Summer, 1904.

During the Summer holidays a new kitchen was built. This involved closing the gap between the lamp-room and clock-tower to form a continuous façade. Above the kitchen, sickrooms, a bathroom and a matron's bedroom completed a considerable extension. What had been the kitchen was transformed into a sitting-room and extended into its present shape. The project had been too much for Gordon Hake, but luckily a local builder proved capable of doing the job. Shortly afterwards the gas-lighting was replaced by mains electricity throughout the school. These changes did not mean increasing numbers: 'We have decided to limit them to about eighty. We so want to be sure that we are doing all that is humanly possible to help each individual boy to the fullest extent . . . to have the necessary strong and good character for their lives after leaving Cothill.' The limitation of numbers did not last. There was an increasing demand for places as the school became more and more Eton-orientated.

J. C. Banks left to run a successful coaching establishment in Sussex. The following term N. A. Keith joined the staff. He had played golf for Cambridge and soon went round the school course in 26, which remains the record. He was a most friendly and pleasant young man and is remembered with affection by boys who enjoyed talking to him during walks. Although he left after some eighteen months to go into the City, he appreciated S.A.P.: 'The great thing about your father is that he never asks one to do anything he wouldn't do himself.'

Alastair Keith took the place of A. C. Phillips, who had retired after 100 terms at Cothill. He has been described as 'a great favourite with the boys and a great motivator in the classroom'. Alan de Piro says, 'I absorbed meticulous, indeed obsessive and often irritating tidiness from him'. Many recall his sense of drama, as when he came into the dormitories one morning, chanting 'Crystal Palace razed to the ground by fire', threw up the blinds and stalked out. In the classroom, Chris Barnett asserts, 'it was really well worth while breaking wind or getting someone else to. Without fail this used to produce a cry of "Disgusting! My dear little boy, you wouldn't do that in your mother's drawing-room, would you?" This was usually followed by a dramatic performance with matches lit and applied to rolled up blotting paper, which was wafted about in the manner of a high priest with incense.'

A.C.P. was replaced as dormitory master by V.K.D.W., who thus added a further onerous duty to his many other activities. Stanley Chattey remembers 'his nightly warning: "Dressing-gowns off, lights out and no more talking" – a phrase often repeated by my family; an admirable title for an autobiography of an elderly author'.

The school closed for 48 hours for the Coronation of King George VI on 12 May 1937. The grounds were opened to the village, with sports and a supper. 340 sat down, and the Rev. H. E. and Mrs Salter gave each villager a Coronation mug. V.K.D.W. had written a poem, 'Vivat Rex', which was chosen by the *Bristol Observer* to be presented to the King to mark his Coronation. More junketings took place when my 21st birthday was celebrated on 12 June. There was an outdoor sit-down supper on the Major Game football field for all the boys, staff and villagers employed at the school. John Rucker recalls what followed: 'Your father hired a travelling fair which encamped on one of the football fields, and for a whole evening we were allowed as many free goes as we liked on the roundabouts, etc. I still remember it fifty years later, and it is a good example of how clever your father was at knowing what gave pleasure to small boys.'

The same term the school joined the Boy Scout Movement. As already mentioned, M. J. Dauglish had had a prejudice against it, and this antipathy lasted until the arrival on the staff of C. (Charles) Wynn. His enthusiasm and knowledge of scouting won S.A.P. over. The Cothill Troop – 24th North Berks – was started on a voluntary basis. There were three patrols, Stags, Hawks and Peckers, and the 'Log Book' of the Stags survives. From it we learn that scouting took place on Sundays and Thursdays on the golf course and in the Marsh. On 20 June there was an Investiture, and towards the end of the term some of the scouts camped out. Wolf Cubs were also started by my sister Diana and her friend Lavinia Holland-Hibbert. The latter kept a detailed 'Log Book', containing such remarks as: 'Bad meeting; too much shouting and inattention. . . . Thorpe will never make a cub, as can't skip.' Lavinia's brother Michael writes: 'Sandy Stirling and Jeremy Thorpe were the favoured Wolf Cubs and captains of the pack. J.T. with a huge round head on a thin body and legs – a description which I have reminded him of since.' (Jeremy Thorpe was subsequently leader of the Liberal Party.) My sister Audrey remembers how his mother made a great impression by wearing a monocle and having a bird of prey attached to her wrist.

Wolf Cubs and a camp fire with my sister Diana, July 1939.

That Summer a successful cricket XI had some notable victories, including one over Swanbourne in which Graham Pearson took all 10 wickets for 34 runs. In the Autumn David Leggett went round the golf course in 29. He was probably the best golfer the school has produced, and he went on to captain Cambridge in 1946. His widow has written: 'Cothill must have been a very super school.... David always spoke with affection of it – a very sound balance between discipline and humane understanding. He also mentioned: cream on porridge because Major Pike liked it; bowls of strawberries on parents' day; special menus in the sick bay; golf matches with Major Pike. Rather a lot of food items, but no doubt looming large in a schoolboy's life.' Tony Holland and his brother Tim would certainly agree. Tony's memories include 'the endless competition in one-upmanship in birthday cakes, with the Palmers having theirs delivered from Huntley & Palmer in shapes such as the *Queen Mary*, and my mother rushing to Fortnum & Mason to go one better'. Gay Kindersley remembers his father brought the cake 'in a small plane. This caused great excitement, but resulted in heartbroken tears from me during my birthday tea when I heard the plane flying off.' When Tim Holland was recovering from an ear operation, his aunt sent him a hamper from Fortnums which included caviare. 'When your mother visited me she asked me if there was anything I wanted. I replied could she persuade Matron to let me have toast instead of bread. Oh, and could I have a lemon?!'

A novelty at the end of the Autumn term was the challenging of an unbeaten soccer 1st XI by an unbeaten Sunningdale School XI. The challengers won, and the occasion proved to be a forerunner of the yearly soccer match between the two schools which has been played over the last 20 years. 1938 started with an epidemic of mild measles which almost every boy caught. This caused considerable anxiety at the time, for in those days infectious diseases were the greatest worry for a preparatory-school headmaster – far worse than Common Entrance. 'We have been public benefactors. The dread measles has been defeated, ... a quiet prayer of thanks is offered up.' Despite measles, a four-boy team came 3/14 in Foster Knowles's inter-schools Latin competition, with Michael Demarest 3/55 in the individual competition.

The Summer term of 1938 was relatively carefree in spite of the threat of war. The 1st XI was only once defeated, Tom Metcalfe being an exceptionally good batsman. V.K.D.W. produced *The Tempest*, played outdoors in stormy weather, 'the high wind, bending the trees in noisy rustling gusts, threatened at times to drown the voices of the actors altogether'. For once he put his thoughts on paper: 'Every fresh play we study, learn and perform not only affords us great fun in acting, but teaches us a sense of poetic values, an appreciation of dramatic situations and the true essence of humour.' He

Another unbeaten 1st XI, 1986. The Berkshire Downs are in the background.

emphasised 'the *esprit de corps* which it engenders, since each player soon realises that he is contributing to a finished whole; the part of the "speechless super" is as real as that of the leading character; while the good-humoured chaff of rehearsals helps to cure self-consciousness'. Nowadays the therapeutic value of school and house plays is recognised, but in 1938 team work was often associated in public and prep schools exclusively with games. My father was indeed enlightened in his encouragement of so much 'play acting'.

The Munich Crisis, and the year's breathing space obtained by Chamberlain, gives a certain poignancy to the last academic year of peace at Cothill. S.A.P. urged everyone to show 'renewed vigour and zest; aim high; dare all for the right'; ending with two verses from Whitman's 'Pioneers, O Pioneers'. The shadow of things to come fell on the scouts. An entry in the Stags' 'Log Book' of 29 September reads: 'We all went into the gym where various masters were getting out the gas masks.' All were detailed to such jobs as fixing valves to the respirators, fixing head-pieces, and packing. 'They were then all stored in the place near the sweets', where presumably they remained until the outbreak of war. Later in the term the scouts were told by C. Wynn that he was leaving, and so with the new year scouting stopped, though the cubs continued. In a debate, the timely motion 'That this House would approve of Compulsory Military Service' was lost by 10 votes to 30. S.A.P. commented: 'We cannot yet be quite sure that the danger is over; the scheme for National Service announced by Sir John Anderson is to be fully considered within these next months.'

The *Magazine* describing the Summer term of 1939 has seven pages missing, and the main interest lies in the highly successful cricket season. Six XIs were fielded, with only one defeat, 21 wins and 4 draws, the 1st XI winning 10 and losing none. Dick de la Hey remembers, 'as part of the unbeaten cricket team, being rewarded with a trip to Whipsnade Zoo, where Dorothy Pike was forced to hurry the 1st XI away from the monkey-house whose incumbents' behaviour had become embarrassing'.

Not everyone enjoyed himself, however. One new boy of that term writes: 'I suppose inevitably it was partly my own fault that I hated Cothill from 1939 to 1941, but there was very severe bullying over this period. I understand that your father and mother could not bring themselves to believe that this was happening at their school.' As he subsequently went to Gordonstoun where he was 'blissfully happy', it is clear that the life of a 'loner' at Cothill was perhaps harder then than now. His opinion that 'small boys are notoriously unpleasant to each other' is a recurring theme among those who have published books about their schooldays in the 1930s. I am glad, however, to have the flip side of the record of boys echoing the song 'Spread a Little Happiness'.

One such was Dick de la Hey, one of a dozen or so new boys in the Christmas term of 1935: 'I think I was lucky to experience the last years of when the going was good. Phillips' atlas showed a large proportion of the earth's surface coloured pink. The Royal Navy when viewed in the *Illustrated London News* in battle array was larger than any other force afloat. Imperial preference was the vogue and the pound was mightier by far than the dollar. Arriving with my trunk filled with the required linen and clothing, I knew nothing of such matters. Hurst, the butler, immaculate and polite as ever, opened the door to my parents and myself and soon I was in the awe-inspiring presence of S.A.P. For the next five years I remained in his and Dorothy's care. I have been aware ever since of my good fortune in coming under the influence of these two people and have always been able to look back on those happy years in their charge.'

6

WORLD WAR II AND BACK TO PEACETIME

By 3 September 1939, my mother had somehow managed to black out the whole school. My sister Audrey remembers yards of velvet and tweed ('we all had our best coats made of them after the war') being used for the front and back doors, as well as a mass of cheaper material. Someone with a sewing-machine in the rose garden was working flat out to make curtains. All windows were painted with anti-blast glue in one day, and in the dormitories and classrooms wooden blinds were fitted each night into specially constructed slats. The result was a most effective black-out, strictly enforced, with a system of heavy inner curtains to prevent light escaping when anyone went to and from outside classrooms at night.

I had joined the Scots Guards from Oxford in September 1938, and as a 'Munich Boy' had served with the 1st Battalion at Windsor. The order for general mobilisation had come through during a Battalion cricket match, and the game was finished before we began to move to Chelsea Barracks. I did my first King's Guard on 2 September in bearskin and tunic, and we were relieved by the New Guard wearing service dress, respirators and tin hats. In the meantime war had been declared, the air-raid sirens had sounded within 30 minutes, and I had taken the Colour down into the very well-appointed shelter at St James's Palace. Some ten of the household were there too, and as doors banged nearby a cockney voice said: 'They're comin' over in their thousands.' However, the 'all clear' soon sounded; it was said later that the Duke of Windsor had returned to England unexpectedly and was off course.

Neither staff nor boys at Cothill were anticipating air-raids, and no special shelter had been provided, although my father had an extensive wine cellar which could have been used for a proportion of the school in the event of a raid. As is well known, nothing of the sort occurred in England until after the Battle of Britain in 1940, and, at first, life at Cothill continued much as in pre-war days, except for food and petrol rationing. Like a good quartermaster my mother found ways of supplementing the rations. Christopher Arnander writes that 'parents with rural properties gave generously. I remember enjoying my first taste of venison at Cothill.' Dick de la Hey recalls that 'the steady stream of military aircraft from Abingdon airfield that flowed around and over the school was a constant source of fascination for the boys and annoyance for the masters. At some stage the machines changed from their beautiful "Empire Air Day" silver livery to the ominous dark tones of camouflage paint.' According to Philip Duncombe, there was in the Autumn term 1939 'a general feeling that our lives were about to undergo a great change, a little "spy fever", and "hunt the conchie" among the staff. Hindell must be a spy (appearance, name, everything about him seemed Germanic to many of us); Waite came top as a conchie for he was artistic and wore a bow tie; Butler was OK because of his one arm, and Phillimore was considered to have done his bit by being shell-shocked in the 1914–18 war.' H. F. Hindell, who is mentioned here for the first time, had joined the staff in 1935. He was a severe-looking man, bald, with glasses and a thin, pale face. Surprisingly, though, he was something of a 'lady-killer'. Known to the boys as 'The Worm', he was an efficient and exacting teacher, who was to serve the school well for another three years. S.A.P. was just 50 and, therefore, too old for military service. Certain of the younger staff had left, but the rest were at their posts and were not expecting the war to last long.

A hint of 'phoney war' is apparent in the pages of the *Magazine* for the Autumn term and for the Spring term of 1940. S.A.P. had written that 'the fighting spirit and morale of Germany is not equal to what it has been in the past'. V.K.D.W. produced *She Stoops to Conquer*, having run out of Sheridan. The 'Senior Dormitory Magazine' reported: 'The play went perfectly and no one made a mistake. The audience of parents and boys was slightly unresponsive compared with the village, but they all enjoyed themselves very much.... Not so many people as usual because of the petrol rationing. ... The play was at 3 o'clock instead of 6 o'clock because of the black-out.'

Wartime transport, 1943. '... we are safer with less petrol'.

The Carol Service at the end of term was held in the New Hall for the first time. Over a hundred Christmas cards were received from Old Boys. S.A.P. wrote: 'After six months of war . . . Cothill has not been adversely affected by war conditions. . . . Let us leave it that we are safer with less petrol.' Food rationing had added 'fresh interest and variety' to the daily menu. It was bitterly cold, snow curtailed all games, but more than 60 boys skated: 'We will not easily forget the wintry beauty of our afternoons, with the sun going down amid the trees – trees exquisite in their covering of ice, snow and frost.' There was an impromptu concert on Easter Sunday and the Pedagogues returned after some years, the cast including my parents and Diana and Audrey in an extended version of Harry Tate's sketch 'Motoring'. A silent film, Edgar Wallace's *The Clue of the New Pin*, included John Gielgud in the cast. The Senior Dormitory gave a puppet show to certain masters and matrons, a comic representation of Lord Haw-Haw broadcasting in English from Germany.

The German invasion of the Low Countries and France in May 1940, the evacuation of the British Expeditionary Force from Dunkirk and the Battle of Britain had all taken place by the time the next *Magazine* appeared in September. In the editorial S.A.P. wrote: 'We see Great Britain truly and magnificently "Great" these days. . . . Churchill's dauntless valour, courage and staunchness . . . telling us exactly how we stand and what we are to expect, with those touches of racy humour that as a nation we so appreciate. . . . All that is best in our Empire is gradually but surely coming to the surface.' Charles Whitbread writes: 'I can see your father explaining to our dormitory the extent and gravity of the German penetration into France; "the tide will turn, will always turn, some time", he said.' During the Summer holidays, under the threat of invasion, the Pike family had played its part in the general defensive plan by making hundreds of 'Molotov cocktails', home-made bombs which were to be lobbed over the rose garden wall on to passing German tanks. The bombs were buried in an adjacent flower-bed where presumably they remain to this day – certainly there is no record of their having been dug up. Boys and masters helped to excavate a hole for a concrete air-raid shelter next to the slides. When it was built, there was room for the whole school and the staff. The *Magazine* reports that during the Autumn term there were very few alerts and no local enemy activity. Mike Cocks writes: 'Black-outs were the order of every night and gas masks had to be kept with one for most of the time, but I only remember two full alarms to go to the air-raid shelter. . . . The one occasion was of short duration, but the other was an all-night affair when the Germans bombed the car-assembly plant in Abingdon – I think it was MG.' Guy Neale remembers spending a practice night in the air-raid shelter, newly-built, to records of Ambrose and

Flanagan & Allen. Robin Wellesley recalls 'the dustiness of the shelter – at first there were just benches and then we had wooden bunks. The sojourn in there was relieved by the sandwiches which seemed to appear when we came out. One night the whole place shook when a "land-mine" was dropped, and in the morning we woke up to find a Whitley bomber in the vegetable garden opposite; it had apparently landed without undercarriage but was otherwise undamaged. I can still remember that the top hatch on the cockpit was open.' Scottie Cheshire is one who has not forgotten 'the bomb which was dropped one evening (during prayers) in the Winter of 1940/41. Subsequently I saw the crater (cycling to Grey Walls) and it was almost exactly midway between the school and Geoffrey [Cheshire]'s house.... I don't recall any broken windows or indeed damage of any sort. But although your father continued as if nothing had occurred, we were all a bit apprehensive and silent – no one mentioned the word "bomb" but we all knew what it was. There had been no air-raid warning and there was no other disturbance before or later.'

Some time in 1940, S.A.P. appeared in the air-raid shelter with an LDV arm-band. The Local Defence Volunteers soon became the Home Guard, and S.A.P. was given command of a company. Bev Stanier remembers that it 'paraded in the evenings in the yard', and Tim Barker, who was staying at Cothill in the Summer holidays, had the excitement 'to be taken round the Home Guard posts at night by your father.... One night you came too and one of the posts was at the top of a very rickety old mill. There was some professional disagreement between you and your father as to whether it was a good site.' All the masters were members of the Cothill platoon, comman-

Air-raid shelter as rifle range, 1969.

Bathing-pool (after renovation), 1939. RAF Abingdon tapped the water supply, and the pool dried up very soon afterwards.

ded by H. R. Bryant. They had a lucky break when the invasion codeword 'Cromwell' was given, and the Home Guard throughout the country stood-to all night, except for S.A.P.'s company. He had been too late answering the telephone. There was plenty of rumour. Lights were seen in the Marsh, a spy had been caught there. Tim Barker reinforces earlier suspicions that H. F. Hindell was really 'Hundell', especially 'when we saw a letter on the masters' letter-board addressed to the "German Master"'. Stanley Chattey writes: 'We came across a trapdoor in a wood, and found below it a concrete dug-out. I realised much later that it must have been one of the hideouts... for the English Maquis' – or was it the spy's?

Writing 30 years later, in the *Centenary Magazine*, in the Summer of 1970, S.A.P. admitted: 'That first year of the war was rather a nightmare and we even played with the idea of evacuation – a ghastly thought! Parents were naturally anxious and jumpy; one big idea being for boys to go to Canada; one or two did so, but Geoffrey Shakespeare (in the Cabinet) came to our Sports Day and told everyone to calm down and that he was leaving his boy with us. ... The air-raid shelter, with a hundred mattresses and bunks, was never used after a few nightmare nights at the start.'

Much more serious in its effect on the life of the boys was the fact that the bathing-pool was never again used after 1940. This haunt of water-boatmen and other aquatic life has already been mentioned and is affectionately remembered by many of pensionable age. It had recently been renovated, but unfortunately RAF Abingdon tapped the water supply, and the pool dried up. It was the only unfriendly act that the school had experienced from them. For the next ten years there was no swimming at Cothill, as it was impossible to obtain a licence to build a pool during that period. In very hot weather boys had to be content with being hosed down by the master on duty. Shortly afterwards the RAF again threatened the amenities when it pronounced the elms a flying hazard and demanded that they should be cut down. Luckily there was such an outcry at this proposed desecration of a local landmark that a compromise was reached and only the tallest trees round the cricket pavilion were lopped.

When the RAF Station had opened in 1932, one obvious effect had been the noise. S.A.P. was quick to react and wrote to the Station Commander the first of many letters complaining that the boys' work was being disturbed, and asking for an assurance that flying over the school would in future be forbidden. Some sort of understanding must have been established, as flying took place well away from the school buildings and grounds, though S.A.P. was quick to write one of his uncompromising letters whenever a plane flew off course. I am told these letters became a familiar feature of the Officers' Mess notice-board. On the other hand, Charles Whitbread remembers when kite-flying became so expert that a message was received from the Station Commander that a kite at Cothill was so high that it might interfere with the take-off of the Hawker Hart (biplane) fighters that were then operating. After those early days aircraft noises became a familiar background to Cothill life. The sound of Wellington and Whitley bombers warming up in 1940 is remembered particularly by Mike Whitbread, whose father used to land his private plane before the war in the field on the opposite side of the road to the cricket ground. Mike Cocks has recalled lying in bed at night in 1941 counting the bombers taking off and counting them as they returned.,

After the war, bombers were replaced by Beverley transports, whose early-morning warming up provided a strange dawn chorus as they taxied slowly round the perimeter in single file, looking like enormous elephants. Abingdon was for a number of years the headquarters of parachutist training. A barrage balloon at the north-east corner of the aerodrome, near the Wootton crossroad, was a landmark until it suddenly exploded with a deafening report. From the basket suspended below the balloon a stream of parachutists could regularly be seen floating to earth. At other times, there were massed drops with coloured flares attached, and many a cricket game has been interrupted. The most dramatic drop was on one Summer evening in 1975. I was having a quick bath when there was a noise outside like a thousand starlings. I rushed to the window to see below me the whole school in full cry running across the cricket field and into the rose garden. A parachutist had landed in the big poplar tree next to the road. This apparition, a huge man wearing bright orange overalls, seemed like a visitor from outer space. He turned out to be a sergeant instructor, and very embarrassed he was, especially when in a very short time a fire-engine and an ambulance arrived from the aerodrome. However, he then gave his gaping audience a lesson on how to take off and pack a parachute in the shortest possible time.

Every year, in September, the anniversary of the Battle of Britain is celebrated by an 'Open Day'. Huge crowds come to see the most modern planes and to watch displays, such as aerobatics by the Red Devils and fly-pasts by helicopters, a Spitfire or a Hurricane contrasting with a Harrier jet. This display continues for most of the day, and the locals, if they can, absent themselves, as the noise is deafening and pets especially are frightened. Cothill boys enjoy a grandstand view from the cricket ground, and some enthusiasts are taken to visit the aerodrome and join the crowds.

My grandmother, Charlotte Williamina, widow of Joseph Armstrong Stenhouse, who had died in 1931, came to live with my parents in the Summer of 1940 when her house in Hayling was requisitioned. She was only

My grandmother and her great-grandson, Nicky Cheshire, 1949. Both died in 1950.

4 foot $11\frac{1}{2}$ inches ('half an inch taller than Queen Victoria'), with snow-white hair, a Fergusson by birth and a Jacobite by instinct. It cannot have been easy for my parents to have my grandmother living with them in the school until her death in 1950. She had her own bed-sitting-room (still known as 'Granny's Room', though now a dormitory), where she played endless games of patience, but she dined with my parents every night, changing into elegant long evening dresses and enjoying her dry martinis. We have many happy memories of her sense of fun, sweet smile, and one distinctive drooping eyelid behind thick glasses.

She brought with her Lovegrove and his wife Maggie. Ideal couples are rare in any walk of life, nowhere more so than in domestic service. Maggie had been engaged by my grandmother in 1906 on a month's trial as a kitchen-maid. Very handsome, she became a superb cook and had married Dan Lovegrove in 1912. During the Great War he had been desperately ill, but recovered to go back to work in the London engineering firm of Andersons. Maggie had been with my mother when I was born, and she and I had a wonderfully affectionate relationship for the rest of her life. In 1929 my grandfather persuaded Lovegrove to try his hand as a butler, and thus began a superb partnership of domestic and every other sort of service, first at the

Maggie and Lovegrove, 1947. A wonderful couple.

Abbey, Sutton Courtenay, then at White Lee Cottage, Hayling, and finally at Cothill, where they settled down to live in the village at No. 3. Maggie busied herself looking after my grandmother, my parents and a succession of parents and Old Boys who came to stay during the war. Only in an emergency did she find herself cooking for the school. Lovegrove joined Hurst, and Cothill became probably the only prep school to have two butlers.

The earliest butler mentioned by Old Cothillians is Argent, who in R. Tomkinson's headmastership also sang Victorian songs at school concerts. In 1927 he was replaced by Newton, who, according to an Old Boy, was 'spare and fair in pinstripes and tails.... He had a white-coated acolyte. ... Their only function in our part of the school was the evening gaslighting ritual when they would come round with tapers.' He was succeeded in 1934 by Hurst, a shortish man, with very black-rimmed glasses and dark hair smarmed back, always immaculate and polite and ready for anything. The 'Scout Log' of 1938 records that when the two school ponies, Tweedledum and Tweedledee, escaped from their field and roamed the golf course, 'Hurst came with some oats and enticed them back'.

Ernie Garton, 1965.

In 1937 Hurst was joined by Ernest Garton, then a young footman in short black coat and striped waistcoat. 'Ernie' soon established himself as a great favourite, with his cheerful manner, his smiling face and his constant laughter. When war broke out he joined the Royal Navy, serving in *Ark Royal* and other ships as a steward, and sailing in several Malta convoys. He survived and returned to Cothill after the war, succeeding Hurst as butler in 1956. In 1962 he left to look after my parents in their retirement, first at Hayling and then at Henley, until my father's death in 1979.

There was a spirit of high patriotism in the school in the Summer term of 1940. The play was *Henry V*, and Guy Neale wrote a patriotic poem, 'This England', which was published in the Autumn *Magazine* – a rare honour in those days. S.A.P. was determined that the boys should not think they were in a backwater: 'We must consider ourselves as very definitely part of the War Effort, training ourselves to be enterprising and brave leaders of the future.' The vegetable garden was enlarged to make the school more self-supporting, logs of wood were sawn and cut by boys to save coal and coke. Two young masters joined in 1940. K. Farnsworth, short-sighted, sensitive and humorous, endeared himself by writing a poem for Diana's 21st birthday and another for my parents' Silver Wedding, both events taking place during that Summer. In 1941 Kenneth was called up for military service. J. E. Hamilton, son of the then Bishop of Shrewsbury, joined the staff straight from school. John had been Senior Prefect at Radley and was an altogether exceptional young man, making a great impression during his two terms' teaching before joining the Coldstream. He was killed in Italy in 1943, having won the Military Cross.

School plays continued to be produced by V.K.D.W. That Autumn it was Sheridan's *The Critic*, in which the distinguished actor Ronald Simpson's son Robin played the part of Puff. Everyone was delighted with the production and S.A.P. wrote: 'Mr Waite is a genius at the game, and has the knack of the few really great trainers of racehorses – that flair for getting the animal to the post on the day at the top of his form and in the pink of condition.' S.A.P. was determined that his 'animals' should strive to be leaders. Quoting in the next volume a poem which ended, 'I saw the powers of darkness put to flight! / I saw the morning break!', he urged that when that morning did break, all who were or had been at Cothill should, 'by their acts and lives and in their conversation, influence public opinion in such a way that the weak spots in our land may vanish and the finer, nobler things increase and prosper'. In the Summer of 1941 he was faced by an exceptionally large list of leaving boys: 'Every term there is a feeling of sadness at losing boys for whom one has no feelings but affection, and yet also one is proud that they are such satisfactorily manly, cheerful, brave and capable young Britons.'

Richard Gooch's scholarship to Marlborough was celebrated by an expedition to Savernake Forest. V.K.D.W. produced *Henry IV, Part I*, last performed in 1934. It was notable for Miles Jebb as the Carrier ('an amusing little cameo of comedy acting which often threw rehearsals out of gear'). V.K.D.W. also started weekly sing-songs for the whole school. 'There were times when we recaptured some of the spirit of old musical England, with such songs as "The Cavalier" to the tune of "Polly Oliver" and the old

Cornish ballad "A Good Sword and A Trusty Hand".' He quotes William Byrd's 'Reasons to perswade everyone to learne to sing': 'It doth strengthen all parts of the chest and doth open the pipes.... It is a singular goode remedie for stuttinge and stammaring in the speech. ... It is the best meanes to procure a perfect pronunciation and to make a goode orator.' Clearly these singing sessions were a challenge and tonic to boys in wartime. According to Michael Stourton, 'his great thing was that someone was invariably flat, and he used to shout out, "Flat, flat, who's flat?" He was remarkably tactful, he never seemed to pick on anyone as the culprit, but made us all feel that we were joint culprits.' 'Old Boys' news' included a Charterhouse item: 'Leonard Figg, had he stayed on one more term, would have been both Head of the School and Captain of the 1st Football XI; so does a war cut into a boy's career and ambitions.' Luckily he survived to send three sons to Cothill and eventually become H.M. Ambassador in Dublin.

A comment and enquiry by S.A.P. on the future of preparatory and public schools in 1942 is apposite to the present day if references to the Empire are amended: 'What other remotely comparable system for the training of our future leaders is in view? What other educational system is so suited for the development of unselfish citizenship, sound character and breadth of vision? If all our best prep and public schools were to disappear, then the Empire would suffer a blow ... that would strike at the roots of our National and Imperial system.' Criticism is acknowledged: 'Too few public-school boys ... have given up sufficient of their spare time ... for actively aiding and sympathising with those less fortunately placed (e.g. by taking an interest in School Missions).'

An important milestone in the development of the school was the start of V-badges. These were described by S.A.P. as 'Badges of Victory, Valour, Versatility, Victory-over-self, Vigour, Virtue, Virility and all other good Vs'. A bronze 'V' was worn on the coat lapel, and it had to be re-won each term by a combination of good work and helpful conduct. Part of the attraction was the V-badge treat, consisting of an extra half-holiday with special tea and a film. From now on parents asked 'Have you got your V-badge?', thus further strengthening the Parent-Boy-Staff triangle. Another milestone was my marriage to Gabrielle, youngest daughter of Edward Woods, Bishop of Lichfield. The boys subscribed generously to a wedding present. Neither of us had at this time any idea that one day we would be deeply involved in the life of the school.

A school debate discussed the motion 'That in the present situation, this House does not consider Democracy to be the best form of government'. It was defeated 15–19. Shortly afterwards Japan bombed Pearl Harbour. The senior school began listening to the BBC 'Broadcasts to Schools'. There were

Gabrielle and I, newly married, early 1942.

three programmes: 'Historical events and personalities 1700–1800'; 'If you were American', from the founding of Pennsylvania to the 'New Deal'; and an Orchestral Concert series. The two last were written up by boys from memory with comments in a special book, which unfortunately has not survived. Five Old Boys were reported killed: David Hardie, Keith Rumbo, Harold Atkin-Berry, Pat Chamier and William Parker.

S.A.P. considered what boys would do when they grew up. Some will 'wish to run some big industrial concern' or look after 'an estate and its tenants'. The problem of making a better world after the war, with the need for courage and enthusiasm, is stressed. Meanwhile boys continued to cut wood which had been lopped from the elms. There were no matches, but two weeks' skating. 'Old Boys' news' highlighted Colin Hodgkinson's winning his Wings and Pilot's Certificate, in spite of losing one leg and the other foot as the result of a crash just before the war – 'a splendid and inspiring example of the best type of Cothill spirit'. The Summer of 1942 saw scholarships gained to Winchester, Eton and Charterhouse. Two cricketers, Jonty Craven and John Lyon, dominated the batting and bowling respectively, the 1st XI beat the Dragon on their ground, but lost both Summer Fields's matches by two runs. The Autumn term saw the first concert appearance of a school orchestra, started by V.K.D.W., 'our maestro, bully, coaxer, conductor and friend'.

1943 started with the boys Craven, Lyon and Craigmile playing in a combined Dragon, Summer Fields, St Bede's and Cothill football side against the Bermondsey Mission boys. Jonty Craven captained the combined XI, which was soundly beaten. The term ended with 15 Old Boys returning to Cothill for Sports Day. A number stayed to dinner, when they had 'a great gossip, reviving many past Cothill incidents and exploits'.

Writing in the *Magazine* on the objectives of the school, S.A.P. emphasised the need for certain rules – the fewer the better – to provide 'liberty, peace of mind and kindness'. To aim at 'an impossible standard of excellence might all be really rather fun, and certainly better than the dull wasting of time by foolish slackness'. General Dick McCreery, who had sons in the school, came to lecture on the Tunisian campaign. He stressed the importance of 'fighting morale', and how in a school, as in the army, a high standard of discipline and keenness was needed.

Robin Wellesley remembers how H. R. Bryant 'took us in rifle drill with wooden ones . . . and on battles which ranged over the golf course, where bunkers became very realistic weapon pits'. Apart from this, the nearest that boys got to battle was 'Roundheads and Cavaliers' in the Marsh, and military tableaux in the desks. The former has been described by an Old Boy as 'an exciting territorial game played one evening in the Summer term in the wooded land lying next to the school grounds. Sachets of lemonade powder were dispensed to both sides beforehand to sustain us through the vicissitudes of seventeenth-century warfare. I wish I could remember how the rules went – ambushes and challenges and prisoners and escapes.' Bev Stanier says that everyone was given a rank in one of the teams, from private soldier to general, with at the summit King Charles and Cromwell. 'It was a mixture of living chess and l'Attaque.' Another describes the desk tableaux: 'A desert tank-battle would entail the whole desk being filled with sand raided from the nearest golf-course bunker. Dinky toys and tin soldiers were arranged with special explosive effects lit up by means of hidden batteries and red-painted bulbs. Impressionable new boys could be "charged" heavy viewing fees, such as half a bar of chocolate or a rather unfavourable swap of their prized Conway-Stewart fountain-pen with 14-carat nib.'

My parents picnic in the woods with Gabrielle. ABOVE *My mother paints, Spring 1943.*

The lawn tennis competition in 1943 saw the first mention of two promising young players, John Ganzoni and Dick Bridgeman. In the following Summer John beat Dick in the final, and S.A.P. noted, 'they might both be seen at Wimbledon one day'. The prophecy was partly fulfilled when John Ganzoni, as Lord Belstead, became a committee member of the All-England Lawn Tennis Club. That he should become Leader of the House of Lords was not anticipated. Dick Bridgeman became a well-known rackets and real tennis player. These two, with Ben Porter and Graeme Anton, in the Autumn, were a squash quartet well above average, not to be matched until nearly 20 years later by Willie Boone and Andrew and Christopher Milne.

Naturalists recorded that a long-tailed tit's nest was watched, that numerous Summer visitors and residents had been seen, and S.A.P. noticed a solitary seagull on 12 August – a rare sight in those days before the proliferation of reservoirs. It was also noted that both green and spotted woodpeckers were seen fairly frequently in the surrounding woods.

One prominent bird-lover, E. H. Butler, retired at the beginning of 1944 after 15 years on the staff. S.A.P., in his appreciation, described him as 'an excellent example of the old type die-hard schoolmaster: punctilious, strict with himself and with boys, somewhat aloof, very critical of slack deportment and offhand manners'. His place was taken by a Mr Mence, a somewhat brash character who taught boxing, and did not stay long. Nick Dawson remembers other birds of passage, such as a Mr Arton, who had a fight with Stuart McCarthy and always forgot to do up his fly-buttons. 'Mr Arding [known as 'Sardine'] used to put up very fussy, very neat notices. On one day he found a stamp and the notice read. "Found a Chile Air Stamp in the chilly air".' He was a diabetic who, forgetting to take his insulin, fell into a coma in the dormitory passage.

H. V. Welch, who joined the staff this year, was to remain until 1957. Henry was 'a round, tubby, short and cheerful man' in his fifties, who specialised in Geography and Mathematics. He is remembered by Paul Whitfield for 'his mercurial temperament – I think we called him "Wibs". However explosive he had been during the week, he was generally good for some extra points on our weekly behaviour charts.' To Julian Shuckburgh, in the early 1950s, he was 'a pleasant man who read us H. G. Wells and E. M. Forster stories in a melodious voice'. He was dormitory master until his marriage to the matron Pixie Parkinson. He coached hockey, wearing a college blazer, and had been, on his own admission, 'quite a player'. Though in some ways a figure of fun, with his strange slang expressions, such as 'I slung him a corker', he was an expert gardener and an authority on Kipling. Friends and ex-pupils remember him with affection as the kindest of men.

But it was on H.R.B. that my father came to rely increasingly as his second-in-command, for he was meticulous in administration and documenting, in his neat handwriting, everything that was going on in the school. Mark Hely-Hutchinson recalls this being extended to 'a multi-coloured chalk map of the D-Day landings, which got updated each day as the news came in of various battles'. He drilled the school every morning after breakfast. According to Nick Dawson, 'We lined up by Groups; if you were late you joined the Barbarians. He also did the films, cartoons mostly. One evening the projector broke down and he led us all in songs, one of which was about Zam-buk: "You can't have any of my Zam-buk when your Zam-buk is done".'

The opening of the Second Front and the Invasion of Normandy in 1944 had only one direct result as far as Cothill was concerned; the cancellation of the Fathers' Match because it was impossible to raise a Fathers' side. Robin Wellesley remembers 'the sky black with tugs and gliders. It was an awe-inspiring sight.' General Alexander paid a short visit to see his son Shane. 'Old Boys' news' included the fact that six were serving in the Navy, 42 in the Army and six in the RAF. One, Franko Seymour, presented the school with two massive wheels taken off a captured Italian merchantman. At the time they were considered the last word in useless presents, but as they could not be hidden away they have ever since been a prominent feature, first outside the football pavilion (before it became a sports store) and now outside the Complex. Few know their origin, but they have acquired a certain totem significance.

Events of this historic Summer included a six-month drought; the arrival of main water; the worst cricket side for 12 years, with five matches lost; a play by V.K.D.W. called *Flight*, about Charles II ('His plots are good cut-and-dried likely plots – things happen naturally and with pace and a nice blending of humour and excitement.'); John Ganzoni beat Dick Bridgeman in the tennis final; poplar kittens and cinnabar caterpillars were found, collected and fed; 18 wasps' nests were destroyed.

Meanwhile, Peveril Sandford, in the 60th Rifles, and Micky de Piro, in the 12th Lancers, had been killed. Both were outstanding as boys at Cothill, at their public schools and as officers. All the Pike family were particularly shattered by Micky's death, as he, with his elder brother Alan, had spent many holidays with us, because their father and mother lived in Singapore. The blow was to some extent softened by a letter from Micky's Commanding Officer: '. . . an outstandingly good officer – always calm, elegant and brave. We all loved him.' Both he and Peveril had been mentioned in Despatches, and S.A.P. was very proud of them. Bev Stanier writes: 'Major Pike was heartbroken by Micky's death. His brother Alan came and taught for a short time. S.A.P. told us about the war in prayers, morning and evening, and reminded us of the school motto. We sometimes sang patriotic songs on our walks, including one called "Boney was a Warrior", nowadays totally forgotten, and must even then have been very ancient, as Boney was Napoleon Bonaparte.'

When VE- and VJ-Days had come and gone, S.A.P. wrote in the Autumn of 1945: 'Shall we grasp the great opportunity given to us so that we mould a finer and a better world for the future? . . . The alternative . . . sinking back again into a state of frustration, disillusion and discord, thus making yet another World War inevitable . . . vastly more terrible . . . the atomic bomb still in its infancy. . . . Be proud to give your best to your country. . . . The ball is at your feet.' A ball of another kind was well bowled by cricket captain John Ganzoni ('The Egg') whose team lost only one match, against the Dragon. 'Old Boys' news' mentions 'the distinct Cothill flavour about Eton Junior Cricket. . . . In one number of the *Chronicle*, 10 Cothill boys are mentioned for cricket successes; this may be mostly due to good sound coaching under an ilex tree on a certain corner of a field in Berkshire . . .'.

V.K.D.W. was showing signs of fatigue, and departed following a breakdown in health. His place was taken by E. H. Butler, who was welcomed back out of retirement; T. E. Dowell stepped into his shoes as producer of plays, his first being *The Knave of Hearts*, in which 'the two pastry cooks were acted admirably, with perfect contrast, by the Dawson twins'. Tom Dowell was tall and thin and wore a light-brown, pin-striped suit. He was a charming, gentle person, with a fine sense of humour, who would have appreciated his nickname '*Ho pistos doulos*', the faithful slave, given him by those learning Greek. James Holt remembers him playing Brahms and Liszt in the New Hall; 'I have liked piano music ever since'. He took on the training of the choir and playing the organ in church.

My sister Audrey provided the main excitement of the Autumn term of 1945 by marrying Christopher Cheshire. He and his brother Leonard lived half a mile down the road at Grey Walls, and Christopher had lectured to the school on his experiences as a prisoner-of-war. The wedding provided an excuse for my getting leave from Germany. I was commanding a company in our 2nd Battalion, which had joined the Guards Armoured Division the previous January. Now we were at Wipperfurth, near Cologne. Audrey and I had met briefly in Paris shortly after the announcement of her engagement, and I had said I would try to provide the champagne for the wedding. I collected two cases from the Division's Eye Club in Brussels, but when I arrived at Ostend there were at least 30,000 awaiting embarkation. Luckily I met an old friend, Philip Pinkney, and with his help I was able to wangle a special pass on compassionate grounds. I arrived home just in time to help in the preparations, and was particularly delighted to see again V.K.D.W., who had been invited to play the organ and direct the choir for the service.

The 1st XI had an undefeated football season. The first match against Horris Hill for over four years provided a highly dramatic start: 'Will any of us ever forget those last hectic ten minutes . . . four goals down . . . we actually scored four quick goals to . . . force a sensational draw. No wonder many a cap was thrown aloft . . . when that fifth goal was scored.' It was *Boys' Own Paper* stuff, and among those who played were John Ganzoni, Bernard Gordon-Lennox and Dan Massey. In 'Old Boys' news', Miles Jebb's victory in the Eton Junior Steeplechase gets the comment, 'Cothill food breeds tough guys'. Sandy Stirling, in a shooting competition, 'got 99 out of 100, just about the best score ever done at Eton'. At this time 50% of leaving boys went on to Eton, where there were over 50 Old Cothillians, and an Etonian Cothill Old Boys' football XI lost to an Etonian Summer Fields Old Boys' XI. The Spring term of 1946 saw bleak weather and no matches, though things improved to allow Sports Day to take place. S.A.P. noted the beginning of an immunity to the horrors of atom bombs, tidal waves, torture, famine, and asks, 'Should we not be more alert and critical of evil? . . . The boys of Cothill must be in the vanguard of the movement towards the building of a brave new world and continue the work of those who so gallantly gave their lives. There is one great society on earth: the noble living and the noble dead.'

The Summer *Magazine* contained a 'formal goodbye to Mr Waite after 17 years'. His contribution to the life of Cothill had been unique in its depth and variety. An Old Boy remembers that he had been a 'hard and impressive teacher' – and that went especially for French. He was appointed Head of Modern Languages at Bristol Grammar School, and went on to make a name for himself as an author and BBC broadcaster in 'Round Britain Quiz'. D.E.P., continuing the Waite tradition, produced a one-act play. The two main parts were taken by Dan Massey, son of Raymond, and David Wells, grandson of Nicholas Hannen – an unusual theatrical double. Dan's cricket is also commented on: 'A painstaking bat. . . . He has perseverance and keenness in his make-up.'

In September 1946 L. M. Swinbank arrived on the staff, and so began a long Cothill career which only ended in 1986. Leonard might never have chosen to come to Cothill, but for the accident of fate that ensured that his application to Canon W. R. Mills, Head Master of Highfield, Liphook, was never forwarded to the Grand Hotel, Eastbourne, where the Canon spent the holidays. I was to hear Mills bewail this when I took a job myself at Highfield for the Summer term of 1947. 'Finest lot of testimonials I've ever seen in my life; must be a first-class man; your father's very lucky.'

Leonard Swinbank as Bursar, Autumn 1978.

L.M.S. has written what he calls a 'Fractional Flashback' of the Winter of 1946/47:

'Teaching staff – male side of – all except Dormo master housed in Masters' Cottage.

'Use of bathroom. Skilfully worked out by Humphrey Bryant on a rota basis. This meant that never before and never since have I been so punctual in climbing out of bed.

'So to the school yard in time to take breathing exercises (usually three) at 7.50 a.m. As I tell the groups to file in to breakfast, I become aware of a reproving stick pointing towards me. It is held by old man Fairbro', whose eagle eye has noticed that one of the boys has *black* shoes on. For Sunday use only, the pairs of *black* shoes should all strictly have been in his boothole. I must rectify the omission immediately after breakfast.

'At the breakfast table the 13-year-old prefects appear so much more knowledgeable than I about school life. The Senior Prefect, Mark Hely-Hutchinson, with a smile on his face kindly fills in some gaps in my understanding. Do I know what marking up means? Nothing to do with him, but he will explain when we leave the room. Under his guidance I duly see that this ceremony is performed by as many as possible, then hasten to the Big Schoolroom to receive more instructions, this time from Dust Phillimore. It is now the ceremony of drawing the partition – unlike the Berlin Wall [until December 1989], opened and closed daily and more than once.

My father with Fairbro', 1937

'After three lessons it is quarter break, and I have to ensure that not only does every boy have *brown* shoes on, but also his cerise cap. Participation in the yard game forbidden unless this is worn.

'A military figure stands by the green double doors with hands gently clasped behind his back – yes, it is the H.M., Major Sam. He sends off a player for kicking the ball above waist height. Most important good ball control on the ground. "Too true", as Nelson Battell has often been heard to remark.

'S.A.P. turns up again to support me as I line the boys up for lunch, checking hands and hair, along the length of the passage.

'At lunch the staff are served from the top table. Lovegrove D. looks after me, ensuring that I receive a helping of milk pudding, usually an alternative on the menu.

'After lunch all the boys receive a skilful lesson in the use of the important words *thank you* and two or three sweets from Dorothy Pike before sitting to read quietly in the Big Schoolroom or to be read an extract from *Brigadier Gerard* by Dust in the Library. Special few to flat-foot exercises.

'Then no football today, but skating on the pond beyond the second green stile. Weather crystal clear – sky blue, golf course not green, but shining white. One boy clearly in a class by himself like Currie or Cousins. It is John Burrell. Silver would as certainly have been won by S.A.P. himself, elegant and stylish.

'As I remove my skates, I notice from the corner of my eye the early beds returning from their walk in the woods in the charge of the new Sister.

'Afternoon school comprised two lessons with tea in the middle as a sandwich. When the snow wasn't there, it meant that it was possible to get in six holes on the golf course with a colleague also not on duty – on that day – provided one carried only one club, a five for preference.

'On weekday evenings, prep consisted of two subjects, Latin and another. On Saturday Bryant showed a silent film in the New Hall – not that the audience was silent. It was the highlight of the week. Any boy who had not pulled his weight was confined to do extra work in the Big Schoolroom, a detested punishment.

'But S.A.P. nearly always allowed the idlers or criminals to return to the main body and attend film part two on Sunday evening.'

The 'new Sister' was Joan Gorringe-Smith. She has added her own recollections of the Spring term of 1947: 'From the first week of my first term we existed in a snow-covered world. Living on the South Coast I had never experienced anything like it before. The most vivid memory of that term was skating in the Marsh. The boys in knickerbockers and red caps, some like John Curries, others sitting on their tails more often than not, but all having the most wonderful time.' Christopher Brett adds a rider: 'The awfulness of the Winter of 1947 inured one to cold for the rest of one's life.'

The following Summer has become famous for the unusually hot and sunny weather and for the batting of Compton and Edrich. At Cothill the annual sports were held in May, postponed from the previous March for the

Joan Gorringe-Smith (Swinbank), 'the new sister', Summer 1947.

first time in living memory. Tom Bowles won the championship, and was 'a splendidly keen and alert captain of a pleasantly workmanlike eleven rather than a great one'. He headed the batting and bowling averages and narrowly missed an Eton scholarship. His sister, Julia Budworth, writes: 'Our Bailey cousins [Richard and Michael] declared that Tom was a professional schoolboy; he had a talent for school. Many Englishmen have it. . . . When he was at Eton I know he looked back upon Cothill as a time of wine and roses.' As a new boy, in his first letter home, he had written, 'This is a smashing school and I am having a super time.'

After a lapse of many years, an outdoor play was produced. A spotted flycatcher nested in the cricket pavilion, though only one nestling survived, and 40 birds were 'ringed'. S.A.P. commented that 'amid the kindliness of nature, this country is in the throes of a crisis [of coal stocks]. As in the war, the solution of our national problems depends on the efforts of every individual' and he urged those at Cothill to concentrate on the one word 'Service'. 'A school is a country in miniature. We are none of us alike. We all have our own way of doing things. We have our own likes and dislikes, our favourite amusements and hobbies. We can all help to make Cothill an even happier place by making full use of these enthusiasms. . . . You will be serving the school, and possibly helping by your example to save your country.' It was with these Pitt-like sentiments that my father prepared to welcome his son.

7
APPRENTICED AS ASSISTANT MASTER

I arrived to teach at Cothill in September 1947. Gabrielle and I had rented Mill Cottage in the nearby village of Marcham, and I used to bicycle to work to save petrol coupons. I was not entirely new to the job, having spent the previous term at Highfield in Liphook. This experience had broken me in and shown me how much I enjoyed teaching boys of prep-school age. It also gave me another school to compare with Cothill, a worm's-eye-view of life in the masters' house, and the opportunity to see how a school worked. The Head Master, Canon Mills, was both rich and snobbish, but he had a delightful and very able staff, many of whom became friends. I was gratified when Mills wanted me to stay for a year at least, but S.A.P. needed a replacement for the Autumn term, as he had been constrained to dismiss summarily an assistant master with homosexual tendencies.

So began my apprenticeship, which was to last for 15 years. Happily this was not suspected. S.A.P. had suffered a slight heart attack after the end of the war, and both he and D.E.P. had written to me in Germany that he was thinking of retiring. It was for this reason that I had applied to retire from the Army, something which was not easy for a regular Scots Guardsman to do. However, thanks to the fact that my father-in-law, Edward Woods, was a personal friend of the Military Secretary, Gerald Templer, I had returned to civilian life in March 1947. Once I had joined the Cothill staff it became apparent that S.A.P. had no intention of retiring, and so I became, as it were, a company commander again, not second-in-command for another year, and certainly not a partner. Apropos my situation, the following conversation is supposed to have taken place at a public school: 'Isn't the Head Master of Cothill a Major?' 'Yes.' 'Isn't his son on the staff too?' 'Yes.' 'I suppose he's the Sergeant.'

My first term might have been complicated by the fact that H. R. Bryant was Senior Master. He had been a great support to S.A.P. for 11 years, and I felt I had to reassure him that I was starting from the bottom and had everything to learn. I need not have worried. He was extremely welcoming and helpful, he showed me the ropes and gave me much good advice. He did not seem to resent my arrival, but it cannot have been easy for him or for the

The new assistant master with Hudi, 1947.

Two generations of Pikes, late 1940s.

others on the staff to have the Head Master's son thrust upon them. Luckily for me I had known most of the senior staff for many years, and 'Dust' Phillimore since childhood. As I was officially known to the boys as 'Major George', and was on Christian name terms with the staff, they gradually began to call each other by their Christian name instead of by surname, though this took time.

My parents were clearly pleased to have me back from the war in one piece and willing to join the firm. However, they found it hard to accept the fact that Gabrielle and I should want to lead independent lives, based on Mill Cottage. Neither of them had any intention of sharing with us the responsibility of running the school; they had been too long in the saddle to let anyone else into the financial and domestic arrangements. I was an assistant master and no more, and this I understood and was willing then to accept. It was later that S.A.P.'s determination to control everything himself led to complications and near disaster. Gabrielle, finding no future in the school, was soon to put her foot on the first rung of the National Federation of Women's Institutes' ladder by becoming President of Marcham WI.

L. M. Swinbank, Old Carthusian, of medium height, thickset and already balding, had twinkling eyes behind horn-rimmed glasses. He and I had been up at Oxford at the same time, but had never met. Now we were to embark on a friendship of over forty years, for I soon realised that behind his quiet manner was a delightfully humorous man. H.R.B. had a high opinion of Leonard's potential, as well he might, since L.M.S. had been awarded the OBE in the war. Desmond Wigan has described him as 'the ultimate tower of strength', and Anthony Weld Forester, 20 years later, experienced 'the enormous conscientiousness of Mr Swinbank'. In these early days he taught boxing to nearly half the school, and Roger Carrington says 'he used to invite us to hit him as hard as we could in the chest; it was like hitting a sandbag'. Donald Fergusson thinks of him 'as a football referee in long shorts', but most others pick on his fondness for rhymes and puns. Thus Johnny Peel on Sports Day, after 'trying to jump chin-high hurdles' was told he had been doing 'the western roll the eastern railway', while Roderick Chamberlain recalls L.M.S. standing in for H.A.G.P. for Latin and Greek and drawing out from Hugo Powell a mnemonic for elisions, 'A beats E, is beaten by O: subscript I and away U goes'. Ten years later he was encouraging a despondent Charles Bland with 'Cheer up for Chatham, for the Dover Straits are in sight'. He left Simon Moffett 'a compendium of acronyms; if you saw some of my computer programs you would see his hand'. He was a benign and patient teacher, but when provoked could suddenly explode into a torrent of unintelligible remonstration, uttered at the top of his voice.

My first appearance in a group with my parents, Summer 1948. Staff, from left, standing: *H. R. Bryant, L. M. Swinbank, G. L. S. Pike;* sitting: *Betty Ellis, Pixie Parkinson, the cook(?), Muriel Wright;* right, standing: *H. V. Welch, T. E. Dowell, H. A. G. Phillimore, Judy Grant, R. M. Preston, R. A. L. Ogston;* sitting: *Nina Hargreaves, Miss Couchman(?).*

We had a good football XI during my first term, losing only one match, to Horris Hill. S.A.P. was not altogether satisfied, however, for he wrote: 'If only we could produce some of the dashing goal-scorers that kept bobbing up in our teams during the "Thirsty Thirties"! Boys who delighted in dashing through to score innumerable goals. . . . Forwards who took a delight in prowling about looking for an opening and who then made straight for goal instead of zigzagging, crabways, from side to side.' One of the high spots of the term was the Wedding of Princess Elizabeth and Prince Philip. The service was listened to by seniors in the sitting-room, and later two short plays were produced by T. E. Dowell, *Shivering Shocks*, with Julian Grenfell as Captain Dallas VC, and *Elegant Edward*, Julian Mitchell and Robin Dixon 'giving us a good idea of two types of burglar, the elegant and the tough and rough', and with Duncan and Freddy Rawson-Mackenzie as 'a couple of efficient policemen'. At the end of term the staff performed a Cothill version of *Cinderella*, written by the matrons, Sister Gorringe-Smith, Miss Parkinson and Mrs Ellis. This proved a great success, particularly with my parents as the front and back legs of a performing horse.

The term had a dramatic sequel. Some hours after the boys had gone home, the telephone rang. S.A.P. answered. 'Guy Aldous here. Did you have an infectious disease at the school? Tom has a stiff neck and is running a high temperature.' It was soon diagnosed as poliomyelitis, and three other boys developed it within 24 hours. Tragically, one of these died a year later, but the others recovered completely. Meanwhile we were all in a state of quarantine siege. Gabrielle and I went down with flu and were nursed by Maggie in the Cothill spare-room – a nasty moment before Dr Hobson confirmed we had not got polio.

L.M.S. wrote to S.A.P. in the Christmas holidays, 'I have asked Joan Gorringe-Smith to marry me, and she, *mirabile dictu*, has accepted me'. My father was appalled, thinking L.M.S. might leave. In any case he did not approve of married assistant masters; it was bad enough having me in Marcham and not in the Masters' Cottage. Luckily, however, the whole family was in the sitting-room when he read out the letter, and we all shouted him down. Leonard and Joan were married the following August and embarked on a happy partnership. Joan, small and smiling, was a vivacious enthusiast who complemented L.M.S.'s reserve with a constant flow of chat. They were to benefit the school in so many ways, not least through their sons, Mark, Bill and Robin, who were all to come to Cothill.

By January 1948 I was beginning to feel confident that I had made the right choice in becoming a schoolmaster. I taught most subjects at different levels in the classroom between the old gym and the garage. I enjoyed taking games and playing squash and golf. It was a busy life, among noisy and high-spirited boys. The prefects seemed giants, looking more grown-up in their knickerbockers and caps than their modern counterparts. First impressions of the school from new boys at this time were mostly favourable. Roger Carrington remembers the post-war austerity, the drain on clothing coupons caused by the requirements of the uniform of excellent quality from Billings & Edmonds, the school tailors. 'It was a kindly, if a little spartan régime. 'Nanny' (or 'Nina') Hargreaves presided over the round table for the new intake; Muriel Wright, 'in a cosy classroom, provided an agreeable introduction to proper work, not least in French'. Her accent, however, was not up to much, for she was overheard by a colleague: 'Now, I want you all to say after me – "Vwolla".' Jonathan Stedall chiefly remembers the dormitories: 'Small boys crying at the beginning of term . . . and the welcome presence of those one or two women on the staff who seemed like angels in that otherwise abrasively masculine world. . . . How we treasured our Dinky toys and swapped them and played with them. I had a collection of Army ones – tanks, lorries and field guns; we fought wonderful battles in the hedges beside the cricket pavilion (my opponent someone called Beeby – does he remember those campaigns?).' There was a fashion of dragging a procession of Dinkies on a long piece of string; another craze was to charge around with the right hand on the nose and the left on the tail, in imitation of a rhinoceros. This was called 'cinching' and was invented by Jimmy Dawnay, who had recently arrived from the USA. Loss of temper was known as 'sueing', and if a boy wanted to get a rise out of another, he would stroke his left palm with the tips of his right-hand fingers, saying 'Sue, sue, sue'. In the long breaks the Major Game assembled in football boots for shooting practice with S.A.P. – a dozen leather footballs were propelled in a non-stop volley at two goal-keepers, those wide of the mark being collected by a squad of juniors standing behind the goal-line. All would be wearing caps, still compulsory at all times out of doors, except during games. Roger Carrington's mother remembers how 'one Sunday morning in church a small boy sitting in front of Sam and Dorothy turned round and said, "I think I am going to be sick". Whereupon Dorothy hustled him out at great speed, but as they started down the aisle Sam called him back: "You've forgotten your cap." An agonized look from the boy, but he got out in time. Later Dorothy said to us, "I could have killed Sam!".'

Memories of my first year included a fine Sports Day in March, followed

Feast, 1973. Shouting at entry of Christmas pudding.

by a very pleasant cricket season, in which the 1st XI lost only one match, to Horris Hill by three wickets. It was captained by John Arthur, 'who started the season as our star bowler and ended the season as almost our most reliable bat'. Philip Harari and Mark Dundas were other successful batsmen. In contrast to modern practice, the first match in 1948 was played as late as 5 June, the last on 17 July. Three boys won awards: scholarships for Jimmy Valentine and Michael Bailey to Eton and Charterhouse respectively; a Head Master's exhibition to Harrow for Gervase Duffield. This was celebrated by a trip down the river: 'Lovely weather, lovely food (especially cherries) and lovely locks to negotiate, and listening in to the Test Match scores' (Bradman's all-conquering Australians). These awards brought the total for the previous ten years to 19. Special mention should be made of Michael Demarest's top scholarship to Rugby in 1938. In 1942 Andrew Iliine won a scholarship to Winchester, Christopher Quantock Shuldham to Eton and Robert Rogers an Open scholarship and Special Bean scholarship for Classics to Charterhouse. Two short plays were performed outdoors, memorable for David Winn's performance, especially his cries of 'I kill, I kill'. He is remembered earlier by Christopher Brett, who writes of 'a particular kindness on my first day at school when I arrived with no money and David, later so tragically drowned, gave me half his'.

Food is arguably the most important part of school life, and there is general agreement among Old Boys and staff that they were well fed. Hugh Stockwell wrote to his parents as a new boy in 1912 about Fathers' Match: 'At lunch I over eat myself. First I had a helping Sammon, then I chicking and tong and then I had Irish stew, and after that the pouding came. First I had cherry tart and then fruit sallaad and then cheese straws. . . . Then we had tea, I had 4 helpings of stroberay and cream and some cake.' The annual Christmas Feast was anticipated with delight from before 1927. 'How we gorged ourselves', writes Franko Seymour, of the 1930s, 'then worked it off with "the masters' rag".' 'The mess caused by the heavy bombardment of masters with paper streamers was prodigious', observes the 1948 *Magazine*.

Of normal school meals in the 1930s, one Old Boy says, 'Only when I went on to Malvern did I realise the excellence of the Cothill food. . . . I often wonder whether your parents did not run it at a loss.' Another speaks of 'huge joints of meat carved at the high table', a third of 'a lovely treacle pudding on Thursdays that usually appeared collapsed from the proper shape of the bowl in which it was made – this was known as "Hag's hat" [after H.A.G.P.'s battered trilby] and was much relished'. There was also stodge and the very welcome milk pudding seconds. Boiled mutton and what one boy called 'Capernaum sauce' was not so popular. Even in wartime, a prospective new boy thought the tea meal 'looked exceptionally inviting – spaghetti, cheese, fruit, and seemingly unlimited bread, butter and jam'. But in the late 1940s Jonathan Stedall was always hungry: 'In our day the forbidden contraband was food. . . . I remember consuming three or four kippers at breakfast . . . since thankfully many of the boys disliked them. . . . I not only stayed alive, but was given the nickname "Kipper".' There have been other criticisms: 'the agony of stewed figs week after week'; an objection to 'eating hot hard-boiled eggs on Sunday mornings'. Sometimes there would be strawberries for tea. S.A.P.'s grace is recalled: 'For what we have received, especially the strawberries, may the Lord make us truly thankful.' One boy, whose parents were food faddists, had to eat brown rather than white bread, and according to a contemporary, 'We all suffered. Food was wholesome in its widest sense, though at times we felt very under-privileged and coveted the bright-red harvest-festival apples in church.' Prefects sitting at the top table have enjoyed such privileges as Carr's water biscuits, Stilton, and Cooper's Oxford marmalade. Leaving Boys' Supper was, as one Old Boy puts it, 'an evening I will always remember, with the rare treat of wine as well as very good food'.

In the Spring term of 1949 the Golf Cup was won by Colin Clive. On one occasion when he was playing below his usual high standard, he was heard to say, 'I must change my professional'. I played with him and others as often as I could, once doing the 9th and the 2nd holes in one in quick succession; the latter feat was witnessed by over half the school standing by the green on their way to the Marsh – a great cheer went up.

H.R.B. did not return for this term. His voice had suddenly failed, and Dr Hobson had diagnosed cancer of the throat. This was confirmed and he went into hospital in London. I visited him at the end of this term and the following Summer, when his brother, a Cowley Father, was trying to take upon himself some of Humphrey's pain. He died in September, aged 44. S.A.P. wrote an obituary which was published in *The Times*. In the *Magazine* he reminded readers how H.R.B. 'threw all his enthusiasm, energy and fine intellect into his work here. He set himself a very high level of conduct and he expected the boys to do the same. With all his kindly tolerance and natural humility he was a strict disciplinarian; and the boys, being fond of him and knowing how fine he was, liked his discipline – and reacted accordingly. So passes away a brave and gallant gentleman and a very fine schoolmaster; we all – grown-ups and boys alike – are everlastingly grateful for all he did for Cothill, and we will try our best to carry on as he would have wished.' His death was a great blow to the school and especially to S.A.P., who was devoted to him.

Old Cothillians who fell in World War II were commemorated with the men of Dry Sandford and Cothill by a tablet in the church (see *Appendix III*). This was unveiled in July by the Warden of Radley, the Reverend J. C. Vaughan Wilkes, at a special service attended by senior boys.

The darker side of school life was experienced by some. Jonathan Stedall recalls that after writing Sunday letters 'we were free to go off into the woods and marshes for the rest of the day. There were gangs and camps; it was the perfect setting for the worst kind of bullying. Although I never suffered badly myself, the savagery left its mark. There were certain boys who had terrible tempers – they were bated. There were fat boys and ugly boys, who, it seems to me now, were learning far too early in life what a cruel and unfair world it can be if you don't quite fit in.' Bill Stockton remembers sneaking on the seniors in his first term, walking into supper amid complete silence, while everyone watched him. 'I learnt a lesson never to be forgotten.' Donald Fergusson, coming from Singapore, complements these memories: 'There were differences between a far-distant colonial background and home life and the closer, more introspective and socially aware ("with one of our gamekeepers the other day", "with my .410...") UK base of the others: it was probably as natural for me to talk about "our servants" and I was certainly teased for it.' He kept up with none of his contemporaries, probably because he was a solitary Rugbeian from a school that at this time had the majority of Old Boys at Eton. 'Wherein lie the faults? With me – certainly to some extent – for temper and being different; with the rest – likewise, for not accepting others' differences.' I wrote to Julian Mitchell, the playwright and novelist, that I was anxious to avoid hagiography and would welcome what I imagined would be a dissenting voice. He replied: 'I'm afraid anything I wrote about Cothill would be unacceptable in a celebration.' To Julian Shuckburgh, who shares my concern about hagiography, 'life at Cothill was eccentric and extremely mystifying for an eight-year-old'. He remembers marching round the playground armed with a wooden rifle and learning 'drill movements like recruits in a private army'. This in fact only occurred on rare occasions as a change from PT, and the rifles continued to be used spasmodically until the arms drill in the services was altered with the introduction of the new rifle. At the time of writing there is one wooden survivor.

In the Summer of 1950 the new swimming-pool was in some sort of working order. It had been designed by Lionel Brett, who omitted to provide a plug-hole, so that emptying had to depend on a pump. The *Magazine* reported

Swimming-pool (completed 1950), Summer 1975.

that 'it proved a great success. All is not in perfect order, e.g. some of the paving-stones subsided... but it was able to be used in time for the June heatwave. The chlorination plant is still suffering from growing pains and needs careful nursing.' The pool had been a large and uncompleted hole for some time, but now, after ten years, Cothill boys could swim again. Donald Fergusson, who had learnt to swim in warm Singapore waters, easily won the Cup this year and for the next three Summers. For the less expert, there were 'informal' swimming sports at the end of the term, organised by the newly joined T. E. B. Jackson. This included 'a backstroke race with 25 competitors all getting in each other's way... so funny that we have quite forgotten the winner's name'. So began the aquatics, to become a yearly feature at the end of each Summer term. T.E.B.J., and subsequently a succession of helpers, notably J. S. Malim and K. Bones, provided swimming instruction. A list would be put up, showing which boys had passed various swimming tests. These started with the 'A' test, the width of the pool, and progressed to 'B' for a length, 'C' for three lengths, 'D' for diving. A half-holiday for the whole school was promised if every boy passed the 'A' test. This was never achieved; not surprisingly, in an outdoor, unheated pool with a very limited swimming season.

H. A. G. Phillimore, known as 'Hag' to the boys, had always been 'Dust' to his family and friends, from a childhood inability to pronounce his second name, Augustus. He was a remarkable eccentric, whose impact on boys and staff was unforgettable, as I now saw for myself at close quarters for the first time. His classroom technique was based on a special combination of 'carrot' and 'stick'. One of the former was a promise to read from an historical novel; the most notorious 'stick' was the 'shifty prod', executed 'fist clenched with the knuckle of a forefinger [the thumb between fingers is another version] to the upper arm of the victim'. If anyone sinned in the half of the Big Schoolroom where Dust taught, he was sent to sit in the back row, which Dust christened 'Rotter's Row'. 'One knew instantly', writes Roger Carrington, 'on entering the class if someone was destined for Rotter's Row. The unfortunate prospective Rotter, on sitting down, was fixed by H.A.G.P.'s gaze in fiercest vein. Very slowly he would approach the boy, bearing the offending exercise book; with a sudden thrust the horror was put in front of him; "Were you trying? – 1 BM" stared from the page; the offender was quickly banished to the back, and more than usual geniality was shown to the rest of the class.' Another ploy described 'was to fling open the classroom door and say "The door is open to Major Pike's study"'. There was more than one occasion when he announced 'Someone is being foolish; we'll do no work'. And the whole class sat there for the rest of the period in petrified silence.

With Dust Phillimore, early 1950s. *Scholarship river treat.*

Out of school H.A.G.P. had for 20 years presided over the sloping 'Minimus' game football field. Here, in the 1930s, according to Dick de la Hey, 'at least 22 of the smallest boys chased in broken file round the field after a football. The two permanent residents, Messrs Tweedledum and Tweedledee, Shetland ponies, enlivened proceedings by trotting up behind laggards and butting them in the back.' One new boy, Johnny Peel, in the 1950s, remembers how, 'during our first chaotic set-to on the football field, he interrupted his losing battle to referee [he never used a whistle] so as to return a stray ball from the senior field and managed, with one impressive kick, to project one of his galoshes clean over the boundary wall'.

He was much valued for his quaint expressions: 'Look sharp, don't run' to boys in the corridor; 'Our dear châtelaine', referring to my mother. Among H.A.G.P.'s colleagues, V.K.D.W. recollects how 'his unsuspected wealth was hidden by a rigid parsimony. On one occasion he entrusted me with a single shoe to be repaired in Abingdon. When asked where its fellow was, he replied archly, "Ah, that one hasn't quite worn through yet".' Another recalls how 'he would sit on the very edge of the most uncomfortable of all chairs, watching all comings and goings' through his ever-open door; doing *The Times* crossword with the shortest of pencil stumps, which he called a 'bleischrift(?)'; or writing letters with a school pen and inkwell, in a beautiful hand, with writing all round the edges. These activities would periodically be interrupted by strange announcements, such as 'No soup on the private side'. He was greatly amused when a temporary colleague told the boys to go to the 'study hall' after lunch, meaning the Big Schoolroom. S.A.P. was surprised when they all crowded outside his study. 'Go to the study hall' became one of Dust's catch-phrases.

In the holidays he continued to entertain favoured pupils. Since his sister Hester's marriage to General Sir Frederick Pile, the flat in Cadogan Gardens had been presided over by 'our Nellie'. Dan Massey writes how Dust 'would ring up and ask if one wanted to "take in a film". One jumped at it, of course. He would arrive on the doorstep in that old Graham Greene mack, black shoes and one of those beautifully faded old suits, and off we'd trot – Tyrone Power in *The Black Swan*, Errol Flynn in anything. I really believe he loved it all as much as I did.'

One who had joined the staff with me was R. M. Preston. He enlivened the Masters' Cottage with the noise of his motor bicycle. H.A.G.P. was indulgent and nicknamed him 'Rootin', tootin', shootin' son-of-a-gun', presumably because he was also in charge of shooting in the converted air-raid shelter. E. H. Butler, who had left his garden to come out of retirement for the second time in 1949 to help out in H.R.B.'s absence, took a dimmer view of the 'infernal machine'. Michael Preston was a large, podgy-faced man in his twenties, a good golfer who took full advantage of the school course. He taught top Maths and bowled fast but well to boys in the nets. I acted as his best man when he married my sister Audrey's Nanny, Lois White, who had looked after Audrey's son Nicky until his tragic death from nephritis at the age of three in 1950. She helped teach the bottom class for some months before R.M.P. took up a senior mathematics position in Norwich in September. Before leaving, he had an amusing altercation with a young man called Brown who came to teach for a term. The latter wore coloured waistcoats, tried to get me interested in Freemasonry, and was extremely pleased with himself. Brown took a low Maths class, but volunteered to examine the top class in Geometry. He not only set an extremely difficult paper – top marks 30% – but wrote a long and critical report, which concluded: 'Throughout the top class there is no trace of the rudiments of appreciation of the aesthetics of mathematics as an exact science and yet a fine art.' Underneath R.M.P. wrote: 'Pompous Rot – they are only 11 or 12, and you sound at least 16', and at the top of the page, 'The examiner thus concludes his first term as a schoolmaster by showing he would be better off continuing his theological studies. He has taken Maths VI, and aspired rather transparently to dizzier heights.' This passage of arms would have appealed to W. T. C. Maynard, who has commented earlier on the 'considerable friction' caused by the system of setting exams for other masters' classes.

R. A. L. Ogston joined the staff my second term in January 1948. Ran was resident piano teacher and choir master as well as a teacher of French and general subjects. He was then about thirty, friendly and humorous, very boyish in appearance and manner. His impressions are of 'a rather overcrowded country house, a splendid feeling of professional amateurishness', something which he feels is nowadays sadly lacking in most prep schools, 'where the chief criticism seems to be all too often the modernity of the amenities'. The Masters' Cottage was enlivened by R. A. L. O.'s presence. He remembers 'Tom Jackson came back one night to find that his bed had been removed and the bedroom transformed into a sitting-room. John Ganzoni [who was doing a stint of schoolmastering between leaving Eton and going up to Oxford], after some especially patriotic remark, found his bed made up with Union Jacks filched from the school flag locker.... Finally, with one twist of a tap, I blew up the Cottage boiler and deprived the staff of weeks of baths.' In a concert given in 1949, R.A.L.O. resuscitated the recorder band and was given credit for 'much patient coaching'. On another occasion, with Bromley Challenor playing the viola, and a violinist Mrs Gotch, he gave a successful recital. He left in the Autumn of 1951 to teach French at Summer Fields, St Leonards, where he became joint Head Master. Subsequently he joined the staff of Summer Fields, Oxford, where he remained until his retirement. Though he came too seldom over to Cothill, his memories of it are happy. 'Those of us who were lucky enough to be there have much to be thankful for.'

Let T. E. B. Jackson introduce himself: 'Thirty-five years of Cothill started with Gabbitas (or was it Thring?) telling me I had no hope of getting the job. I arrived for my interview on a blisteringly hot day on foot, having walked from Frilford Heath. Sam and Dorothy always gave that as the school address as they thought it sounded blustery and healthy. It didn't help being told that there was a golf course in the grounds, for when I dropped into the 19th of the Frilford Club the barman thought I was a lunatic. He had never heard of any school. A woman then misdirected me, and it was not until I was almost half way to Oxford that a cyclist told me where to go.

'Sam surprised me by answering the door in co-respondent shoes. He made me welcome, finally calling Dorothy away from a fête which she was organising, in order to meet me. By the time I left I had the impression he thought I was a prospective parent. He eventually wrote, addressing the envelope to T. M. Hill, offering me the post, and expressing the hope that I would be prepared to run the choir. Those who have heard me sing will not be surprised to hear that I declined.'

Tom found the Masters' Cottage 'a wonderfully happy and friendly place in those days, despite the fact that we all addressed each other as Mr so-and-so. Christian names came later'. He was shown the ropes by young J. J. Ganzoni. Described by T.E.B.J. as the liveliest member of the Cottage, John was heard to say to the bottom class: 'I haven't time to explain the Trinity now, so get on with your work.' When he came down from Oxford, he taught for some years at Selwyn House, Broadstairs, before succeeding his father, Lord Belstead, and starting his political career.

Another to join the staff in 1950 was A. K. Reid. Arthur was a Canadian by birth, though educated in England, and had had considerable success as a playwright in the period immediately before the war, especially with *People in Love*. He was a large, cheerful man in his forties, with fingers stained by nicotine. Why he chose to become a prep-school master remains something of a mystery, for, as Richard Ryder points out, 'his teaching prowess left plenty to be desired. A normal practice of his was to conduct lesson after lesson from 'Quiz' and 'They Saw it Happen' books. Instilling the basics of subjects into children was not his forte. Quiz questions were less demanding for him as well as his pupils.' This is not altogether a fair criticism. He taught certain subjects conscientiously, but was handicapped by having to teach every subject. His chief contribution to the life of the school was a succession of boys' plays that he wrote and produced, and his hilarious Christmas pantomimes acted by the staff after the Feast. Richard remembers that the plays were 'skilfully and wittily written. Their craftsmanship and reception must have given him enormous pleasure. Indeed, he never seemed more relaxed and happier than when accepting, over glasses of Pimms and packets of cigarettes, the plaudits of parents in the garden after school plays.' He disliked and avoided taking games; instead, as T.E.B.J. recalls, 'he gardened endlessly, then, at the end of each year claimed a disability pension from the Canadian government for a bad back'. He remained on the staff until 1962, enjoying a 'special relationship' with my mother, whose cry of 'Where's Arthur?' would herald a gardening session in her herbaceous border.

Gardening as a minority hobby for boys is first mentioned at the beginning of the Great War. Michael Snow says there were four plots on the south side of the school. Three or four boys shared a plot, prizes were given and invariably won by the group that included the Sutton brothers, of Suttons Seeds fame. The 1930 *Magazine* records dormitory gardens still flourishing. By the late 1930s they were cultivated by syndicates of friends. In both wars there was much satisfaction derived from growing food from seed. Graham Rogers writes: 'to this day I get enormous pleasure from vegetable growing – far more than from flowers'. After World War II gardens reverted to individual enthusiasts and there were periodical complaints about the shortage of

Gardening, Summer 1987. At bottom of car-park, once Dust Phillimore's Minimus football pitch.

them ('Many people want gardens but there is no room; there are about 25 gardeners and 15 gardens'). In 1982 a Gardening Club was formed, encouraged by members of staff. Gardens were moved to the bottom of the car park, where H.A.G.P.'s football ground used to be. Here, 'from the staff-room window [in the Complex], avid gardeners clustering busily round their burgeoning plots look like so many little blue bees buzzing round an irresistible honey-pot'. Now gardens have once again moved, this time to the front of the Bungalow, recently enlarged to house some thirty boys, where Muriel Wright once tended her roses.

On the 19/20 June 1951 the school was inspected by HMIs for the first time since 1930. The Inspectors reported that there were 101 boys as compared with 55 in 1930, and that the fees were 80 guineas a term, as compared with 50 guineas in 1930. They noted that the Head Master had been joined by his son, described as 'an important acquisition to the staff and already a teacher of considerable ability'. The Head Master's 'dignity of manner and his sincere desire to maintain the highest standards are constantly reflected in the achievements of the school; his wife makes an inestimable contribution to the life of the school and together they have built up a tradition of which they can be rightly proud.' The Inspectors thought the system requiring all members of the staff to teach all subjects placed a heavy burden on most of them, and suggested that 'better results might accrue from a more modified system of grouping which would allow some masters to teach their specialist subject at more than one level'. (This was not taken up until 1962 after S.A.P. retired.) It was noted that there was 'no study of Natural History and that this side of the boys' education seems somewhat neglected'. The sad fact was that after A. C. Phillips's retirement there had been no one on the staff with enough knowledge or enthusiasm to encourage the boys to revive the interest in caterpillars, moths, chrysalises and butterflies that existed in the 1930s. Anthony Gill recalls how then 'there used to be rows of cages, jars and boxes, with various denizens of the Marsh, placed along the window-sills. Cinnabars were popular, but the most interesting to me was the puss moth, that grew quite large and then built a fine chrysalis and eventually hatched. One year some boy got two huge chrysales from South America and I remember the terrific excitement when one of the butterflies that had a wingspan of five or six inches began to emerge. It was a fantastic blue, I think a morpho from Brazil, and it was released in the Marsh, to die presumably of cold or lack of proper vegetation to eat.'

Another criticism by the Inspectors concerned the general presentation of written work in English; 'it is not tidy and the handwriting is poor'. Latin and French were considered to be well taught, the latter 'as a living language in an enlightened manner'. The physical education was well planned, the grounds were acknowledged to be excellent, particularly 'a large area of hard playing surface which is available and is of great value'. They noted that 'considerable emphasis is put on the moulding of character as one of the school's aims', and concluded their report: 'This school continues to perform its function admirably. There is a genuine desire on the part of those in charge to do all that is possible for the general welfare of the boys and to provide them with a suitable education. The achievements in both these respects are noteworthy.'

What the HMIs did not see was the everyday life of the school. 1951 was Festival of Britain Year, and boys were urged to collect, make models and draw with inventiveness and skill, and there was never any reluctance on the part of the majority to do any of these things. The *Magazine* also reported 'an outburst of journalism among a small group of right-wing intellectuals, and several newspapers were in open competition, vying with each other to procure the services of the star reporters and contributors. ... Roving reporters pestered boys and staff with all manner of questions on every imaginable subject.' A gallup poll found that cricket was more popular than football and that the favourite pudding was apricots or fruit salad, with treacle tart a close second. There was a craze for golf among juniors.

Next term the standard of tennis improved, thanks to the coaching efforts of J. J. Ganzoni. A poor cricket 1st XI needed to learn three lessons: '(1) Bowl straight and to a length; (2) Use the feet to get to the pitch of the ball; (3) Remember Jack Hobbs's saying that there is no excuse for bad fielding and that it is only 20% natural aptitude.' Messrs Ogston and Reid produced *Noah* by André Obey, in which Jonathan Stedall 'made us feel the goodness and faith of Noah, on conversational terms with God, while John Yorke brought out the feminine concern resulting from such a violent change of home and scene'. In September 1951 H. N. A. Shelton joined the staff as Music Master; he is remembered for his enormous enthusiasm, his success in training the choir, his producing reams of cyclostyled new music every week, and his selling three school pianos at *7s.6d* each. Tall, thin and saturnine, he would flap his arms like a great bird over S.A.P. in his study as he made endless requests to further the musical life of the school. It was to escape from these sessions that S.A.P. would plead the need to go and change his shoes, much to Hugh's puzzlement. The football 1st XI was successful, largely due to Seton Wills, outstanding at centre half, and Tom Aldous in goal. Guy Fawkes's Night fireworks included 'a device that sent out hundreds of whistling squibs and caught the lighter by surprise'. This was almost certainly L.M.S., whose 'Swinny bombs' (buried mortars) were a special feature of the annual fireworks, which took place on the football field until the building of the Complex in 1972. The term ended with the first of A.K.R.'s masters' pantomimes after the Feast. This production of *Cinderella* introduced the pattern to be followed in the years to come: slapstick, puns on boys' names, H.A.G.P. in drag, and songs. The main chorus was 'Each Cothill boy's a Prince Charming. / Although his behaviour may be / Revolting, disgusting, alarming / He'll end up as nice as can be', to the tune 'Oh what a beautiful morning'.

The following year, 1952, A.K.R. wrote and produced a special Masque, to celebrate the 75th year of the school and the 25th year of the *Magazine*. Both dates were in fact two years too soon, as the school had been at Cothill since 1879 (though founded in 1870) and the *Magazine* was started in 1929. However, A.K.R. seems to have been given dramatic licence and the excuse for a party proved stronger than S.A.P.'s sense of chronological accuracy. The Masque was performed in front of the parents on Fathers' Match day and at a special Old Boys' reunion. It 'showed the growth of the school in a series of imaginary episodes, while bringing in a large number of names of people connected with the school'. The first Head Master, C. W. Carles, was seen outlining the aims of the school, leaving the boys to choose their first Head Boy by means of a fight behind the stables. Then followed scenes from the Diamond Jubilee and the Great War, with Smith Minor reappearing from the Front as Major Smith. The first part ended with two brothers heralding the arrival of my parents (song: 'We like Pike'). In the second part the story of the school was told by commentators in pairs in between episodes. Two of these took the form of boys conversing with the ghosts of Julius Caesar and Alfred the Great, the first appearing in 1930 as the result of a Roman coin being dug up in a bunker on the golf course (this in fact happened), and the second in 1942 when the country was in danger. The last scene showed a group of boys of all ages telling of their dreams for the future, and 'the serious and comic were most skilfully balanced'. Charles Cropper had the closing line: 'When I grow up I want to be a spiv.' Written in verse, and as the author said, mainly to amuse, 'the underlying feeling throughout was of pride in the school, of continuity of effort and traditions and of a desire to "build a future to fulfil the past"'.

Earlier in the year S.A.P. had written of the original launching of the *Magazine*: 'We felt that the boys still at school would benefit by being given a printed record of their various activities and that it would also keep our Old Boys at the public schools in touch with our life at Cothill. . . . The *Magazine* has grown in size and scope to a certain extent, but it remains quite an unpretentious affair and not much more than a School Diary.' S.A.P. goes on to say how he has formed the habit of writing a personal note to Old Boys at public schools when sending them a copy of the *Magazine*, 'to send our affectionate good wishes and to extract a letter of acknowledgement in return. This latter object has, naturally enough, been only partially realised.'

Not surprisingly there was an excellent turn-out on the Old Boys' Day, though a telegram was received from '66 disappointed Etonians', who were unable to come because of quarantine for polio. Everyone was delighted to see V.K.D.W., Miss McMillan and Mrs Fulton (formerly Miss Spokes) and greatly appreciated a telegram of congratulations and good wishes from Miss Hames, Matron from 1894 to 1925. My parents were given two cigarette-boxes and a fund was started to help finance a new Hobbies Room. In thanking all Old Boys, S.A.P. wrote: 'We pray that the vast majority of our Old Boys will look back on their years with us as happy years and that they will feel they benefited from the Cothill "atmosphere" and teaching which we will continue to strive to make not only helpful and constructive, but also fully worthy of the type of boys that come to us – for only the very best is good enough for Cothill.'

Cothill House Magazine. *The first photographic cover, September 1969. The production not quite the 'unpretentious affair' of my father's day. The Sports Day illustrated was the first to be held in the Summer term; marking 'the death of freezing March afternoons'.*

The school listened to the broadcast of the funeral procession of King George VI and afterwards to the service from St George's Chapel. A few boys went up to London with their parents to see the Lying-in-State and the procession. The Coronation of Queen Elizabeth II in 1953 was attended by Charles McCreery as page to Lord Alanbrooke. He noted that when the peeresses put on their coronets, 'some were so small that they had to be kept on with hair combs and elastic'. A.K.R. wrote a Coronation Pageant, which involved twenty scenes and half the school. 'Everyone knew his lines, ... everyone was audible, and frequently outstandingly funny and moving.' A special song, 'Gold bless the Queen', was written by Arthur Rucker and set to music by Julian Shuckburgh. S.A.P. wrote: 'England is very much back on the map. Everest conquered, the Ashes regained, and a lovely and good Queen on the Throne.'

A casualty of Coronation year was A. C. Phillips, who died in February. His contribution to the life of Cothill from 1903 to 1937 has already been described. Many Old Cothillians must have had their special memories of him, like Tim Bailey's: 'He used to come and stay with my family in the holidays, arriving in an open Morris tourer. We would go out for a day's golf

A. C. Phillips on a Henley picnic, June 1933. Cigarette in mouth as usual.

– he had a wide, sweeping swing, reminiscent of scything a hay field.' Or Hugh Barrett-Lennard's: 'He supervised the Minor Game cricket. He sat under a may tree in a deck-chair with a very old-fashioned canopy over it, smelling of citronella to keep off the gnats. It was remarkable to watch his extraordinary conduct of the game, without having to move from underneath his canopy.'

He would have been particularly delighted with T.E.B.J., who was at this time inspiring boys to make full use of the new Hobbies Room, and wrote in the *Magazine*: 'Last term's plaster moulding absorbed over $1\frac{1}{4}$ cwt of plaster. Comets, Dolphins, Weevils, Frog Herons and Vampires – not the forming of a Natural History Society, but model planes. Mark Lakin's Dolphin glided the full length of the golf course before crashing into the trees by the Major Game.' A marionette theatre was started and other activities included Billy Dulles's artificial hand for David Cunningham when he fractured his arm, and six-foot candle stands prepared for the Carol Service. T.E.B.J. ended by wishing everyone 'a very Hobby New Year'.

T.E.B.J. had been 32 when he arrived in 1950, a spare figure of medium height, with thick brown hair, which has never shown a sign of greying or diminishing. His thin, ascetic-looking face and piercing blue eyes commanded instant respect from the boys, who soon learnt that behind a mask of ironic cynicism was a warm-hearted bachelor, who was to spend his working life looking after others; first his father before he died of Parkinson's disease, then his totally deaf mother with whom he shared a bungalow in Dry Sandford, and all the time the boys themselves. Though a self-confessed agnostic, Tom has lived the most Christian of lives.

Simon Moffett writes that T.E.B.J. deserves a chapter to himself: 'His special talent with us was his absolute authority and yet he could talk to us at our level. He drew magic pictures and cartoons. He told stories. He had the gift of being able to come to a mathematical problem and see the difficulty that the pupil had and change the approach, to enable the boy to see past the problem. I always hoped I could get some magic from being near him.' To Robin Leanse, coming into the school at the age of 11, 'he was a really important and interesting individual, almost a phenomenon. I remember the intensity he brought to focus on problems of one's work and behaviour, and the clarity with which he praised or blamed. Oddly, the irony in his outlook enhanced my feelings of respect for him.' His discipline was absolute. David Hannah was told on arrival: '"Watch out for Jakes, he blows people up." ...I had a momentary vision of his planting dynamite under a boy, and I began to wonder what kind of people Cothill contained.'

Tom Jackson, early 1970s. The kitchen and sick-room in the background had been built in 1935 and joined the clock-tower to the main building.

Desmond Wigan was one who knew him in a double capacity, as 'a superb teacher and a great friend and mentor as a colleague'. He has called him 'the world's most indefatigable punster'. He loves writing letters in verse and playing about with words; David Way soon found himself addressed as 'Straight and Narrow' when the morning letters were given out. David hymned him before leaving with a four-stanza poem in the *Magazine*, which included the lines: 'At times, he buys for ungrateful boys – / Super puzzles, and brand-new toys, / His words and deeds, and clever wit, / Drum-in maths just bit by bit.' According to the Greenwell brothers, addition and subtraction were taught 'by the decimation and joining up of two Mars Bars'. Charles Gooch writes: 'He used to set us mind-twisting puzzles, with prizes of Mars Bars. One end-of-term we walked into his classroom to find something written in code on the blackboard. Once decoded, it told you where the Mars Bar was hidden.'

In the middle of the Autumn term of 1954 Muriel Wright had to leave to look after a sick sister. For 26 years she had presided over the bottom class. Many new boys will echo Jonathan Stedall: 'She was gentle and kind and reminded me of home.' S.A.P. wrote of her: 'One seldom saw her ruffled or perturbed, and her calmness and patience were of the utmost value to all in her class.... A new boy soon realised that she was a guide, mentor and friend.... She set herself a high standard and she expected her small boys to

'Mummy' Hall, 1972.

do likewise.' He appreciated especially her recounting the amusing remarks made to her in class, and 'her unfailing loyalty and friendship'.

Luckily for Cothill, she was succeeded by another exceptional teacher, Barbara Hall. Married, living in Abingdon, with two sons, she was a large, smiling Scotswoman, in her late thirties. She recalls her early days: 'I was immediately made to feel part of everything by Major and Mrs Pike. The masters were so friendly and encouraging. . . . Here I was drawn to the boys, they were so warm and, I felt, needed a motherly figure in the bottom form, having come from loving homes.' For the next thirty years 'Mummy' Hall was to give new boys the start they needed. They remember how she taught them how to address their letters home, which did not stop one of them addressing his 'To our Mummy'; how she read their letters to them because they could not read their parents' handwriting; how she would receive posies of the Head Master's snowdrops from her flock. Every year she produced a short, class Nativity Play, 'and was lucky enough to be the wardrobe mistress for school plays (how I will never know. I do not enjoy sewing, nor had I any idea where to begin each new play) and to be able to enjoy the fervour in the Library as different characters prepared to go on.' Something that touched her particularly was 'the warm feeling when boys rushed to tell me they had done well in their Common Entrance'.

James Holt, who had arrived as a new boy in 1945, has sent the following note about the circumstances of his entry to Cothill, written by his mother: 'How to choose your son's prep school. The Mama goes and looks at the school and is shown round. She counts the number of loos, which is satisfactory. Bids goodbye to the Head Master and returns to London. After some persuasion she manages to get a promise out of her husband to go and look at the school. They visit together and are given tea in the sitting-room. The head and the father spend 45 minutes talking fishing. It is then time to catch a train back to London, so father and mother make their adieus with thanks – the future is amicably arranged after a look at the calendar – and a successful future is embarked on.'

Jim Bellew 'can still see that Spring afternoon [in 1930] in front of the school, the driveway packed with cars arriving with trunks and boxes. Cars large, upright and square, luggage-racks mounted on the back, behind the spare wheel. There seemed to be hundreds of boys with red caps dashing around looking for old friends or with some terribly important task to perform.' Tony Findlay, after his parents said goodbye, recalls 'being at a complete loss for anything to do. We ended up walking endlessly and aimlessly along the downstairs passages. Conversation was limited to "Hallo, what's your name? Where do you live? How old are you?"' Elder brothers are seldom much help, but Johnny Peel, 20 years later, 'spent the first week clasping the hand of my cousin throughout the day and crying myself to sleep in the company of an earless donkey ("Der Mumy and Dady, I am very homsick")'. In the 1960s, according to David Way, 'The new boys are assembling. There is tea in the Pikes' drawing-room. We eye each other. Our parents chat away among themselves. Major Pike moves around a lot and has bushy eyebrows and a moustache. Mrs Pike is very tall and elegant. I am asked a few questions and answer shyly.'

Later that day the parents of new boys need reassuring. John Hannah remembers how he and his wife left David, 'a diminutive figure, looking confident but probably very apprehensive. . . . Gabrielle rang up half-an-hour later to say that he had in fact dissolved into tears, had been given a slice of chocolate cake and was now happily watching a film.' More recently, Bill Stockton, coming back as a parent, comments on 'the magnificent way the pain of leaving James for the first time was eased; he was really welcomed as a new boy and Rachel was wonderful.' It was at this stage that Muriel Wright and Barbara Hall gave new boys comfort and confidence to face the future.

The Spring term of 1955 was free from illness, but with not enough snow for Winter sports, walks became tedious and there were only two games of hockey. After football 'sixes' had been played off without a hitch, the *Magazine* concluded: 'We came to the calmer waters of sports practice in almost springlike weather. The flags and the white lines looked gay in the sun, but overcoats and sweaters were worn without too many cries of, "Oh, sir, I'm boiling". Mr Swinbank's revolver scared the wits out of the three school dogs, the judges crowding round the tape disentangled some horribly close finishes, and only one hurdle was broken – and no necks, although one small boy caused some alarm at his attempt to perform the "western roll". A pleasant fortnight, unlike anything else in the school year, with its relaxed atmosphere and its promise of various end-of-term pleasures.'

8

FAREWELL TO S.A.P.

After ten post-war years, the school was unchanged in its essence. There had been little modernisation; boys were encouraged to make their own amusements and television was almost unknown. Indeed it was only now, in 1955, that a second-hand 'talkie' projector was bought, with some help from leaving boys' contributions, and its popularity increased as we discovered a wider variety of suitable films. A craze for making balsa-wood aeroplanes had been preceded by a rash of model diesel engines. T.E.B.J. reported: 'We soon found that noise, and noise alone, was everyone's objective, so a new rule was made: no engines were to be run until they were mounted on an aeroplane ready to fly. This resulted in mass production. Roller-pill runs were cleared from desk lids. Blueprints, so richly studded with glass-headed pins that they looked like war maps, took their place. The smell of diesel oil was superseded by that of pear-drops emanating from the balsa cement everyone was using. Eventually one plane did fly, its final crash being received with more applause than its actual lengthy flight.'

Academic standards were sound without being brilliant and Common Entrance failures were rare. Bapji Jodhpur remembers: 'Cothill prepared me for admission to Eton in a no-nonsense and matter-of-fact manner. When I received the news that I had passed, there was much cheering: "What's all this noise?" boomed the daunting figure of Major George. When it was explained, he thundered, "No occasion for rejoicing, it's only as expected".' The best results were probably achieved in Mathematics, Classics and French. T.E.B.J. proved to be an exceptional teacher of Mathematics, but, under the system of 'setting', he could only take one class. Similarly in Latin, H.A.G.P.'s love of the Classics and his skill in teaching them could only be appreciated by the top class. HMI had detected 'much energetic teaching in Mathematics and a good standard at the top of the school', and had commented on the 'scholarly precision' with which Latin was taught up the school. Although there was no attempt at cramming, one future scholar remembers how H.A.G.P. would 'cover odd bits of the blackboard with allusions and odd quotes which could have got us through "O" levels at the age of 12'.

Bapji's mention of a daunting figure with a thundering voice gives me the opportunity to say something of my life as S.A.P.'s second-in-command. I was recently asked by the mother of two Old Boys, 'What would you have done if you had not had the family business to go into?' I had no clear answer; by 1947 it seemed that I had a duty to help my parents to bring the school into the post-war world. From the first I had a full teaching programme, learning as I went along, with the help of holiday courses in Oxford. Bicycling holidays in France improved my French. I tried to pass on something of my enthusiasm for History and English literature to senior boys, but soon realised how difficult it is to teach either of these subjects. I met all prospective parents when they were shown into my classroom and then socially afterwards. I became assistant editor of the *Magazine*, with special responsibility for 'Old Boys' news', and began a friendship with Jack Hooke, owner of the Abbey Press in Abingdon, a delightful man who somehow deciphered the handwritten 'copy' my father and I sent him.

At this time S.A.P. was 67 years old. He continued to hold all the reins, and although we discussed future entries, he and I seldom talked finance. He seemed to have made a complete recovery from his heart attack and appeared very fit, though there was a hiccup when he suddenly developed spondylitis after a fall and had to wear a collar. This enraged him so much that he forced himself to walk further and further every day until he was able to throw the collar away. Before long he was even playing golf again. I had in the meantime relieved him of certain duties such as taking morning prayers before breakfast, followed by breathing exercises. I had taken the morning

PT in the yard, c.1912.

PT period, which included games such as 'O'Grady Says', since H.R.B.'s death, and the drill display remained a feature of Sports Day.

I visited all our rival schools with various teams, making special friends with Geoffrey Bolton, John Evans and Pat Marston of Summer Fields, the Stow family of Horris Hill, Harold Evans of Swanbourne and Joc Lynam of the Dragon. S.A.P. was too much of an individualist to take much interest in the Incorporated Association of Preparatory Schools (IAPS), but I had become a member in 1953 and was extending my acquaintanceship with prep- and public-school headmasters. They were a friendly lot in Number 10 District, and they ran a good collection of schools. Among them the Dragon was (and still is) a law unto itself, with its huge size, scholastic record, free-and-easy manners and a go-ahead attitude towards change; almost 'This is the way we propose to do it, and we recommend others to follow suit'. Summer Fields, so different in atmosphere, with a fine scholarship record for Eton, was somewhat grand and very hard to beat at cricket. Horris Hill was then primarily a Winchester school, with a reputation for toughness and Spartan conditions. Our boys always got on particularly well with theirs, admiring their all-round excellence, especially their near-invincibility on the football field. My father and 'Daddy' Stow had been friends for years, vocal supporters of their respective teams. My parents were also very fond of 'G.B.' (Geoffrey Bolton), that gaunt and formidable Summer Fields figure with a heart of gold; they were two of the very few who called him by his Christian name.

What sort of impact I had is hard for me to say, as most Old Boys are either too shy or too tactful to give much indication. My nickname, at one time, was apparently 'Rubbery' (because of my somewhat bouncing walk?), but later became 'Toff'. Toby Pryor wrote to Peter Glossop of an earlier period: 'I do have a soft spot for Major George because he was the only teacher in the whole of my distinguished academic career ever to award me 10/10 for anything. . . . I once drew a triangle with a circle in it and it was absolutely perfect. Bless him for that one item.' Chris Palmer-Tomkinson remembers 'your own house-colour socks on the football field which I thought must have been incorrectly knitted by your mother as the colours were a mis-match'.

My sister-in-law Janet, married to the well-known engraver Reynolds Stone, sent two sons to Cothill. The elder, Edward, now a distinguished painter, was a withdrawn and silent little boy when he came in 1949 after an unhappy time at a previous prep school. Soon, however, he blossomed, grew more confident, showed promise as a left-arm bowler, but found his work difficult and left early to be coached by J. C. Banks in Sussex before going on to Eton. Edward's younger brother, Humphrey, had arrived in 1950, aged seven, a diminutive figure in cut-down trousers. He describes himself as an acutely shy small boy. 'It was a credit to the school that I was able to develop happily minding my own business but learning to get on with my peers.' He recalls 'the pleasure of rushing through the woods where badgers made their setts; bird-watching on the golf course, and green woodpeckers disappearing round the pine trees; growing mustard and cress in a place that the other boys wouldn't detect; queuing up to see Matron to have cod-liver oil and malt every morning; being shown how to fold a pair of socks by Miss Hargreaves; the smell of "Ma Dep" as she entered the Dining Hall ['She uses scent', he confided to his mother his first term].' Three things about S.A.P. stick in Humphrey's mind: 'his alarming purple nose; how when watching the high jump, his right leg would go up as the boy leapt into the air; and his lectures on achievement, that second best was not good enough.' Janet appreciated the 'Edwardian country-house charm in the private side of the house, and hospitality to match. Sam was wonderfully kind and helpful to a homesick son, with Dinky toys in his study, and Dorothy was so pretty, with a particularly engaging smile. Their harmony and devotion to each other created a unique happy family feeling in the school.'

Humphrey Stone's last Summer term was to be in 1955. As Captain of the cricket XI 'his length and direction were immaculate, and on several occasions he seemed to hypnotise the opposing batsmen into making all sorts of weird shots'. Summer Fields, in particular, have reason to remember his three years in the 1st XI, where his slow bowling proved their undoing on a number of occasions. Another to leave this term was John Woolmer, with a scholarship to Uppingham. He had arrived as an eight-year-old with a great reputation as a chess player, having already played for Berkshire. He had won the school chess competition every year since then, and was to become, for some years, a mathematical don at Winchester. While there he was ordained and is now the enthusiastic Vicar of Shepton Mallet. He was clearly one who profited from S.A.P.'s lectures on achievement.

There were two special aids to this achievement; Good Marks and the Good Work List. The latter dates from the setting up of the V-badge system in the war. Weekly Reports were produced for every boy in Latin, Maths and French, and depending upon these a boy would be placed on the Good Work List, read out on Saturday mornings. If he was on this list for three successive weeks he would be awarded his V-badge, and would then have to maintain his high standard. Probably unique to Cothill were the Half-term Reports on a boy's progress sent out to parents, together with a Half-term Order. This involved a lot of work, but it was considered beneficial to keep parents up to date with their sons' general progress. Comments were kept short and were written on a single report sheet. Thus for a new boy in the bottom class for English: 'He reads well and is working hard'; '4th out of 7' might prove reassuring when the Head Master could add, 'A very good half-term – well done'. End-of-term Reports were fuller, with a separate sheet for each subject, stapled together in the form of a booklet. Most parents turned at once to the Head Master's report. An early one from S.A.P. in 1927 contained the comment: 'This boy is inclined to be frivolous at the wrong moments.' Daphne Gough says 'some of Sam's reports were wonderfully characteristic of him, his highest praise being "sensible". "Piers has had a sensible term."' One tried to keep reports as much like a letter (or postcard) as possible, commenting on success rather than failure, and hoping to develop a seeing eye and the ability to 'get the boy right'.

S.A.P. wrote a letter in his own hand after a boy's last term and I continued the practice. Among those that survive is one written to Rosie Harley about her son Tom. After commenting on work, health and games, I have added: 'He became increasingly responsible as a prefect and dormitory captain. He succeeded in keeping himself reasonably clean, his table manners were not quite so jungly and he is learning to laugh at himself. In fact he is really becoming quite civilised.' Marigold Freeman-Attwood, the mother of Robin and Harry Wedderburn, feels that Cothill was a place where education was put above learning, where you were a person first and small boy second, where competition was stimulating and fun but not ultimately important.

In the Summer term of 1955 T. M. E. Dawson joined the staff. Tim and his twin brother Nick had been boys in the school from 1942 to 1946, two grinning, black-haired, piccaninny-like identicals, whom no one in the school except my mother could tell apart. They were inseparable, wore the same clothes, played games with great enthusiasm. Strangely, in view of their subsequent success as cricketers and footballers, only Tim in his last year was in the cricket 1st XI and also the 1st XI goalkeeper. ('Dawson mi. improved in marked fashion and towards the close of the season was safe and cool' in goal.) Neither of them was a prefect, as they left young to go to Eton, where they were exceedingly happy. They had just finished their National Service with the Rifle Brigade and had decided to go in for teaching. They hoped to run a school, which they eventually did. The story goes that they now tossed a coin for who was to go to Cothill and who to Sunningdale. As Richard Bird says, Tim's arrival at Cothill 'must have lowered the average age of the

Guy Fawkes's Night, 1969. The bonfire after the fireworks.

staff considerably'. He was very strict as he was so near in age to the boys; he made a great deal of noise, especially when bellowing 'All in'; was effective in class and a great asset on the games field and as a groundsman. I remember him also in various rôles on the stage, singing 'Look for a Silver Lining' and reciting 'There was an old woman who swallowed a fly'.

The Autumn term saw a successful football season for the 1st and 2nd XIs, with 10 wins and 3 defeats, two of those inflicted on the 1st XI by Horris Hill. L.M.S. had taken over the Major Game ('with imagination and infectious keenness') from S.A.P., who had coached them for nearly 30 years. Writing about the game, the latter notes: 'Cothill football has made a very definite mark at Eton . . . where Association football has recently had a renaissance. There are usually two or three Cothill boys in their 1st XI. Association football is outstandingly a team game – possibly more so even than cricket – but both games help character-building. To play soccer well one needs courage, unselfishness, intelligence, fitness of body, alertness of mind, enterprise, daring and the knack of taking full advantage of the opportunities that come one's way.' Clive Craigmile, Tom Bowles and Nick Dawson all played this year as Old Etonians in the Arthur Dunn Cup.

The Autumn term was always S.A.P.'s favourite, and he wrote of what a boy might look forward to: 'The crisp fresh mornings with their gentle mists hanging in the trees and slowly fading away. The lovely and varied colours of the leaves during October and early November – the conker season – mushrooms – fairy spider webs glistening – instructive and exciting weekend films – extra periods off when a Saint's day turns up – fireworks – group senior and junior six-a-side playground football matches, based on the rules of the floodlit Wembley contests.' It reveals the child behind the man, his appreciation of the beauty of the place, his understanding of what boys enjoyed and looked forward to, the importance of treats and excitement.

One of the treats was the annual Guy Fawkes's display. David Dundas, aged 10, wrote: 'First of all, a big ray of light spread all over the trees, red and green. Then three or four red rockets sped high into the air. After about ten seconds the whole display goes zooming up into the air with a terrific bang. Of course sooner or later I suppose it has to rain. And it did. It came down in torrents. Everyone rushed in to gaze from a window in the New Hall. But after a minute or two out we went. Now all the fireworks start again. Another rocket is lit. Is it going to work? No! it goes phut, and Major George lights it a second time. Now is it going to work? Well, it does, though it shoots off towards the fifth game pitch. Now I think it is Major George lighting the Niagara Falls. They look really lovely against the dark blue sky.' This gives some idea of the remarkable displays that Messrs Brock provided in those days, at a very reasonable price.

In 1956 the Rev. J.S. Reynolds became Vicar of Dry Sandford, and so embarked on what Richard Bird has described as 'a long [27-year] uncompromising incumbency'. Many will remember counting the number of times he cleared his throat during his sermons. It is said that he stopped in the middle of one of these because he suddenly spotted a boy in the pew in front of him eating a hard-boiled egg. According to Richard, he wore Newmarket boots under his surplice, for he walked everywhere, being unable to drive a car. John was at this time a tall, prematurely bald, Victorian figure in his late thirties, evangelical and legalistic in his churchmanship, with a beautiful speaking voice, a sensitive nature and a ready sense of humour. He did not find it easy to adapt to the boys, who were seldom able to appreciate until later in life his wide scholarship and dedicated ministry. To go round a church with him is a stimulating experience, for he is an antiquary and genealogist of repute.

That Summer A.K.R. produced *The Tempest* (starring Mark Fisher), the *Magazine* account commenting on 'the wizardry with which the former transformed a stage into a magical island'. The 1st cricket XI had a good season; 7 wins and 1 defeat. Peter Wigan and Garth Wood were the stars, the former scoring the first Cothill century – away against St Andrew's, Pangbourne – since Harold Porter's in 1900. The Spring term of 1957 saw Walter Quantock Shuldham's 51-year-old long jump record of 14 ft 6 in. beaten by Robin Bailey, and Alan de Piro's quarter mile equalled by Hugo Powell. Films included *The Lavender Hill Mob* and a V-badge showing of *The Lady Vanishes*, which frightened the younger boys. (Even greater fear was caused by the showing, some years later, of Alastair Sim in *A Christmas Carol*, which makes one wonder how today's boys, nourished on television, would respond to these films.) It was in this term that the first mention is made of a television set, given by Colin Vandervell's father, the creator of the Vanwall racing-car.

A contrasting form of entertainment was a Latin play performed by the nine-year-olds. It was the product of M. Lamprill, a cheerful and energetic young man, who had recently joined the staff. He wrote in the *Magazine:* 'It is good to have some Latin inside you; and it was to realise this object pleasantly that this small play was written. Vocabularies were made of words not known, correct accenting practised, parts zealously learnt outside lessons. The performance was a strange mixture of drama, fine acting, numerous loud promptings, bawls of "light". The whole class took part, some in several rôles.' Michael was on the staff for not more than two years, but he achieved fame as the originator of a variation of the game of 'He'. For many years boys continued to play 'Lamprill' without realising anything about its origin. T.E.B.J. says: 'He was a splendid man. One day he was arrested walking across the airfield. When asked by the duty officer what he thought he was doing, he said he had never been up in a plane and hoped for a ride. He got one, and at the end offered to pay for the petrol. He wanted to learn Arabic, for some reason or other, and got Sir Reader Bullard (ex-Ambassador to Tehran), who lived close by, to give him lessons. He left without any luggage (I ran him to the station).'

Two other masters, C. H. Gibson, an Old Boy, and D. Edwards, joined the staff straight from their public schools. Clem Gibson had been captain of the Eton cricket XI in 1955, and David Edwards had been in the Winchester XI. During their relatively brief time at Cothill before going on to higher things, both of them added to the gaiety of life generally and to the standard of games in particular.

In the Summer term my sister Diana married Archie Heyman, a charming, good-looking man, who had kept wicket for Cheltenham and remained boyishly enthusiastic about all games. He had been a boy at Cothill during the Great War and he had sent his son Peter to the school in 1952. Shortly

My father with the teaching staff, 1956. Standing: *G. L. S. Pike, H. A. G. Phillimore, T. M. E. Dawson, T. E. B. Jackson, R. E. Langhorne;* sitting: *C. H. Gibson, J. R. Vassar-Smith, D. Edwards;* foreground: *A. K. Reid, S. A. Pike, L. M. Swinbank.*

after this his wife had died. Peter writes: 'I vividly remember your poor father having to tell me the sad news . . . and feeling that I ought to cry, but was too well prepared in my own mind to cause Sam too much embarrassment. All the boys were exceedingly kind to me, particularly one of the McEuens who was in charge of my dormitory at that time.' Archie had remained a widower throughout Peter's time at Cothill, watching him develop, according to Peter, 'from being a frightened little boy who periodically fainted in church into Head Boy reading the lesson to the whole school. You and the rest of the staff must have done a good job at character-building in my case, as I am sure was true of many others.' Since Archie's sudden death in 1969, Peter has been a great solace to Diana.

Peter Heyman's mention of reading the lesson reminds me of the occasion some years later when Charles Guernsey failed to get from me the verses to be read the following morning in prayers. Not to be daunted, he began reading from where the previous reader had left off: 'The Lord said unto Joshua, Make thee sharp knives and circumcise again the children of Israel...'. After a few verses in this vein he finally ground to a halt, and afterwards apologised to me for causing embarrassment. Whereupon Michael Edwardes-Ker piped up: 'Oh, don't worry, sir. They've got to learn sometime.'

Later in the Summer, on the Sunday after Fathers' Match, Blackie the jackdaw appeared. 'No one knew where he had come from', according to the *Magazine*, 'though certain boys were under suspicion, since he was always seen on their shoulders. He attended classes and cricket games, jumping up and down and squawking protest when the ball came near him. A favourite occupation was throwing pumice-stone and soap out of the bathroom windows. For variety he would fly off with magnifying glasses and other bright objects which were usually found in flower-beds. We never discovered where he spent the nights. Then one day, just before breathing exercises, we saw that he had a companion – presumably a jilldaw.'

A feature of the end of every Autumn term had for many years been the dormitory Christmas decorations, or 'Dormo decs'. In the *Magazine*, T.E.B.J. described how 'Somewhere about half-term things begin to stir. New boys mystify their parents with demands for "crepapper", and the long, thin, flat parcels start arriving.... As the term wears on ... lockers bulge with coloured paper chains.... "How many has your dormo got? Ours has 117".... Major Pike's supply of string and drawing-pins is gradually depleted.... At last the day comes when the decorations can start going up. The staff is pleased, "keeps them quiet". The dormitory master is wiser. He knows what to expect... chariot racing in number 10; the fight for the ladder in number 5; determination of number 11 to coat their walls with glue; the indignation of number 1 when told that six-inch nails are not permitted even in the plaster.... Three days pass, order reigns.... "Our dormo is to have a play".... Tableaux are very vivants. There are Marys, Josephs, and shepherds and lambs, and stars which stand still and stars which shoot upwards. Everything is planned in great detail. Even so there is the inevitable last-minute rush.... The judging is over... there is peace, but only for a while. ... Clearing the decs for action, that mad tempestuous moment when everything is torn down and thrown away.... Then, when Nina [Hargreaves] has finished retrieving the belts, and ties, and socks, and dental plates, which are invariably carried to the incinerator with the general litter, all is over. Another happy year has nearly ended.'

A sad event was to cloud the end of this year, however; Lovegrove died after a painful illness, aged 72. For the last 17 years he had been the school's major domo, a distinguished-looking figure in short black coat and black tie. He answered the front-door bell, waited at meals, shopped in Abingdon, fetched visitors from the station, looked after the petty cash and PAYE. After his death, S.A.P. wrote in the *Magazine*: 'He took such a great pride in Service – in unselfishly serving others and putting loyalty to his employers before self-interest. Nothing was ever too much trouble and he certainly did not keep to normal trade-union hours. He set himself a very high standard of work and conduct and we, as a family, were on our guard in case anything we said or did failed to meet with his entire approval.' But he had a wonderful sense of humour, looked like Stan Laurel, and in his own cottage was a lively and generous host.

In the Spring term of 1958 Duff Hart-Davis lectured on his journey to Russia with his godfather Peter Fleming, Ian's elder brother and a well-known writer and traveller. This was the first journey by car to be made by two Englishmen to the USSR since the war and the description of it was enthralling. Maths I put on 'When the π was opened', written, directed and inspired by T.E.B.J. 'Old Boys' news' revealed that at Eton Henry Berens was the first Old Cothillian to be Captain of the Oppidans during the Pike régime. Henry, with Seton Wills and Henry Lopes, formed a Cothill triumvirate in Pop. Not all Old Cothillians were particularly distinguished, but one Etonian, not himself a Cothillian, told his father at this time that they were nice chaps, extremely friendly towards each other and very loyal to their prep school. A partial nominal roll of boys in the school appeared in the *Magazine* in the form of a rhymed 'Cothill Alphabet'. It contains the lines: 'I for the idle and ignorant "who?" / J for Jodhpur and Jourdain, only two. . . .'

Bapji Jodhpur has sent his recollections of 'An Indian at Cothill': 'I was a small boy aged eight, thousands of miles away from his home in an entirely alien environment. . . .

'One of the first and most vivid of images to remain in my mind is as the train from Paddington Station slowly gained momentum and I bid a final farewell to my mother, my aunt and uncle, and in the background Mrs Scott, whom I had only just met over lunch and who was to become my English mother-figure – a role which I discovered later she was admirably suited for. But at this moment I had eyes only for my mother and I knew, as she knew, we were both desperately fighting back our tears. A show of public emotion is conduct unbecoming to a Rajput. Once out of sight, the impact of this momentous parting finally hit me and left me in a state of inanimate suspension....

'The four years in between that first day at Paddington and the news of my passing out of Cothill to Eton are filled with several haphazard images. Looming large above them all is the patriarchal presence of Sam Pike, with his kindly face dominated by a large red nose. He was, as all good Head Masters should be, held in awe and affection. Afternoons spent crammed into his study listening to BBC's educational and classical programmes were an important and formative part of my introduction to the Western cultural scene. Dorothy always appeared to me a little more formidable, but the ice was broken on those long warm English Summer evenings when we were allowed to sketch and paint in her delightful garden. Cream buns and cucumber sandwiches also fit into this picture somewhere, but I'm not sure exactly how....

'About half-way through my first term, for a change I heard some coherent and catchy music being played on the piano in the Junior Common Room. I had never seen the boy before, but stood there to listen to his music. He looked at me, but didn't say a word until he had finished. He then turned to me and said, "You must be my black brother. I am Andrew Scott". Andrew, one of my guardian's sons who had missed part of the term, had heard about me from his parents. Though sadly both parents died while I was still in England, the Scott children remain my family in England. Outside school I learnt from the Scotts the nuances of English life that helped me so much to enjoy fully my time in England.

'I soon fell into the routine of the school, but there was one aspect of life that none of us could reconcile to, and that was the early morning ritual cold bath.... That ritual and the dormitories fell under the charge of Mr Jackson, or "Jacko" as he was known to us. Imagine my surprise when the first words he uttered to me were in Hindi. He had had an Indian army background and had picked up many phrases which he would try out on me from time to time. He also used the Hindi honorific suffix and called me Jodhpurji when he was in a good mood....

'Cothill was at that time one of the few prep schools in England to boast a golf course, which provided us with a bona fide excuse to break bounds, when we would disappear over the fence into the woods, ostensibly looking for lost balls. In retrospect I wish I had taken that early introduction to golf more seriously, as it is a game that I am still trying to master. Thanks to Jacko I also got an opportunity to play hockey now and again. It wasn't a game played regularly at the school, but was the game that I played better than most of the boys, being the Indian national game. Though I learnt to enjoy the other games, I never did excel at them at Cothill....'

R. E. Langhorne and his wife Jean left in the Summer of 1958 to teach in the West Country. Robin was a smiling, toothy man, in his thirties, exceptionally enthusiastic and competent in the classroom and on the games field. His memories include 'the hour's Latin [first period in the morning], with nine- and ten-year-olds in the partitioned Big Schoolroom, with Dust in the other half – how scared I was, particularly at first, of raising my voice. Dust would freeze, his head on one side, his arms crooked in a characteristic gesture and a look of inexpressible hurt and disapproval on his face. . . . Back I would go to the task of trying to teach. . . . I always remember that ineffably neat translation of "He was killed by an arrow" – "Sagittabatur". Dust never uttered a word of censure and was always so kind and welcoming in my early days in the Masters' Cottage. Arthur Reid and Tom Jackson made up the quartet there in 1954. Arthur had the ability to appear infinitely experienced and yet never patronising.' Robin will never forget a highly successful two-hour party given by A.K.R. when the only strong drink was an inch of sloe gin. Another abiding memory was when 'Sam drafted me in to keep order in a dancing class when the lady teacher had difficulty with recalcitrant youth. Sam looked in half way to see what sort of job I was making of it. Allen ma., or was it Allen mi., was wearing ink-stained corduroys and braces and was dancing man to my lady. We made such a graceful couple.'

He remembers 'enough gin to put me at my ease' before dinner on his first day; 'your father leaping about in the Autumn, catching his twelve falling leaves [for 12 happy months]'; one of the Milnes-Gaskell brothers emerging from S.A.P.'s leavers' talk on the facts of life and remarking, 'that seems a

Autumn leaves, 1976.

Cricket match, early 1960s.

very sensible arrangement'; T.E.B.J. announcing, with a very worried expression, 'I want to lay my hands on a Trollope'; Fathers' Match 'with strawberries and cream and Dorothy's lovely roses'. He ends: 'Please include somewhere what a welcoming place it was and what a benign influence your parents were on staff, pupils and parents.'

Hobbies were renamed 'make and mend', with work on mowing pitches, building foundations for a coconut-matting cricket net, filling potholes in the yard, making new Snob wickets. A.K.R. produced *The Lady's Not for Burning*, 'an ambitious choice, which made considerable demands on the principal players', Ian Brown and Nicholas Chance, both of whom left to recover at Marlborough. There was an end-of-term novelty. 'A poster in the Big Schoolroom announced that P. W. Gough, R. A. Chamberlain and J. M. R. Powell were soon to star in "As It Was In the Beginning, Is Now, and Ever Shall Be", a new comedy by the budding playwrights R. A. Chamberlain and J. Bradbury. We therefore looked forward to the performance with eager anticipation, and were not disappointed. In brief, the three-act play dealt with the penalties involved – decapitation, electrocution and projection into outer space – by those unprepared to pay their taxes in the past, present and future respectively.' Roderick Chamberlain recalls 'with undue pride writing it, aided and abetted by James Bradbury, who now heads Lucas's electric motor-car development team. I remain hugely pleased with the line "All serfs, tides, omos, persils and other detergents of ye realm shall pay a tax of ye three groats on ye she goats". . . . Arthur Reid's amazing pun scenes in the masters' plays were a fair challenge – there were always an unexpectedly large number of boys named in these tongue-twisting sessions.' Among special treats that live in his memory are 'G.L.S.P. reading *The Cricket Match* and *Poets at Play* and the school holiday when I scraped an exhibition to Radley (I nearly drowned ducking for apples)'.

A tantalising tailpiece to the Summer term says: 'We received a visit from two of the "original" Old Boys, who had been in the school under its first Head Master, Mr Carles, in the 1880s' – no names or details are given. As already mentioned, unfortunately no written records survive of C. W. Carles's headmastership. The boys' names on the Dining-Hall boards begin only in 1894 under M. J. Dauglish.

The Autumn term produced no football stars, but a workmanlike XI, which beat Summer Fields 5–2 at home, but was beaten by them away 0–3, 'out-kicked and out-run'. A variety show was produced 'by boys for boys'. David Dundas and James Bradbury, 'in top hat and tails, regaled us with a medley of tunes, as the "Dixie Duet". Then came the "Slick Sextet", the Cothill skiffle group.' A.K.R.'s production *Babes in the Wood* saw 'Swinny, Jacko and Jodge in their best slapstick form and that is high praise'. The hardy annual 'Here's to Crime' was sung and H.A.G.P., in a red wig, recited 'The Owl and the Pussy Cat'. Of the difficulty of keeping the pantomine a secret, S.A.P. wrote: 'One unfortunate (or is it fortunate?) master has to be left out of the production and to hold the fort and be "masterful" elsewhere, i.e. he has to keep a hundred boys quiet in one room without their guessing that the one and only rehearsal is going on elsewhere and if one hears a shout from afar one hurriedly drops a book or coughs to smother it. Another tricky problem is to know how far one can go to say a firm "No" to go "Round the corner". So spare a thought for this "stage manager behind the scenes"; he has his humble part to play.'

In March 1959 Audrey married Hugh Parry after divorcing Christopher Cheshire. Hugh was a tall, wavy-haired Welsh solicitor, who had negotiated the divorce, and had been from the first impressed with Audrey's lack of bitterness. He was a recent widower with a young son John, and while Hugh was to prove a devoted husband and affectionate step-father to Tim and Sue, John was absorbed into a happy home by Audrey. In 1960, twin daughters, Margaret and Jane, were born. Sue has memories of staying at Cothill over the previous years: '. . . going into classes with the bottom form; meals at the top table and feeling very embarrassed walking out first. . . . Tim and I fell through the pavilion roof and made a hole in it. Grandoo was extremely cross and I think we had to write lines.'

Carpenter's shop under A. S. J. White, 1968.

In 1959 a Mr Stock came to teach carpentry and to be general handyman. He was an outstanding instructor who helped to stimulate the boys' enthusiasm. The carpenter's shop had been a happy centre in the life of many boys since the days of Mr Short, whose kindly reign had continued until about 1925. Chris Barnett remembers the smell of glue, the hard work of making coffin stools in elm ('Perhaps to get some muscle into our feeble little "war-baby" arms'). He was one of many who absorbed a love of joinery and acquired a skill in DIY for which he has always been grateful. No power tools were used; boys learnt to do a job properly by hand, and the periods of only 45 minutes ensured that no one was bored. More than one Old Boy regrets not learning carpentry and wishes it had been compulsory.

Films were a common feature of the Autumn and Spring terms. Raphe Palmer is reminded of an occasion when T.E.B.J. was showing a 'Carry-On' film. 'In one scene there were some girls doing exercises and a piece of clothing came off, very suggestively. Coincidentally the projector malfunctioned. It then restarted after missing out this scene. Five minutes later a similar scene began. Again projector malfunction! Then Jacks mysteriously got a bad headache and the whole showing then ceased. Censorship à la Cothill!' The lists of films shown in the fifties make nostalgic reading, including such classics as *The Count of Monte Cristo*, with Robert Donat, and *The Wooden Horse*. There is also mention of 'a never-to-be-forgotten adventure serial in eight thrilling, exciting, nail-biting parts, *The Snake-skin Belt*'. One wonders where T.E.B.J. had dug that up.

Cricket, c.1912.

In the Summer of 1959 parents were reminded that boys could go out on two Sundays, but no more. The *Magazine* highlighted World Refugee Year, with the Queen as Patron, at 'a fitting time, twenty years after the outbreak of World War II, for all of us to give our sympathy, and think how we can help this great movement of relief' for the half-million refugee children scattered over Europe and the Middle East. There was a brief revival of arms drill with the Lee-Enfield (L-E), Cothill model, wooden, mark IV. 'Group instructors did their work well, the final "battalion parade" was extremely impressive. Our spies tell us that the L-E will be in use at all public schools for some years to come.' Cricket was played in hot weather, standards improved, though 'the "Under-Ten" match against Summer Fields was a very one-sided affair, our opponents having two potential Bradmans who clouted our tired and rather erratic bowling. By contrast our batting lacked spirit and revealed little promise.' Many afternoons were spent in the swimming-pool, but 'alas, not all the boys in the school can swim yet'. An Old Boys' cricket match took place on a scorching Sunday. 'Several wet-bobs were press-ganged into playing, cricketing clothes were provided for some who had been too modest to bring their own.' Peter Wigan captained the Old Boys' team, the school 'appeared over-awed by their opponents and completely failed to do themselves justice' under Christopher Wigan's captaincy. An item in the scorebook reads 'Wigan P., l.b.w. Wigan C. 0'. As Peter had just got his XI at the age of 15, and was to score 58 in the first innings at Lord's, his wicket was a considerable scalp for Christopher. Meanwhile, the same term, Desmond Wigan made history at Eton by being the first boy to win the Queen's Prize for both French and German.

The 1950s ended with 'a craze for flying kites. Several school ties, illegally used for decoration, were lost over the Marsh.' Another jackdaw appeared and stayed about a week, during which time it disturbed every class and removed a number of fountain-pens before it suddenly vanished. John Hanmer, an Old Boy who had been on the staff for a short time, left to become a racing commentator. Mary Curtis arrived as o/c Music. She was an attractive 35-year-old, with a quiet voice and glasses. She taught the piano and singing, but unfortunately could not play the organ. This task was undertaken by a local, Mrs Fuller, who did her best to cope for Sunday services, while Mary Curtis coached the choir. It was an unsatisfactory compromise, but in other respects the musical life of the school flourished. Congregational singing was as hearty as ever and visiting teachers taught a variety of instrumentalists who combined to form a small orchestra.

Peter Shakerley and others mention singing during the Great War. H. K. Kefford, a popular young master and a good cricketer, played the piano and encouraged everyone to sing, 'however unmusical they were' (according to John Thomson). Sing-songs out of the *Scottish Students Song-book* were popular on Saturday evenings instead of prep. Solos were sung in church: 'I well remember my first solo effort', writes Chris Barnett, 'being plied with Friars Balsam on lumps of sugar by old "Hatter" [Miss Hames].' His cousin, Evelyn Hulbert-Powell, 'scraped away on his violin more like Jack Benny than Kreisler. I believe he was allowed to keep his violin as a POW.' Throughout the 1920s and 1930s Miss Spokes taught the piano. Peter Carter remembers her 'counting the beat, "one, two, thee" (she couldn't pronounce her rs)'. In later years piano lessons seem to have been painful memories for all but the most gifted. In the early 1950s Humphrey Stone recalls ' "Shelly Bag's" [Shelton's] despair at my poor playing. "Monumental" he nicknamed me, which was meant to be a pun on my name, as I sat pondering the next note.' Ten years later Wold Palmer echoes this: 'How much I dreaded piano lessons, as I had never done any practice. I should have quit when I passed Grade 1 on a rickety old piano in the Randolph Hotel.' Ten years later, Charles Gooch remembers 'piano lessons with Miss Bitterling. She used to brandish a ruler and crack me over the knuckles when I played a wrong note. She would get very annoyed with me for saying "what" instead of "pardon". I was never cured.'

For over 20 years Bromley Challenor came out from Abingdon to teach the piano. 'I first had Martin Williams as my boss and taught in what is now the Prefects' Room, but in those days stuffed birds of prey glared down at me from their glass cage and boys kept tame mice in the room, . . . bearable in the

Orchestral group, 1968, in the Music Room, built single-handed by Fred Hughes.

Winter but in the Summer overpowering. During that time a pupil (I think Welsh) said he had not done any practice during the holidays because thieves broke into the outhouse where the piano was kept and burnt it.' A grey-haired, serious-looking bachelor, Bromley had a quiet manner and rather dry teaching methods which hid great skill as a jazz pianist.

An orchestra had been started in 1943 by V.K.D.W., who wrote a 'Pastorita Symphonique' for what S.A.P. described in the *Magazine* as a 'highly successful concert', probably because he played the triangle. In 1969 we started a band which played at the Carol Service, consisting of two clarinets, an oboe and 12 recorders, which were not universally appreciated. Charles Smith wrote in *The Cothill Scene*: 'Recorders should be chopped into matchwood – noisy, high-pitched and squeaky, they give me a headache.' Musical appreciation had begun in the 1930s with S.A.P.'s Sunday recitals in the study, played first on a fibre-needled EMG gramophone. Light classics, Caruso and Chaliapin, Ravel's 'Bolero' ('it goes on like this for ever'), Schubert's 'Marche Militaire' ('Each one of us caught the rhythm and began to conduct imaginary orchestras. Your sister Audrey was waving her arms about with the best of us'). Graham Rogers remembers how in the war it was his 'only contact with classical music; . . . a time when one's fellow students had to shut up and listen and no one could spoil it'.

My father with the choir outside Dry Sandford Church, 1954.

The weekly Sunday service at Dry Sandford Church has continued to provide the choir with opportunities to lead the congregation and sing anthems. For Michael Knutsford, between 1935 and 1940, 'The choir played a large part in my life at Cothill; . . . plain but friendly intimate Victorian church – vestry smelt musty; matins looked forward to as a change from School Hall prayers (rather monotonous at times); V.K.D.W. in white surplice. . . . Easter, March 24, I sang three solos, . . . my parents were in church, and three days later I left to start at Eton in May 1940.' Andrew Loyd, in the mid-1970s, had been up late on a Saturday night for an illegal swim, and was yawning in church: 'You most generously took this as singing with great gusto and congratulated me at the end of church on singing louder than the rest of the choir put together.' In the 1980s, under S. A. H. Johns, unaccompanied medieval and Renaissance music was sung in church, and in April 1987 the choir toured Germany, giving concerts of British music. Clearly, 'The singing will never be done'.

The 1959 football XI was considered by S.A.P. to be potentially unbeatable: 'The writer has not seen a better, more assertive and lively forward line for some years.' My father was over-optimistic. It was beaten twice by Horris Hill in 'most exciting and bustling games', but otherwise lived up to expectations. Cothill was to be the first school to which Prince Charles paid a visit as a member of the Cheam Under-11 team. The Head Master, Peter Beck, telephoned S.A.P. to warn him: 'We're on our way, Sam.' 'Oh yes.' 'Not to make any fuss, you know, no publicity.' 'No, of course not.' He was at first completely nonplussed, not knowing what Beck was talking about. When the Cheam side arrived, the bar of the Fleur de Lys had somehow filled up with reporters, but they co-operated in keeping the visit private, and little, if anything, appeared in the papers. Prince Charles and Richard Ryder (later a prominent member of the Conservative government) were rival captains of the teams, Cothill defeating Cheam 9–0. C. J. Boothroyd remembers how H.R.H.'s detective 'had to run up and down the touchline to be adjacent to him at all times, which is perhaps why he played left-back rather than centre-forward'. H.R.H. was a somewhat lonely figure off the field, standing by himself in the yard. The scene reminded me of the Max Beerbohm caricature 'Dons of Magdalen at great pains to incur no imputation of flunkeyism' towards his great uncle when Prince of Wales.

The leaving boys organised a concert. It 'included community singing, three sketches ("The Craze to End All Crazes", "Night Operations" and "The Execution of Mary Queen of Scots"), piano solos by Lim ma. and Montgomery ma., piano duets by Hay ma. and Wedderburn, a tune by Young Recorderists conducted by Miss Curtis, singing by Shuckburgh who accompanied himself on a guitar, Lim mi. as a snake-charmer, a Western Brothers act by Eccles ma. and Jourdain, a song duet by Jourdain and Lim ma., and a playlet, called "The Turnippers", produced by Mrs Hall and enchantingly acted by the whole of her bottom form. Wedderburn and Hay filled the intervals with impromptu tunes at the piano while Millar acted as compère.' 'Old Boys' news' gave details of scholarships by John Woolmer and Richard Bradbury to Oxford and to Cambridge by David Boyle; also the election of two MPs, Robin Balniel and Jeremy Thorpe.

1960 began with epidemics of chicken-pox and mumps. Three members of staff (including T.E.B.J.) contracted the latter and half the school had one or other, sometimes both concurrently. 'We were filled with admiration for the magnificent work done by Sister and her team, and all patients will be grateful for the efficient and cheerful nursing they received.' The Sister was Flora Daniel, a widowed New Zealander in her fifties, a fine figure of a woman, with white hair, a smiling face and an authoritative manner. According to T.E.B.J., 'she epitomised Snap, Crackle and Pop'. Richard Ryder says of her: 'If Sam Pike had written out the ideal qualities required of a prep-school Sister, I doubt whether he could have improved upon those possessed by Mrs Daniel. Firm, yet sympathetic. Efficient, yet tolerant. Conscientious, yet unfussy.'

For those still in school that Spring term, the *Magazine* reported that 'one of the main attractions was the gradual emergence of the old and very dilapidated carpenter's shop into a classroom. Mr Boothroyd and Mr Vassar-Smith worked like beavers, under the guidance of Mr Stock, and the final result, with pink walls, skylight and large northern windows, was ready by the end of term. Several boys, particularly Brunton and Jourdain, gave excellent support.'

The classroom was for C. J. Boothroyd (nicknamed 'Bottle' by T.E.B.J.), who had joined the staff from Harrow in the Autumn term of 1959. Tall, thin and intense, Chris, at 19, was already a very competent teacher. Out of school he turned his hand enthusiastically to everything ('I still have Sam's testimonial, in which he made great play of my abilities with a motor-mower'), started a Printing Society and courted and eventually married a beautiful assistant matron, Ann Matthews. Two Old Etonians, P. C. Glazebrook and D. Wigan also joined. Peter was a studious-looking young man in glasses, always immaculately dressed, a Christian Scientist with a chuckle. Desmond had just left school and was employing his linguistic skills before going up to Oxford. 'Both were immediately made use of, Mr Glazebrook with hockey and shooting, Mr Wigan with boxing and golf greens.'

In the Summer, there was a whole holiday for Princess Margaret's wedding ('an extra TV was hired'), and the V-badge treat consisted of 'a barbecue luncheon in the rose garden, with large quantities of strawberries. Mr Reid and others worked very hard to produce steaks and sausages, and the

A V-badge treat, early 1970s.

weather played up well. In the afternoon there was a treasure hunt and swimming.' The cricket XI, 'despite its three defeats, was a distinct improvement on recent years', beating Horris Hill on their ground, while against the Dragon, also away, 'Guernsey's innings was a little gem. . . . We played here the sort of attacking cricket that the Dragons play, and we very nearly beat them at their own game.' For the boys' play, A.K.R. 'concocted one of his special mixtures of sketches, songs and recitations, much of it original, on the subject of animals. These were connected by verses, spoken by commentators, and well over half the school took part in *Brouhaha*.'

The football 1st XI was distinguished by the performance of the captain, Freddy Lim, the elder of two Chinese boys from Singapore. He 'showed unprecedented improvement in one season . . . turned a side without a colour into a team which tried to play football and often succeeded'. He not only gained his colours, but 'was awarded his "star", an unusual honour'. A.K.R. produced *Aladdin*, 'a Masterful Production', involving Mrs Twanky Reid, Grand Vizier Boothroyd, Sorcerer Phillimore ('on a flying saucer complete with spelling book'), Aladdin Jackson, Sultan Swinbank, Drip-Drip Vassar-Smith, Princess Glazebrook. 'This transformation of staid schoolmasters into bizarre characters' was much appreciated by the audience. 'Mr Phillimore's Sorcerer really held the play together, but all remembered their parts, and Mr Glazebrook's operatic soprano skit, followed by the "Palace Rock", was one of the highlights.'

There followed an epidemic-free Spring term of 1961, with mild weather and a perfect day for Sports, on which day an exhibition showed 'fossils, stamps, coins, paper models which ranged from serious Archimedean solids to animalia and modernistic sculptures'. There was a craze for the game diabolo; the school pony had to be put down. Among 'Old Boys' news', Francis Pym won the Cambridgeshire by-election, Charles Palmer-Tomkinson won the British Skiing Championship, Alec Montgomerie won the Army Skiing Championship, Nick Peto reached the final of the Army Rackets Championship, Mark Hely-Hutchinson rode in the Gold Cup at Cheltenham, while Pat Upton and Bob McCreery had several major successes under National Hunt rules.

The celebration this year of Nelson Battell's Silver Wedding is the right time to describe two remarkable siblings who served the school for a combined total of nearly 80 years. Nelson, who died in 1985, was intimately bound up with the start of every boy's school day, for it was he who, since 1931, in T.E.B.J.'s words, 'poured tepid water into each of the hundred basins in the dormitories long enough before the first bell to ensure that it was cold before

Nelson Battell and May Bedwell, 1967.

the boys got up'. 'Batty' kept the school running, the clocks ticking. He kept the radiators radiating and the boilers boiling. He cleaned the boys' shoes (they do their own now). He kept the footballs blown up and studded boots and shoes. He swept all the classrooms before breakfast, and was a familiar sight sitting on his motor mower or marking out the playing-fields.

He was a short, thick-set man, with an habitually worried look on his face. Deafness isolated him, but anyone who took the trouble to talk to him was rewarded by a dazzling smile. He had plenty to worry about, for it was to Batty that everyone turned whenever a pipe burst or a drain was blocked. In his early days he had to wind up the weights to make pressure for the petrol-gas, maintain two boilers run on coke, and supervise the water supply, which was pumped up to the school by windmill and an auxiliary engine from a well a quarter of a mile away, near the San. According to his sister May, 'Many times he worked into the night and early morning to keep it going. The windmill helped and he used to pray for wind.' No one was ever more conscientious or more willing to help, nothing was too much trouble. He seemed never to stop working, not a moment was wasted. The tower clock has never gone again since he retired.

Nelson's sister, May Bedwell, started working at Cothill immediately after her marriage to Jack in 1934. She served a period of probation when she did most jobs in the school, and was put in charge of the Masters' Cottage in 1935. She would arrive at 6.30 a.m., call the masters with tea and shaving water, go over to clean S.A.P.'s study between 7.00 and 8.00 ('he always had a cheerful word and a joke for me'), then return to brush out the masters' studies by 9.00. After that she made the beds, cleaned all rooms upstairs, three times a week she scrubbed the staircase. She did all the washing and ironing, looked after the masters' clothes and reported to D.E.P. on any deficiencies, such as H.A.G.P.'s patched pyjamas and non-existent dressing-gown.

She worked every day, including Sundays, for *6d* an hour, without holiday pay. Luckily she was short and sturdily built. One week she put in 96 hours. She would bicycle home three times in the day, coming back to give the masters afternoon tea, and again in the evening turning down their beds and putting hot-water bottles in if needed. Spring-cleaning took place twice a year, when everything was washed, books taken out and dusted. She even took on repainting the woodwork, indenting for paint when needed without having to refer to D.E.P. This routine continued until 1940 when her mother died and her father came to live with her and Jack. From then on she worked until 2 p.m. This was to last until 1962 when Gabrielle asked her to look after the private side of the school. Here everything was kept spotless, in contrast to some other areas before her amazingly high standards percolated through. She retired when we did in 1976, but she came once a week to keep us spick and span, until recently, when arthritic pains in her legs became too severe. In her late eighties she remains as cheerful, pretty and smartly dressed as ever.

In the Summer term of 1961, A.K.R. revived *Daggers Drawn*, which the *Magazine* described as 'a series of scenes... all vaguely connected by a dagger theme', ranging from the death of Marat to a duet 'Mack the Knife'. Nicholas Scott remembers being cast as Marat, 'with Sebastian Horn as my faithful valet Pierre and Simon Meinertzhagen as Charlotte Corday.... Dress rehearsal went well and we were confident of turning in a sound performance on the day and so we did, that is until the moment of attack, for on the cry "*à moi Pierre, à moi*", the enthusiastic Horn took to his heels and collided full tilt with the wooden tree, thus reducing the moment of tragic death to one of farce, greatly to the amusement of the audience. I naturally bore this with splendid fortitude.... There was one major drawback to the part, of course, which was that after the play the actors were allowed into the garden to drink a glass of Pimms with the parents, and this was naturally a position of envy. Not so much in my case, as my outfit consisted of one extremely skimpy towel because I had to spend the entire play seated in a tin bath-tub. It was most humiliating to parade oneself in such an outfit, particularly as most of my friends were in splendid Roman togas etc. from the previous sketch.'

At the end of term J. R. Vassar-Smith left to join his father at St Ronan's. Never one to do things quietly, he frequently threw a boy out of his classroom, once right in front of a visiting prospective parent. John himself has written: 'I must have come after National Service aged 20, in 1956, through Tim Dawson. I did one term, then left for the Summer. T.E.B.J. said "Good riddance to bad rubbish", and he was right, for I went home and learnt how to use my voice to achieve the desired results. I returned for the Christmas term and the next five happy years.' J.R.V.-S. has always looked absurdly young and remains as boyish as ever. T.E.B.J. became a special friend and is godfather to both of John's sons.

I have already referred to the darker side of school life as recalled by Jonathan Stedall. Homosexuality is one aspect of this that always gets publicity in the press and in books. It is assumed to be not uncommon in boarding-schools. When I went to the 3rd Guards Club Dinner in 1948, General John Marriott's first remarks, when we met in the lavatories, were uttered loud and clear in his distinctive high-pitched voice: 'Hallo, George, how's the school? No buggery, I hope.' It was said as a joke, with a giggle, but to my father it was no laughing matter. He was always on his guard, though he was caught out when he employed, against family advice, a music master of very doubtful ways, until a boy wrote to his mother, 'The piano teacher rubs my bare knees. Will you send some long trousers?'

A short time before S.A.P. retired a letter arrived from the Head Master of Eton, Robert Birley. It was a warning to preparatory school headmasters of what he termed a 'very dangerous homosexual', whom I call 'X.', who had been visiting certain public and preparatory schools in the Windsor area. He was described as extremely plausible, passing himself off as an Army officer, of medium height, with a moustache. He was apparently an expert cat burglar, clever at moving across country. The letter gave his car registration number, and warned everyone to be on their guard.

A few days later, while we were watching a football match, T.E.B.J. pointed out to me that a man was walking towards the school from the direction of the golf course. I went to meet him, but he changed direction and walked quickly past the Bungalow, and along the road towards the school. I ran to the front drive, saw a car in the gateway, recognised the number-plate as X.'s, but was too late to prevent his reversing into the road and driving off through the village. The alarm was raised among the masters and later that evening T.E.B.J. and Hugh Parry spotted X. in the Fleur de Lys, followed him out into the pouring rain, but lost him as he doubled back behind the Masters' Cottage. S.A.P. was taking no chances, and a watch was kept along the dormitory passage from the matrons' sitting-room throughout the night by a rota of masters. Nothing untoward occurred.

Soon afterwards, however, we learnt that X. had visited at least one Old

Cothillian at his public school, posing as a new master. When he was finally caught in one of the public schools, brought down by a flying tackle from a housemaster, he had on him a list of potential victims, with their prep schools. One of our younger Etonians had chanced to meet him in a railway compartment during the holidays. This boy got into serious trouble over money and Birley wrote to S.A.P. that he would like to discuss the matter with me, and not S.A.P., as I had been up to him my last two Summers at Eton. I found R.B. in his study with the boy's housemaster, and was given details of the misdemeanours to which he had confessed. These included various sexual activities in the Cothill grounds with other boys, the implication being that they had been inspired by X. R.B. was understanding, commented on original sin, but advised stricter supervision.

S.A.P. was naturally extremely upset when I reported back. He had never had occasion to discipline any boy for such behaviour, and prided himself on having a 'seeing eye'. Most prep-school boys are experimental in matters of sex, but only rare early developers are sufficiently interested to want to go into the bushes. Strangely enough, D.E.P. had been concerned about this particular boy in some instinctive female way, and now we were all made aware of the damage that X. had done to him and felt a heavy weight of responsibility for the outcome. The whole matter was made more unfortunate because the boy's parents were close friends. They never said a word of criticism, but they did not send their second son to Cothill. X., in the meantime, has served several prison sentences, and when these have been completed, schools are telephoned by the police: 'X. is out', and the chase starts again.

When I was Head Master, one of my assistant masters came to see me in my study in great distress. He said he had been 'window-shopping' in Oxford the previous evening, and had then gone into a public lavatory. On coming out he had been arrested by the police for soliciting. He assured me the whole thing was a mistake and that he was innocent. I believed him and told him he could keep his job until the case came up before the Oxford magistrates. On the appointed day I attended the court. The magistrates found the accused guilty, but an appeal was lodged and I decided to keep him on the staff until it was heard. When the Recorder of Oxford ruled that there was no case to answer I felt vindicated.

The main event of the Autumn term 1961 was D.E.P.'s illness. Early one Sunday morning Sister Daniel came over to No. 7 while we were still in bed: 'I don't like the look of your mother. I think she has had a stroke.' I hurried over to the school to find her lying in bed. Dr Strode diagnosed a cerebral haemorrhage. The day before she had been running upstairs, now she was partially paralysed, unable to talk clearly. There followed weeks of slow recovery, during which time my mother was looked after by Maggie with the same loving care she had shown at the time of my birth when the two were alone in the cottage at Hayling. For my father it was a terrible shock, and he found it very hard to carry on alone. Ernie, the butler, Philip, the Irish footman, and Lang, the cook, all did their best to rally round, but without my mother's supervision, standards fell.

Another milestone was the retirement of Dust Phillimore. This was duly noted by 'Peterborough' of the *Daily Telegraph* (one of his old pupils): 'Few men can have coaxed more unwilling small boys through the Common Entrance examination into Eton and other public schools. Through all his years at Cothill he showed inexhaustible patience, whether instructing eight-year-olds in the rudiments of cricket, or showing twelve-year-olds the first steps in Greek.' A successful football 1st XI was defeated only once, by Horris Hill ('they generously admitted they were lucky to beat us on their ground'). 'To sum up, a gay, enterprising, very well-coached XI, always fun to watch and probably one of Cothill's best teams in the last twenty-five years.' The shooting in the air-raid shelter received a boost with the arrival of a new rifle given by some of the previous term's leaving boys. There is a cryptic reference in the *Magazine* to 'the near-arrest of the shooting master and the rifle's three-week stay in the local police station'.

The Spring term of 1962 saw the arrival on the staff of a young scratch golfer, A. (Tony) Le Page, a tall, quiet Scot, who unfortunately stayed only two terms. A number of boys improved their golf considerably. Willie Boone won his first Senior Squash Championship, when he defeated Toby Weller-Poley in 'a tremendously exciting match. . . . Boone showed himself to be a promising left-hander, hard-hitting and extremely tenacious.' After Sports Day a concert and singsong included 'the novelty of the percussion band, as solemn a bunch of early beds as ever you saw'.

In S.A.P.'s last term Jamie Gough won the top scholarship to Uppingham. It was particularly gratifying for my father, as Jamie's grandfather, the actor Leslie Banks, had been one of his oldest friends, both of them serving in the same battalion of the Royal Berkshire Regiment in Salonika. To celebrate, the school was given a whole holiday and held a fête: 'From nowhere, and from nothing, stalls sprang into being on and around the tennis courts. There was bingo, the ring on the electric rod and miniature golf. Aunt Sallies, darts and mug shies. Walking-toy races, ping-pong balls bouncing in jam-jars, skill in swatting mice shooting out of drains. Treasure hidden in a map. Hit the target and soak a master. There was even an obstacle race in which Jamie won an x-ray at the Radcliffe Hospital. Strawberry tea in the rose garden.' A successful cricket 1st XI owed much to Richard Ryder, who 'captained the side very well, setting a splendid example in every way'. He and Richard Fawcett bowled well throughout the season, particularly against the Fathers and Horris Hill.

Thirty-five years is a long time to be Head Master of a school, but for many it seemed almost inconceivable that my father would ever feel that the time had come for him to retire. However, my mother's illness and only partial recovery had made retirement an imminent reality. In the Easter holidays, when Gabrielle and I were in our Welsh hideout, an envelope with S.A.P.'s writing was brought by hand up the track. To our amazement the letter announced he was retiring at the end of the following term. It was the culmination of years of wondering what the future held, and was totally unexpected.

When we had digested this on our return home, I asked V. K. D. Waite to write my parents' 'Vale'. This duly appeared in the Autumn *Magazine*: 'I still have the first letter he wrote me before I travelled by train to Abingdon for an interview at Cothill. "You might very well suit me. But you say nothing about Latin. I must have someone who can teach well and *keenly*. If you like the country you will like this place ... it's a delightful spot."

'As a result of that interview I had the privilege of working with Sam Pike for some 17 years, and over that period I never knew his outstanding qualities as a schoolmaster to vary. First and foremost among these qualities I would place his unswerving loyalty to the ideals he always set himself and his staff. ... Cothill was not just a part of his life; it *was* his life. ... Dorothy shared to the full his devotion to the school. ... I grew accustomed to her doing anything and everything. ... Perhaps the greatest tribute has already been paid to them by the fact that Old Boys kept on returning to Cothill to see them and their old school. ... Sam and Dorothy have loved their life at Cothill ... they will go surrounded by a flood of warm affection. ... '

My father and I with my mother in the last group she was to appear in just before her illness, Summer 1961. Staff, from left, standing: *C. J. Boothroyd, H. A. G. Phillimore, L. M. Swinbank;* sitting: *Flora Daniel, Ann Matthews;* right, standing: *T. E. B. Jackson, D. Wigan, J. R. Vassar-Smith, A. K. Reid;* sitting: *Mary Curtis, Barbara Hall.*

PART II

Autumn 1962 – 1990

G. L. S. PIKE

A. D. RICHARDSON

9
NEW BROOM

My father's sudden decision to retire was the result of my mother's cerebral haemorrhage which had incapacitated her right side, so that she could get about only with the help of a walking-frame. Without her active support my father was clearly both unwilling and unable to continue running the school, and the previous six months had taken their toll. There followed three months' financial and legal negotiations, during which S.A.P. considered accepting an offer made by J. V. P. Thompson, a Radley Social Tutor, to buy the school for £60,000. However, I made it clear that I could not work as a partner with Thompson, and my father finally declined the offer, with some regret as he rather wanted the cash. It was eventually agreed between my solicitor and my father's, J. B. Rosher, that S.A.P. should retain the freehold, but that I should rent the school from him for £3,000 a year, plus a consultant fee of £1,000. In 1962 this was a large amount to find.

The take-over at the end of July could hardly have come at a more awkward time. Gabrielle had recently been elected Chairman of the National Federation of Women's Institutes. This was a full-time job which committed her to being away in different parts of England and Wales during the week. She has recently written of those days: 'Sam and Dorothy hated the thought, not only of retiring, but of leaving what had been their home for nearly forty years. We knew we should have to be moving in directly they left, but Dorothy made it quite plain to me that she would dislike any changes we might make, and indeed much resented my measuring for curtains and suchlike. It was lucky that I was away most of the time, finishing up with a trip to Russia, returning literally the day before we were due to move in.

'We found a dirty, almost derelict school. As Dorothy had been an invalid for months, there had been no supervision of the domestic side of the school. No daily, it seemed, had done her stuff. All cupboards were crammed with junk or broken glass. Painting and papering had to be rushed jobs, as the removed furniture, carpets and pictures had left gaps and dirty marks. Ernie, the invaluable school and personal butler, and indeed the only person who knew all about the place, had gone with Sam and Dorothy, and we were left with Philip Colwell, an Irishman of great unpredictability, in his place.

FROM TOP LEFT TO RIGHT *Philip Colwell*, 1965; *'Gran' Gerring*, 1967; *Sadie Bungay with one of the famous tea urns*, 1973; *Gwen Wallis turns down our bed*, 1971.

... Luckily, on the very day the removers invaded, the sun shone as the packing cases were dumped in the drive and in the rose garden. An American friend was visiting us, and he was delighted when Philip asked where he should lay luncheon, and I replied "in the rose garden". That was the first of many happy meals there, with Philip trailing out with crockery, cutlery and drinks galore.'

Philip, in striking contrast to Ernie, with his rapid walk, was slow, shambling and bald. He was to work loyally enough for Gabrielle and me during our early years, but his standards of cleanliness were not high. Having told Gabrielle that he would never leave her, he was to disappear suddenly, without a word, during the Summer holidays of 1969. Since then the domestic arrangements of the school have been in the more efficient hands of dailies. Of these, Gwen Wallis, 'Gran' Gerring, Lizzie Brakespeare and Sadie Bungay deserve particular mention. Sadie, who is an exceptional organiser and valued friend, is now in charge.

My father's final term had been clouded by sadness and uncertainty. He had not shown me the books and I had only a vague idea of the financial situation. Clearly I should have insisted on seeing detailed accounts and discussing them with S.A.P. However, relationships between father and son are never more difficult than where money is concerned, and my father, as owner of the school, had the whip hand. He wanted me to succeed him in carrying on the school, but perhaps he doubted my capacity to do so. Certainly he never put me fully in the picture. This emerged in all its grimness in early September. S.A.P. had, for 35 years, put all the accountancy and auditing in the hands of his wartime ex-signaller, J. R. Cholmeley. The latter was honest and conscientious, but he did what he was told. Now he had to come clean and admit that there was an overdraft of many thousands of pounds. Worse was to follow when several local tradesmen, having been kept waiting for months on end for their money, refused to supply the school until they were paid. The cash-flow situation was bad enough; worse still was the prognostication for the future. S.A.P.'s entrants had been written in a pocket-sized notebook by hand, and soon it became clear that half the boys in it were unlikely to materialise.

At this point the NFWI came to the rescue in the person of Sylvia Gray, owner of the 'Bay Tree' in Burford. She suggested to Gabrielle that her accountants, Wenn Townsend of Oxford, should be approached. Their chairman, Harold Gray, duly detailed an assistant, John Rogers, to go through the accounts with Cholmeley before the beginning of the Autumn term. Rogers remembers that 'the next few days revealed the seriousness of the situation; when the final account was drawn up it showed a hopelessly insolvent position.... Arrangements were made to meet the Manager of Barclays Bank at Abingdon to enable the school to open.' He recalls 'sitting down to prepare a budget for the Autumn, Spring and Summer terms, a discipline that was necessary but which everyone was loath to accept at first'. The immediate cash-flow crisis was solved by an interest-free loan from a great friend. Another great friend had already given me, in 1960, £10,000 because, as he put it, he had made an indecent amount of money on the Stock Exchange and wanted to help the future finances of Cothill. Without this money the school would probably have had to close. I could never properly repay such generosity, but it enabled Gabrielle and me to carry on, and in turn to help deserving cases in the form of reduced fees. I did this for a number of years until the formation of the Charitable Trust in 1969.

Adrian Richardson drinking tea and watching cricket, Summer 1967. Note the silver kettle admired by Pat Savage.

Meanwhile the school had to function as though nothing was amiss. During the Summer holidays I had engaged two masters, one of whom, A. D. Richardson, was eventually, in 1976, to become Head Master. Adrian and I met for an interview at Bennett's wine-shop-cum-bar in Fishguard, because his parents lived near Haverfordwest and our holiday house was nearby. Somehow this very tall, fair-haired 19-year-old seemed to me just the man to teach Geography. I remember his father saying to me later, when Adrian decided to leave after a year to seek his fortune in London, 'Don't you agree with me that he has the makings of a good schoolmaster?'.

I had sent a letter to every present and future parent explaining the new situation, reaffirming the school's aims and outlining certain changes. Chief of these was the reorganisation of the curriculum. The school was now divided into classes, instead of being set for each subject, and the timetable was rearranged to allow masters to teach their special subjects to several classes instead of having to teach a variety of subjects to only one. This meant that boys were in the same class for everything and no longer was the whole school doing the same subject at the same time. A smooth transition was made possible by L.M.S., who worked out the new timetable. As the *Magazine* editorial of the following term put it: 'No two classes have arrived together to find an empty classroom. . . . Mr Jackson has so far shown no sign of wilting under the strain of taking four Mathematics classes.' T.E.B.J. also undertook teaching gym and producing most of the *Magazine*. He comments: 'The old system worked after a fashion [and had done so since at least 1894], but a lot of the staff had difficulty keeping one page ahead of their classes. I knew my French was bad, but it was only years after I gave up teaching it that I discovered just how bad it was. At Malvern I heard myself in a language lab. I blush now with shame when I think of all those whose pronunciation I must have ruined for life.' His extra work-load had its compensations: 'My pay was doubled the term you took over.' He was made head of Mathematics, while L.M.S. was responsible for Classics.

Other changes included the removal of the pots from under the boys' beds. These survivors of a past age were smelly and unsightly, and the need to empty them raised domestic problems. The existing lavatories proved equal to nocturnal needs, and if there was any increased inter-dormitory traffic, the gain outweighed the possible risk of sexual peccadillos.

The challenges that faced us were many. Chief was the fact that numbers were falling and bookings were at best problematical. In the eyes of the world, my father had continued too long as Head Master, and young parents hesitated before sending their sons to a school run by a 74-year-old, however fit and young-in-heart he and his wife might be. Once my mother had been forced to give up her side of the management, things had begun to slip, and as Leader Fairbrother remarked, 'Your father was "farming for leaving"'. Everything therefore depended on attracting new customers, as too many of the new boys of the immediate future turned out to be no more than names in a book. The place began to look tidier, though from the beginning there were problems with the roof. When heavy snow came in that first Winter, the dormitory ceilings leaked like sieves and buckets were placed to catch the drips. Showing prospective parents round was therefore a chancy business. At first Gabrielle came round too, but soon found that she could contribute more after the tour of inspection by dispensing refreshments and chat in the sitting-room without the fear of telling the mother the opposite of what I had just told the father. Her WI duties and commitments meant that from the first she had to do two jobs, but she was always at home at weekends to say goodnight to the 'babies', and to take their Friday-evening period. She remembers that 'even with the acute worries there was some fun, such as my cleaning out the boys' lavatories when they were in church and before prospective parents were due to descend on the place'.

The school cook, Lang, was adequate, but his personal life was unconventional. He lived in the San, and, as T.E.B.J. puts it, 'excited gossip by changing his wife once a week or so'. Matters came to a head when Gabrielle visited the San unexpectedly and found it full of school provisions. After his departure Patricia Fairbrother, who had been assistant cook for the past six years, took over. So began 25 years of magnificent service, during which time she was to provide imaginative food and run a happy kitchen. A school, like any army, 'marches on its stomach', and this aspect of the boys' welfare has been exceptionally well taken care of. Seven years later, Pat was interviewed by 'our reporter', John Stephenson, for the boys' periodical *The Cothill Scene*: 'She said she liked it here very much, especially the kitchen, which had a homely, comfortable atmosphere. Her specialities are trifle and paella. Scrumptious!'

It was now that Joan Swinbank returned, after raising her family, and took charge of the housekeeping. The health of the school was in the hands of Sister Daniel, whose outstanding qualities have already been mentioned. She became a tower of strength to Gabrielle and me, as she had been to my father, especially during my mother's illness. Always immaculately turned out in starched uniform, she inspired confidence. She provided much-needed continuity and gave Gabrielle such valuable advice as, 'Don't tell the boys not to get up when you come into a room'. The school doctor, Christopher Strode, had been appointed some two years previously. He was a nephew by marriage of Fred Hobson, and he too provided continuity as well as expert diagnostic skill and medical care. A delightful bachelor, with a fund of amusing stories, he is still looking after the school and us. Not the least of the advantages of Cothill's geographical position is its proximity to Oxford, with its many hospitals.

Pat Fairbrother, 1967.

With the prefects in my first term as Head Master, Autumn 1962. The old football 'strip' is being worn.

In this our first term, Gabrielle's niece Phillida Stone, studying art at the Ruskin School in Oxford, came over twice a week with her friend Diana Hand to take drawing classes for about 50 boys. A.K.R. followed his Summer production of *Oliver* by a combined masters' / boys' entertainment. According to the *Magazine*, it consisted of 'singing, or rather shouting, sketches by boys, the happiest item by masters being "The Dispensary", where the new matron, Mr Swinbank, held sway, armed with an outsize syringe'. It was A.K.R.'s last fling. He was bidden a formal farewell: 'We shall miss him in so many ways – his friendliness, the debonair way in which he produced a succession of highly successful plays for boys and masters, the familiar figure in the garden, his never-failing thoughtfulness for others.' Arthur retired to his cottage in Amberley, where he died in 1979.

A shadow was cast on the events of this term by the financial position of the school. Luckily the redecoration and improvements had been undertaken and paid for by Gabrielle before the full extent of the difficulties was realised. In addition to the periodic overdraft and sundry creditors, there was also the annual income for S.A.P. to be found. Unfortunately my sisters and brothers-in-law did not appear to understand the problems, their attitude being summed up by Archie Heyman when he remarked, 'but you're sitting on a goldmine'. Their sympathies appeared to be more on the side of the older

Hilary Bray, Vice-Chairman of Governors, at the Centenary celebrations, June 1970.
Brian Costeloe hedge-planting to replace dead elms, Spring 1980.

generation, and perhaps they felt, unconsciously, that they had lost a base and with it a sense of security. We were saddened by this lack of support at such a critical time.

Happier memories of the Autumn include two visits, from Hilary and Jenny Bray and from Ruth Scott. During the first, C. W. B. Costeloe came to be interviewed for a teaching job. An Irishman from County Cork, with a wartime Oxford degree, he had just retired in his mid-forties as a District Commissioner in Tanganyika after its independence. He had a charming, studious face and a quiet voice, and we took an instant liking to him. He joined the staff the following term and remained on it for the next 25 years, apart from a year's absence to take a Diploma of Education. Brian often spoke of the impression the Brays had made on him at that first meeting. As always, Hilary and Jenny's influence had been beneficent; both were financial benefactors of the school, as well as wonderful friends.

Ruth Scott had for the past fifteen years been the mother of four Cothillians, Jim, Ian, Andrew and Nicholas, the last still in the school. She had become a great friend of two generations of Pikes, with her husband Archie, but now she came to stay by herself. As usual she was both funny and wise, with many useful bits of advice for the new Head Master, but only when he asked for them. One such concerned the matter of telling leaving boys the facts of life. 'Tell 'em everything, keep it light and have them all into your study together.' (This I always did; whether it was helpful or not, I have never discovered.) Ruth was killed a week later when she fell asleep driving her car near Newmarket. I had to break the news to Nicholas.

The Spring term of 1963 produced the most arctic weather since 1947. A blizzard blew as the boys returned to school, with fathers staggering through the front door looking like snowmen ('Can't think how I shall get back'). Somehow the school bus arrived from Oxford Station, and there was a full complement by prayers. It was so cold that Sister wrapped each boy in a blanket in bed. The next morning we borrowed 24 new shovels from the RDC and these proved invaluable during the next two months, for the gangs of boys who cleared the snow from the yard and the reeds from the pond in the Marsh. This had frozen over for only the second time since 1947, and some 20 boys learnt to skate, while the rest of the school towed a variety of sledges through the woods to the quarry, where a toboggan run was improvised under A.D.R.'s supervision. Raphe Palmer has 'clear memories of skating on the frozen pond in the woods – playing "He" and hide-and-seek. It's odd now that I can hardly skate at all.' Perhaps not all that odd, as since 1963 most winters have been mild, and there has been no skating at Cothill. Another to join this term was D. H. Stevenson, who came for one term before going up to Cambridge. His mother was an old school friend of Gabrielle's. Dennis was an exceptionally able young man, a good violinist, and something of a wine expert. He has since become a millionaire business consultant and Chairman of the Tate Gallery Trust.

Later in the term Gabrielle would take boys tobogganing, and we organised cross-country running in the snow, which melted in time for 'sixes' to be played and Sports Day to take place. The *Magazine* comments that 'even the golf course became playable, and so, thanks to a complete freedom from infectious diseases, the normal Spring-term programme was completed after all. The only casualty had been hockey.' Two portents of things to come are also noted: 'Mr Thompson from Radley brought over Howard Palmer and other prefects to give some basic instruction in Rugby football to future Radleians and others going to Rugby-playing public schools.' Willie Boone led a squash team of five to beat New College School.

For some members of staff the 'great freeze' was not such fun. C.W.B.C. in particular had a hair-raising time getting to work each day from the cottage he and his wife Thelma had rented at Wootton, near Woodstock. Finally everything there froze up and they were without water. A solution was found by moving the assistant matrons and Mary Curtis from their Bungalow into

George Fairbrother and the MG, 1976.

the main building, and putting the Costeloes in their place. Here they remained until the end of the Summer term. The Bungalow then became the home of George and Pat Fairbrother. I persuaded George to leave Pressed Steel, Cowley, and follow in his father's footsteps. So began over 25 years of loyal service as groundsman, chauffeur and security officer. His lean figure became a familiar part of the Cothill scene, and he dealt with all manner of problems with cheerful competence.

C.W.B.C. recalls his early memories. 'Ninety boys, all boarders, with classes rarely exceeding twelve. . . . Dyslexia was not mentioned. We did not play rugger. As in most schools, games were played and adjudicated with a refreshing amateurishness. There was no school office or secretary. An accountant arrived with his wife on the penultimate day of the term. He paid the bills and the staff (who were paid termly). . . . The Common Entrance exam was not constantly being modified and one knew what to expect. . . . A barber paid regular visits. During the day boys would be summoned from lessons; their shorn return always caused much merriment. All meals were prepared in the school kitchen, vegetables came mainly from the school garden. The food was good, plain and plentiful. Traditional boarding-school favourites featured regularly – "dead baby" enriched with golden syrup, "Ganges mud", tapioca, beloved of some, tarts and custard galore. I mourned the passing of rolled neck of mutton, known as "hedgehog" [impossible to carve with a blunt knife]. . . . Once and only once we had grilled herrings. . . . At the end of the meal it became perfectly clear why so many baskets of remains were taken up after the feeding of the 5,000. Meals were served on well-scrubbed tables by Irish lads; . . . their smiles compensated for their lack of finesse; ... large thumbs so near the surface of the stews were as thick as their lovely brogues. ... After the "great Winter" ... the snowmen remained in our fields till April.'

John Goodrich, who had spent his first year under my father's headmastership, had found leaving his parents painful, and feels, looking back, that he was far too young. 'I remember your becoming Head Master as an improvement. I appreciate the warmth and kindness you showed me. So far as I remember the more Victorian rituals such as cold baths in the morning were stopped by you.' Simon Moffett, two years older, agrees with John that he will never send his children away. 'From the habit of being away from home young, I have lost the need for going home at all, and only now begin to feel the need to let my children know their grandparents. ... I wonder how many boys were affected in this way.' Both are nevertheless grateful to the school. To John, 'Cothill was a good school of its kind, well run by you and with a lot of dedicated teachers – and I also made friends ...'. Simon 'loved the woods and grounds. Nature was very present. ... I don't remember any horror stories. ... The magic in your classroom behind the gym for me was the wind-up record-player and the 78s, notably "Shadrach, Meshech and Abednego" [by Louis Armstrong].'

A contrasting view of school life as a boarder comes from Mark Swinbank: 'I started as a "mature pupil"(?) and of course being my father's son I was considered to be a spy. It took me well over a year to put a lie to this situation.' When he left in 1963 he was Head Boy. His most vivid memory is of '100 plus boys marching round the yard with wooden rifles'. Mark's two younger brothers, Bill and Robin, followed him as boarders. Bill was athletic, a speedy right-winger and the holder of the school long-jump record. Robin lists several 'invaluable facts' he learnt at Cothill: '(1) Great Britain will never be an oil-producing nation. (2) Use the personal pronoun "tu" only when speaking to your wife, family, very close friends and your mistress. (3) If you start with a penny and could double it every day you would be a millionaire within a month. (4) Very expensive thermometers break when taken out of boiling water and plunged under a cold running tap by mischievous young scientists. (5) Ragging in the dormitory can prove a very painful experience.'

From the earliest days there does not seem to have ever been an excessive amount of caning at Cothill. As far as I can find out only the Head Master ever used the cane; Kit Wilson's story of being beaten for poor fielding probably involved senior boys. Gully Nickalls writes of 'an orgy of flagellation' from 'one of the assistant masters' during a particular three-week period in 1910, and this may well have referred to the joint Head Master, F. Knowles, who was to leave under a cloud soon afterwards. But M. J. Dauglish is not remembered as being in any way sadistic. Caning (or 'the whacks') was always on the bottom, a part of the anatomy designed to take punishment; unlike the hand which can be permanently damaged. There is no record of public beatings, or of 'swipings' with a birch on bare buttocks.

Pat Halsey writes: 'In 1916 I was captain of a dormitory. In it were two large and very broad beams. Jim Knapp-Fisher suggested that these were gods, Batagar and Behomegar, and that worship and sacrifice should be paid them by the flicking of our elastic garters on to them. This caused much excitement and noise and M.J.D. walked in. Next morning I, as captain, was summoned to his study and beaten. I remember my screams!' John Thomson was beaten twice; 'when M.J.D. had finished the second caning, he said he thought the particular punishment was unjust, but that I had been boiling up for a beating for some time. I certainly behaved better after it.'

Chris Somers remembers being beaten by S.A.P.: 'It fell to your father's lot to beat me my last term for ragging in dormitory. Then he had to do the same thing to my son his first term. I'm sure there aren't many headmasters who've had the privilege of doing this to father and son. (In spite of this I'm all for the cane being retained. It did me no harm!)' Several others agree with the last sentence, if the beating is not too severe. Johnny Banks says it was a moment of pride when he showed off the cane marks in dormitory. When it came to my turn, I limited the punishment to rare cases of bullying, and extreme insubordination. Marc Piercey says he was beaten by me 'on a number of occasions' but I hope and think he exaggerates. Andrew Loyd remembers 'the relief of how little it actually hurt'. Corporal punishment is now illegal in the maintained schools and discouraged by the IAPS. A.D.R. has not beaten anyone for five years. When parents ask him about it, he says it is 'the deterrent that is never used, like the atom bomb'.

In the Summer of 1963, the first 'Long Leave' was introduced after the Fathers' Match. Boys had never been allowed out for a night during term time. The generally accepted view had been that any break in school routine would be bad for work, would interrupt school matches, would make it hard to get started again afterwards and would expose the school to infectious diseases. Also it was not at all certain that parents, having got rid of their children for three months, would welcome the idea of having them home again in mid-term. But now there was a general agreement among local preparatory schools that some sort of a break was needed, at least by the staff. The boys therefore went home for two nights. Those without parents in Britain stayed with relations or school friends, while a small number remained at school with Gabrielle and me. This leave was extended subsequently from an annual to a termly event, the length gradually being increased. Boys were also allowed away from school for Saturday night on two set weekends, one either side of Long Leave. Nowadays a long half-term break is taken for granted, but then there was an air of exciting innovation, and the experiment was generally popular.

In the Autumn term the school was inspected by HMIs. It was only 12 years since the last inspection, but a new Head Master made a good excuse for another visit. Looking back, I wonder that the school achieved such a good report, for the staff has never been weaker. A.D.R. had left at the end of one year to work in the City; C.W.B.C. was away taking his Dip. Ed.; one master took to his bed for the two days; I had to take on the teaching of Geography to the top class, never having taught it before. Desmond Wigan had just rejoined after coming down from Oxford. His broad grin, enthusiasm and knowledge of French made up for his lack of experience. Other new staff were D. R. M. (David) Dalglish and a retired schoolmaster, V. F. Ball, who came in daily to teach Latin, but died after only one term.

The report noted that the new Head Master, 'though naturally desirous of introducing some of his own ideas, has been careful to cause no sudden and violent changes in the strong traditions of the school'. They pointed out that 'his wife has been called upon to shoulder the cares of the domestic side . . . at a time when she was already committed to filling the distinguished and onerous post of National Chairman of the NFWI'. The Inspectors considered the grounds and outdoor facilities 'exceptionally fine', but were not so impressed by 'a number of somewhat cumbersome locker-desks', though they admitted that these were 'objects of veneration and a source of pride to their occupants'. L.M.S. and T.E.B.J. were appreciated for their abilities and for providing 'a strong thread of continuity. . . . While there is, perhaps, no very distinguished teaching there is no lack of schoolmasterly qualities.' Mathematics owed much to T.E.B.J.'s 'progressive scheme and careful organisation'. The report noted that Science was not taught, and that Art was in abeyance, owing to lack of proper accommodation. Music, however, was recognised as being 'a very strong feature in the life of the school' and 'some sensitive singing was heard'. The main criticism was of 'some of the work of those classes immediately above the youngest one'. The conclusion was that 'this is a school of firmly established reputation and traditions, which the new Head Master has already shown his capacity to maintain'.

Dancing, Spring 1974.

The death in April 1964 of Kay Kirwan, the dancing mistress, suggests a word on the Cothill dancing tradition. The earliest mention is in the Great War, when a Frenchman, Monsieur Gautier, taught the lancers and Sir Roger de Coverley as well as ballroom dancing in a hall in the village, according to Guy Halsey. Gerald Hamilton remembers him after the war, 'immaculately clad in tail coat, grey waistcoat, cravat and pearl pin'. Dancing was part of the curriculum, though John Thomson was so clumsy that he was let off; 'instead I was sent to exercise the pony which Tomcat kept for his children'. Peter Rowley says Gautier and the boys wore white gloves and pumps until 1927, after which M. Gautier disappeared and dancing became an extra on Thursday afternoons, and a very unpopular one. John Rambaut recalls 'the futility of being taught to dance while football was going on outside the tall glass windows'.

After World War II, Mrs Kirwan persuaded my father that the whole school should learn dancing. This was not appreciated by all the boys or the staff, and even H.A.G.P. was gently mocking in his references to 'Terpsichore'. However S.A.P., a keen dancer in his youth, persuaded at least a minority of boys that all good athletes were good dancers – 'light on their feet, you know'. There was also the added incentive that the Dragon had large dancing classes, and anything they could do, we could surely do too.

Kay Kirwan had been a first-class teacher of all kinds of dancing, and at her death she was succeeded by her pretty and equally gifted assistant, June Esau, whose grandmother had been born in Cothill House in the 1860s and who had started teaching at Cothill in 1960. 'I remember my amazement at the standard of dancing which was very high. In particular Robin Eccles and a Chinese chap called Freddy Lim. Over the years we had some excellent dancers, but these two stand out in my memory.' The music was supplied by a succession of pianists of varying competence, until in the early 1970s John Lynam came over from the Dragon to provide a never-ending stream of dance music, which he played by ear, in only one key, but with a splendid sense of rhythm. He even took over the teaching when June was abroad for a term. Also taught were country and Scottish dances, so that the young were given some idea of the pleasures of dancing before the ubiquitous disco engulfed them. Prizes were given at the end of each term, and many Old Cothillians must have memories of competing round the New Hall, in gym shoes because the floor was so slippery. Nicholas Scott writes: 'Dancing classes are never to be forgotten and I remember winning the waltz in my last Winter dancing the female part with Charles Stokes. Can't dance the blessed thing now for love nor money.'

After 1976 I continued to oversee the dancing classes and it was not until I had finally retired from teaching in 1981 that A.D.R. bowed to the majority view of the staff that the time would be more profitably spent by having an extra prep. Whether this was a benefit in the long run is debatable, but *tempora mutantur*. Later June Esau wrote: 'The best time was when John Lynam joined the team and between you you managed to disrupt the classes while *you* hummed the "golden oldies" and *he* played them regardless of their relevance to the job in hand. Like you I miss those Tuesday evenings and especially the old 78 records and the wind-up gramophone.'

W. J. H. Liverside ('Liver Sausage'/'Squidge') joined the staff at the beginning of 1964. He had been a friend of mine since 1929, when we met as boys in Sutton Courtenay and went shooting together. My grandparents had recently bought the Abbey, and the Liversidges lived just outside the front gates. Their house was a delightfully friendly place, and Bill's sisters, Anne and Mary, were my first female dancing partners, to a gramophone and such tunes as 'Tiptoe through the tulips'. Already nearly six feet tall, he went to Radley when I went to Eton. We met again at Oxford, where he distinguished himself particularly as an oarsman at St Edmund Hall. He became an assistant master at Bishop's School, Cape Town, and after serving with the South African army, he was appointed Deputy Head Master of the Duke of York's College in Nairobi. While on leave just before Kenyan independence, he told me that he was resigning and would like to join the Cothill staff. Thus began a very happy association, which greatly benefited Cothill geographers and cricketers, as he was a qualified MCC coach.

In 1964 Robin Dixon had made history for Britain and Cothill by winning the two-man bobsleigh Gold Medal with Andrew Nash in the Winter Olympics. He was invited to present the prizes at the Sports Day that year. The *Magazine* produced its first illustration, a photograph of Robin handing the Sports Cup to Nicholas Bell. Afterwards the bobsleigh was on show in the squash court. This Sports Day also included 'a little light relief given at the end by the Shakers, who were obviously considered "the fabbest of the fab" by the screaming fans who invaded the stage'. Whether this school pop group would have been approved of by HMI is uncertain, but they would certainly have welcomed four boys taking part in the *St Matthew Passion* with other schools in the Oxford Town Hall. Three classes were taken to the OUDS production of *Twelfth Night* at the Playhouse and the school orchestra took part in the North Berks Annual Music Festival. Meanwhile, the stone-floored squash court was producing future rackets players in Willie Boone and Christopher and Andrew Milne.

A nine-year-old Charles Bland blasted off in the *Magazine* against seniors in 'It's Too Jolly Well Unfair': 'I cannot bear them; there are so many privileges for seniors; radios all the term, going to plays, watching television in Major Pike's sitting-room. Seniors, I agree, should have one or two privileges, but having nine, ten or perhaps even eleven is really going too far. Mr Glazebrook is always at the seniors' service. He will give them their garden as soon as they ask for it, but we juniors have to wait ages before we get one, and by that time it is too late to plant any seeds. . . .'

In the Summer term Leader Fairbrother and his wife celebrated their Golden Wedding. Richard Fawcett completed four years in the 1st XI and two years as captain. With his fast, left-hand bowling 'few opposing batsmen were good enough to touch his more dangerous ball'. 'The well-kept lawn of Summer Fields, bordered by flowers on one side and boys on the other, was the scene of an entertaining afternoon's tennis which resulted in a 5–2 victory for Cothill, led by the Milne brothers.' I took the five Colour Caps to see a day of Lords Test Match against the Australians.

D. Wigan produced *Julius Caesar*. The reviewer picked out Robin Leanse's 'convincing performance as Mark Antony and the brilliantly-staged crowd scenes. . . . It was no cardboard battle on the plains of Philippi, but a flesh and blood affair.' He concluded that it was 'a suitable contribution to the Shakespeare year'. Later in the term, seven boys learning Greek went to Bradfield to see a performance of *Hippolytus*. P. C. Glazebrook and Mary Curtis left, both having served five years on the staff and having contributed greatly to the teaching of English and Music respectively. They had also combined to produce the first Cothill Gilbert & Sullivan, *The Pirates of Penzance*.

P.C.G.'s success as a teacher of English was appreciated in the HMI report: 'There is evidence of enterprising and sensitive teaching which evokes a good response from the boys, particularly in the discussion and writing of poetry, which is not always a very strong side of the English in a preparatory school.' P.C.G. writes: 'In 1963 BBC "Radio for Schools" programme "Listening and Writing" was introduced in warm, reassuring Northern tones by Ted Hughes. It was a programme in which he presented contemporary poetry, including his own. I used to record the programmes on tape and use them for in-class discussion, appreciation, leap-off points.... When I sift the numerous memories I have of Cothill, I have to admit that there are a good many where the young inmates must have found me a Disappointing Adult.' He cites his failure to recognise a Boeing; suggesting an improvement to a budding clarinetist ('Here, *fortissimo*' – 'but sir, I'm not on that page, I'm on this one'); and being asked by a very tiny George Howard, 'When will you be on that board, sir?', as he pointed to the War Memorial in the Dining Hall. 'Cothill in those days had the happiest atmosphere of any school I know. Still has, I shouldn't wonder.'

Gwen Stevens ('G.S.'), 1970.

My father had never employed a secretary, but I soon decided that with the amount of teaching I was doing and in the cause of greater efficiency, Gabrielle and I needed one badly. After two false starts, a middle-aged angel from heaven appeared this year in the shape of Gwen Stevens, known to all as 'G.S.'. She had worked in a solicitor's office in Abingdon, and brought with her a sense of order as well as a great expertise in typing and shorthand.

For the next ten years she lightened our burdens and stimulated our everyday routine. She would dissolve into peals of musical laughter at my feeble jokes, and the dictating of letters was liable to be interrupted by a discussion on some passing thought, often of a theological nature.

The Autumn *Magazine* commented on the great activity at Cothill, where 'the New Hall is being redecorated, the Library turned into a Senior Common Room, and what was Mrs Hall's classroom is the new Library. It is over thirty years since the New Hall really was new. The builders are also converting the gym into two classrooms, and the additional space will enable us to go ahead with plans for a Geography Room and a Science Laboratory.'

G. N. Georgano and Daphne Stewart joined the staff. 'Georgs' was in his twenties, bespectacled and with an old-fashioned manner, somewhat reminiscent of H.A.G.P., and a habit of nodding his head. He was a patient teacher and extremely popular with the boys. He wrote several illustrated books on the history of motor cars, but was unable to drive one himself. Daphne was a charming and attractive married woman in her forties. She remembers the staff joining in the entertainments and concerts 'with great gusto . . . hard work to prepare . . . but they delighted everyone with their lack of inhibition'. She particularly recalls her first post-Feast concert – a joint effort by staff and boys, compèred by T.E.B.J. 'George brought the house down when he appeared on stage outrageously disguised as a yokel in smock, kerchief, gorblimey trousers and a battered hat, clutching a bottomless bucket filled with straw. Together we performed "There's a hole in my bucket, dear Liza . . .". And when I finally chased him round the stage in mock exasperation trying to hit him, the audience was delirious with joy.' There were other songs ('Messrs Liversidge, Costeloe and Pike became "Three Birds in the Wilderness" and caws-ed much amusement'), sketches, dance ('Miss Scott and Miss Yates . . . with their can-can') and slapstick. The Feast had 'lived up to its magnificent tradition. The snowmen welcomed us. The ceiling glittered. Pat Fairbrother's delicious cooking melted in our mouths. The plum-pudding roar deafened us. Three hundred crackers cracked, and another happy memory was born.'

Gabrielle attended the funeral of Winston Churchill in Westminster Abbey on 30 January 1965. The whole school watched on television, and later the prefects were taken to Bladon to see the flowers on his grave. 'The carpentry shop was turned into a playroom, with ping-pong table and a billiard table. Part of the garage was walled off to accommodate the carpenters.' John and Peter Goodrich won the Senior and Junior Squash Championships respectively, the former eventually winning a Blue at Oxford as a freshman. Among Old Boys, Michael Leigh coxed the winning Oxford Eight, Ben Leigh won the Grand Military at Sandown. In the Summer term an undistinguished cricket XI recorded few wins, but there were a variety of treats and outings; the choir visited Coventry, Kenilworth and Stratford with Hilary Davan-Wetton, who had come for a year to teach Music after taking a degree at Oxford. His enthusiasm and fine musicianship made a great impression, as did his wife Jane's ability as an Art teacher.

We were greatly saddened by the death of Ian Scott while on active service in Aden. He was a delightful and amusing young man whose death was a terrible blow to his father Archie, only three years after Ruth's death, and it shortened his life. Ian's fiancée Val subsequently married a Scots Guardsman John Arthur, already mentioned as a cricket captain, and so a Cothill connection was maintained. In Cyprus the four rifle Company Commanders of the 1st Battalion Grenadiers were all old Cothillians: Bernard Gordon-Lennox, Fitz Abel Smith, George West and David Fanshawe. According to David, S.A.P. told him it was due to cold baths and deep breathing before breakfast.

After the end of term, on 31 July, my parents celebrated their Golden Wedding. As I wrote at the time: 'The New Hall was the scene of a luncheon party for over a hundred guests, their ages ranging from four to eighty. As it was the first time my parents had been back to Cothill since their retirement and their move from Hayling to Henley, there was a high degree of anticipation and speculation. Would they like the various alterations and redecorations? Would the garden be looking up to standard? Would the weather be kind? But we need not have worried. It was a great moment for them, for us and for all the relations and friends who came to celebrate. Messrs Phillimore, Banks and Waite were confronted again by a number of Old Cothillians whom they had once taught in a school of only forty boys. They, with Cothill parents, saw again Fairbrother, Battell and others of the staff and village. Speeches were made, toasts were drunk. Walter Somers presented an antique corner-cupboard and a cheque from over two hundred and fifty Old Boys. A magnificent three-tiered wedding-cake, made in the village by Mrs Johnson, was ceremoniously cut. Photographs, formal and informal, were taken. Only one other person in that party had been at the wedding in 1915 – Maggie. She had kept her original invitation, which she now gave back, as it were symbolically. For over fifty years she has been in turn nanny, cook, and always beloved family friend and counsellor ("What you need, Mr George, is a good meal"). To her, as to us, this gathering of all ages marked the full turning of a wheel. It was a wonderfully happy occasion, and we all hope that the golden bride and bridegroom will now frequently revisit us to see how things are getting on at Cothill, for we value so much their wise judgement and helpful comment. A school, like a human being, needs regular

My parents married 50 years, 31 July 1965.

nourishment – physical, mental and spiritual food to keep it strong and help it to grow with a true sense of mutual dependence. By the example of their fifty years together, S.A.P. and D.E.P. have contributed yet again towards this goal.'

R. H. L. Armitage ('Dillo') had joined the staff in the Summer. He was a serious-minded, bespectacled, rather academic-looking, married man in his early thirties. As an athletic Old Wykehamist, Richard seemed a natural choice in the Autumn to take over the running of the football from L.M.S. He reminded the boys: '(1) The ball must be brought under control quickly and skilfully. (2) Never be still, always keep alert and moving. (3) Weak kicking is no good at all.' Two others to join the staff were N. S. Lachlan, tall and thin and recently retired from teaching Classics at Radley; and M. J. H. Williams, round and cheerful, who took charge of Music.

Gabrielle was appointed CBE in the 1966 New Year's Honours, in recognition of the Golden Jubilee of the National Federation of Women's Institutes and her own contribution to various branches of voluntary public service. A JP since 1961, she had sat on several Government Commissions and was now a public figure. An award of another kind was Orlando Gough's top scholarship to Harrow, where he was to become a legendary all-rounder.

Flora Daniel now had to retire for family reasons, much to our regret, after ten years as Sister. She was much missed, but luckily Joan Swinbank agreed to take her place, while continuing to supervise the housekeeping. Joan thus returned to a post she had occupied before her marriage in 1948. She had not lost her touch. An example of her style was when, at the end of one term, we salvaged Simon Greenwell after I had heard him fall from the roof of the school, bouncing to the ground via a ladder and a flat roof. All J.S. said was: 'He's all right, he's yelling.'

I have made little mention of assistant matrons since Vera McMillan in 1927. In the late 1930s there was Edith Norton, who looked after the linen-room, where, according to Ben Stanier, 'the clothes were in cupboards of quite incredible neatness'. She was joined by Margaret Wisnom, of whom Michael Stourton writes: 'I remember the young and pretty matron who was very nice and kind to us boys.' Margaret's own comment on the school is: 'There was a total segregation of the male and female staff, though we did find ways of getting round this.' All assistant matrons lived in the Bungalow until 1963.

Joan Swinbank's original assistants had been Betty Ellis and 'Nanny' Hargreaves. The latter was short and square, with dark hair drawn back and tied in a bow, and a red smiling face. T.E.B.J. says she told the boys 'to wash their hairs [*sic*]'. Richard Bird considers she was 'the only socialist in the entire school'. According to Roderick Chamberlain, 'she sang all the WWI songs, so Arthur Reid could script a scene for the school play'. Betty Ellis was thin and dark and spoke with a lisp. She would work late into the night in her eyrie in the linen-room. Pixie Parkinson, who had been a wartime colleague of my sister Diana, joined in 1946. She was a vivacious and friendly girl, who became Sister in 1950 for one year before marrying Henry Welch.

When J.S. returned in 1966, her senior matron was Suzanne Holmes, the daughter of a well-known Abingdon citizen and baker. After her, there was 'a motley selection', to quote Joan, 'from the very good, such as Jenny Pether and Renée Harwood [who had jet-black hair and looked like the witch in the Flook cartoons] to the eccentric Rosanne Edge-Partington. Andrew Loyd dismisses the whole lot as 'all those dreadful matrons. The only one I can remember, apart from Viner, was Reynolds, who saw a first-day cover of Sir Joshua and claimed he was an ancestor.'

In 1966 a weather station was started by Class 1, for the first time since A. C. Phillips's retirement, with 'a Stevenson's screen in which they kept a maximum and minimum thermometer, a wet- and dry-bulb thermometer and a barometer. Beside it is a rain gauge.' Three periodicals appeared. The best of these, *The Cothillian*, was edited by Anthony Weld Forester. He has sent me a copy of a 'special edition', hand-written in block capitals. In it Jamie Summers produced a regular cartoon called 'Fred Penguin'; various exciting stories, with such titles as 'Gripping Fear' and 'Awful Accident' were interspersed with poems, crosswords and comments on the craze for go-karts and Snob played two months earlier than usual. It included such local news as the arrival of a donkey: 'There was great havock [*sic*] among the new boys as it escaped four times on its first day. . . . If you see a donkey coming towards you, don't panic, take it quietly and you won't get hurt.' The animal in question had been given by Janet Stone, and was called Rosetta. She soon settled down and by the end of term, according to the *Magazine*, 'was already a favourite with everyone, including those who had their ties and jerseys eaten by her. It is hoped she will co-operate in carrying the food for the Summer picnics [in a 'jaunting car' produced by Penelope Betjeman].' According to T.E.B.J., though, 'no boy would ever admit to liking the donkey, however much he did, for he knew that doing so would land him with the job of looking after it'.

Rosetta takes the 'jaunting car' down into the quarry for a picnic, Summer 1971.

10
'THE WORLD OF A CHILD'

Jonathan Stedall had been a new boy in January 1948, and on his own admission not a very happy one. It was therefore a pleasant surprise when he turned up with John and Myfanwy Piper on Sports Day 1964. Some months later he told me of a series of films that he and A. N. Other were planning for BBC 2 under the general heading 'The World of a Child'. There were to be six half-hour films, each featuring a child with a contrasting social background; he suggested that one of them might be a boy in a preparatory school. Why not Cothill?; the BBC would pay £100 for the privilege. I agreed in principle and, as a first step, it was decided that Jonathan should meet a number of 11-year-olds, watch them at work and play and short-list three possibles for the star part. After some close observation and unofficial tests, the boy David Rolt was chosen, the consent of his parents obtained, and the matter cleared with the IAPS to allay any fear of undue self-advertisement.

In the Autumn *Magazine* of 1966 I wrote: 'The first three weeks of last term were dominated by the TV team from BBC 2 – Jonathan Stedall (Old Boy and producer), Bill Baines (assistant producer), Charles Stewart (camera), Tom Fred Sharpe (sound), Elizabeth Barron (continuity). Little did we know, when we agreed to submit ourselves to the public gaze, that we should make five very special friends.

'The first afternoon was none the less a bit of a shock, especially to the unwarned parents of new boys. Fathers tried hard to look unselfconscious when heaving trunks out of car boots; the Rolt family had their baptism of fire when the entire crew squeezed into the car, filming and recording as they travelled from home to school. We all tried hard to obey the only rule – not to look at the camera. By bedtime it was apparent that we were going to have a fascinating experience. How would we stand up to living "with no more privacy than goldfish"?

'We need not have worried. In the days of sunny weather that followed we realised how lucky we were to have these delightful people about the place. We soon got used to being filmed in prayers, in class, during meals, in dormitory. Everything was done with a minimum of fuss and disturbance, there was no script, rehearsals consisted mainly of the crew watching and letting us

School Film, Summer 1966: Film crew ready for an early morning shot.
Jonathan Stedall and Charles Stewart filming, on a rare occasion when a tripod was used.
C.S. was an expert with his hand-held Belgian camera.

get used to them. Charles with his wonderful portable camera, accompanied by Tom Fred, earphones on head and tape-recorder over shoulder, roamed around the grounds, taking shots of everyone and anything. They were undeterred by the hazards of flying cricket balls and the constant interruption from aircraft.

'From the first day the members of the crew identified themselves with the life of the school, and soon they were on Christian name terms with most boys, who were encouraged to ask questions and examine equipment. We learnt such jargon as the difference between "synch" and "wild track" and began to understand a little about how a film is made. When we were finally left to our devices we all felt strangely flat. But we have many happy memories of talks and games and picnics with five highly-skilled professionals who enriched our lives by their friendliness, humour and unassuming competence.'

Jonathan Stedall has written of that time. 'It was, of course, an extraordinary experience to be back at Cothill after 14 years' absence. It seemed a very much nicer place than I had remembered. Certainly George and Gabrielle seemed to have a very relaxed and friendly relationship with all the boys, their parents and staff.... A jungle had, it seemed, evolved into something more like a safe and orderly safari park.... It struck me, however, after that time spent filming, despite the atmosphere of gentleness I never remember from my own school days, that the absence of girls was a very great lack. ... The Sunday Summer outing to the woods and marshes that we filmed was truly idyllic. We saw no signs of gangs or bullying. Boys gathered wild flowers; others flocked around Gabrielle's donkey; some just lay in the grass and talked of home...'. David Way has described these Summer picnics: 'Buckley or another "trusty" is allowed to lead Rosetta, who is harnessed to a special cart, on which are loaded the picnic provisions – "keep hot" bags of sausages, large-scale jugs of orange juice, sandwich-spread sandwiches, apples and cheese. The crocodile winds its way slowly through the woods, destination quarry. Here the food is gulped down, the adults are left drinking Guinness, ranged out on rugs, and the real business of the day starts. Exciting games are devised; boys roll down the quarry sides, boys are pushed down, boys jump down. Others play "Bang-bang", imagining that they are in the desert and tracking down their enemies. Occasionally teams are assembled for a game of scrub football. Sometimes – often – blood is spilt and a boy is led back, howling to school for treatment. So the afternoon goes on, until at last the Duty Master rounds everyone up and we set off on the journey back.' Peter Cooper 'can still hear Jackson's voice droning "Early Beds" across the playing-fields at 6.30 pm on warm Summer evenings, demanding us young mortals to stop having fun'.

Sunday outing with Rosetta, 1966.

Of the various unorganised games played over the years in the yard, Snob, a form of stump cricket, appears to have been played only at Cothill and Marlborough. No one seems to know why it was so named, but the essential item in the game, from the earliest reference by Michael Snow in the pre-Great War period, was the 'white, chamois-leather-covered ball' mentioned by Mike Atkin-Berry (who adds, 'There was no score, no point, but great fun'). These Snob balls were specially made; their great virtue was very little bounce, so that a good eye, correct footwork and a 'straight stump' were needed to hit them. Bev Stanier, writing of the 1940s, describes how 'you queued up to bowl and if you got the batsman out you batted yourself. It was a brilliant game, terrific practice for the real thing and ought to be encouraged by the MCC.' After World War II, however, the supplier of Snob balls went out of business, and old tennis-balls had to be used instead. The added bounce on the hard surface of the yard encouraged cross-batted slogging. More than one prefect enjoyed climbing on to the roofs to retrieve their ball and perhaps find an extra one in the process. Although the game was no longer such good batting practice, it involved boys of all ages for many hours and taught them to bowl overarm. As late as 1980, James Ferguson-Davie, aged nine, wrote in the *Magazine*: 'I like playing Snob in the Long Break. ... It is exciting.... Sometimes you can be sent off for roofing a ball too many times and you can also be sent off for being vicious to a player.... All the windows of the buildings are covered with metal wire to protect them.' Not long afterwards the game was discouraged by cricket purists and sadly allowed to disappear.

'Do you still play little footer in the yard?' asks John Stubbs. 'My brother trod on the football his first day and it burst.' This occurred in 1920. The special little leather ball continued to be kicked about the yard in the Winter after breakfast and during the morning breaks. S.A.P. tried to encourage a dribbling game, but without much success. With the introduction of plastic footballs there was less damage to tiles. By the 1970s, according to Harry Rogers, it had become 'an incredible game; the origin of the rules unclear. Basically numbers per side were unlimited. . . . One day Danny Dixon did for yard football what Ellis did for Rugby by bouncing the ball and running with it.'

The game of 'He' has always been popular and there have been many varieties of it. A particularly hazardous form was 'Chain He'. It involved everyone who was 'caught' having to join the catchers, forming an ever-increasing chain, the ends of which swung round, often forcing the outside boys to be run off their feet, for it was 'not done' to break the chain. Other varieties of 'He' were given special names, such as the eponymous 'Lamprill',

Snob, mid-1960s.

and 'Cockyolly Bird'. 'French and English', too, appeared in new guises, such as 'Cavaliers and Roundheads', 'British Bulldog', 'Caesar', 'Chivvy' and 'Chariot'. These varied from ordinary 'Tag' to very rough lifting runners off their feet. Also there was a highly dangerous jumping game played in the bunker of the 8th green and known as 'Grand National'.

The small boys' appetite for shooting each other never seems to diminish, and 'Bang-bang' continues much as Jonathan Stedall remembers it in the 1940s. 'Endlessly we played it; no more than hide-and-seek with cowboy pistols, and we loved it. Is it harmless to play with guns at that age or not?... I am still confused on the issue.' No such doubts seem to trouble today's young, with 'street fighting' round the air-raid shelter, squash court and Complex. Weapons may be nothing more complicated than a pointed finger, but the noises become increasingly realistic, though opinions differ about the sound of a laser gun.

The quieter games centred round the bunker on the old 9th green and the line of elms on either side of the cricket pavilion. Toy soldiers and Dinky toys were displayed among the Arthur Rackham-like roots and tree stumps; forts and earthworks proliferated in the sand bunker. Paul Whitfield recalls how, in the 1950s, 'inspired by *The Colditz Story*... a group of us decided to tunnel out to freedom from a sandy bunker. Naturally the thing collapsed and we were all in trouble for the orange sand on our clothes.' Twenty years later another group, described by Harry Rogers, 'drew up full-scale plans for the defence of the school when/if it got attacked (presumably deploying Cozzy's three .22 rifles used by the shooting team)'.

World War II produced a craze for clubs. Chief among these was the 'Eagle Club', founded in 1944 by Nick Assheton. It had its headquarters at the 'Hollow Log', a large tree-stump between the football field and the golf course. The 'Log Book' shows that Nick as President received 5/– in wages; two gardeners (Bill Player and Tony Drake) got 2/*6d*; Dan Massey and David Gordon-Lennox 3/– each as recruiting officers, and recruit Julian Mitchell 1/–. Angus James founded the rival 'Hooray Gang', the object of which was to harass the 'Hollow Log'. There was a pitched battle, resulting in a victory for the 'Eagle Club', and the 'Log Book' contains a formal 'Peace Treaty' duly signed by both leaders.

Besides the School Film, events of that memorable Summer term of 1966 included the setting up of a dark room by N. S. Lachlan, whose enthusiasm was the driving force of the Photographic Society. A very successful party was given in aid of Enterprise Neptune. This was the start of a National Trust project, chaired by the Duke of Edinburgh, for the buying of coastal areas of outstanding beauty and interest throughout the country, and Gabrielle was on the board. Some 600 guests invaded the school and over £600 was raised. The cricket season was an improvement on the previous Summer, with some good 1st XI results, due to an outstanding performance by Orlando Gough. He scored 415 runs, with an average of 51.86, and took 33 wickets, at an average of 7.02. This is almost certainly a Cothill record. He was to play for Harrow at Lords, while two other members of the cricket XI, Wold Palmer and Michael Barnard, were to play for Radley and Malvern respectively. A performance of *Macbeth* was produced by R. H. L. Armitage. As the reviewer wrote, 'Everything depends on the two main characters, and here we were lucky to have intelligent and sensitive boys to fill the bill, Orlando Gough and Adrian Hopkinson; they were able to interpret the characters. Leslie Banks would have appreciated his grandson's sleep-walking scene, while Hopkinson spoke his soliloquies with a real feeling for the poetry and stood up well to his towering wife.'

A very delightful and unusual Old Boy, Neil Montgomery, was tragically killed in a flying accident while at Charterhouse. During his last year at Cothill he had become an expert on classical mythology, keeping up a regular correspondence with Robert Graves and producing a complete 'family tree' of gods and goddesses. Another unusual Old Boy had a musical triumph, as the *Eton Chronicle* described in its report on the Organ Society Open Night: 'Robin Wedderburn – clearly Eton's finest musician – then took the floor to tell the audience that he had written a bad piece of music and was about to perform it. A few minutes later he played the final chord to a completely spellbound audience; for Toccata for Organ by Wedderburn is a truly magnificent piece. . . .'

In the Autumn term A. D. Richardson rejoined the staff after a four-year absence. He had come down from London at weekends during the past year to help out with weekend duty, and had eventually been persuaded to exchange the unhealthy life of a London insurance broker for the clean air of Cothill. Thus was he put on course to become Head Master nine years later.

The same term J. S. Malim joined the staff. He remembers his first interview: 'At the front door, to my amazement, I was met by a butler, but was soon gathered up by G.L.S.P. I came away determined to work at Cothill, though I had met no one save a man with a parrot and a film crew.' Jeremy ('Mallet' to the boys) had taught at Sunningdale with the Dawsons for two terms before going to work in London. He is a natural schoolmaster, a rotund, bespectacled, smiling figure, who quickly established himself as a competent teacher even before he obtained his Diploma of Education. More

Jeremy Malim, early 1970s.

important, he showed that he possessed the essential qualities of imagination, understanding and compassion which have made him an outstanding carer of boys. He has described the nine years spent at Cothill as being 'merged into one joyous time (though there must have been "down moments") which stemmed entirely from the atmosphere which was encouraged and engendered by the "management" and reflected in the staff and the boys'. He was particularly appreciative of 'the quite exceptional domestic staff, who were all so nice and so seemingly devoted to service'. This was reciprocated by them and by the boys, among whom Marc Piercey will always be indebted to J.S.M. for launching him on his journalistic career via *Sports Special*. 'He was without doubt the most popular master among the boys.' Other Old Boys will remember trips to Wales, when he annually took a party to our Pembrokeshire cottage. It was he who introduced Rugby football ('despite some mild Carthusian/Etonian opposition'). His regular theatrical productions gave great pleasure to casts and audiences. To many boys' parents his approachability and the warmth of his hospitality in the Masters' Cottage are a particulary happy memory.

On 31 October the film was shown on BBC 2. By a happy coincidence the school was on Long Leave, and many boys and their parents saw it. I had a preview in a tiny room at the BBC. The only other occupants were Jonathan Stedall and John Betjeman. At the end John burst out: 'How envious Joc

3.5

THE WORLD OF A CHILD

Six films . . . Six children . . .
Six worlds . . .
5: In Cothill House—
a boys' Preparatory School

DAVID ROLT

'Going back in the car I hardly ever talk because I'm thinking about school and cold baths and things like that.'

Produced and directed by
JONATHAN STEDALL

Radio Times, *31 October* 1966.

Lynam will be!' Ten hours of filming had been reduced to half-an-hour. There was no commentary, only boy and staff noises, with 'over-talk' by me and others. The action centred round David Rolt and friends, at work and play, eating, gossiping, ragging (with a specially staged pillow-fight). It was a shock to see and hear myself warning the school, on the walk to church, not to get run over ('No strawberry jam!') and roaring from the rear, 'Keep to the path, that boy!' But there were some memorable scenes, such as T.E.B.J. taking the letter-writing session in the Big Schoolroom ('No love? No kisses?'), and a very small Richard Vivian having his hair washed in the bath. I felt that the Stedall touch had done us proud and I was delighted with the result.

The only public reaction came from *The Guardian*: 'The clear message of last night's "The World of a Child" was that if you want your son to have an intelligent, integrated, sympathetic and practical education you ought to send him to Cothill House in Berkshire. It was hard to be sure whether it was the boys or the teachers who most clearly displayed what can be done by the combination of education and affection. Of course, there were off-beat moments: my favourite one was when a master was reading (surely a generation too late) from *Winnie-the-Pooh* and we had a shot of a boy peeping at his copy of *From Russia with Love*, which was not at all by A. A. Milne.'

We received many private comments in letters, such as: 'A very good programme – very fair impression' (Old Boy, public-school master). 'We thought the film superb, a tribute to both subject and producer' (Old Boy).

'Family atmosphere and general feeling of happiness shone out . . . the dormitory scenes superb. . . . I should hate to be filmed teaching or taking prayers' (public-school headmaster). 'It all seemed almost too good to be true – we look forward so much to seeing the school' (prospective parent). 'I thought it gave a very representative picture of a first-class school. It can do nothing but good to the IAPS image' (preparatory-school headmaster). There was only one abusive letter; from an Old Boy when he saw the *Radio Times* announcement and photograph of David Rolt: 'I am surprised that schools like yours have not been abolished long since.' I answered, 'Make sure you see the film', but heard no more.

In the Spring term 1967 I was entertained by nine Old Cothillians at Trinity, Cambridge, a memorable reunion organised by Roderick Chamberlain. We had a superb dinner and afterwards I was told exactly what they all thought of me and the school in a flow of apocryphal and scurrilous reminiscences. At the end I was helped to my taxi in a haze of good wine and goodwill, feeling that there was a lot to be said for 'the other place'. Easter was spent at school. Class 1 had listened to the complete recording of the *St Matthew Passion* during Scripture lessons. On Good Friday I took 35 volunteers to the first hour of the service at Marcham taken by the Rev. Brian Goodrich, and we were greatly inspired by the experience. Brian was at that time Vicar of Chieveley, near Newbury, and had done an exchange of duty with the Vicar of Marcham. He was an exceptional pastor who had been ordained relatively late in life after being Assistant Chief of the Singapore Police. He and Audrey had sent three sons to Cothill, of whom Peter and Simon were still in the school. He was as effective on the golf course as in the pulpit. He and I played as regularly as we could at Frilford and during these games we would 'talk of many things'. On Easter Day there was a chocolate-egg hunt for the whole school, 600 eggs having been hidden all over the school grounds. David Way writes: 'These were eggs and "fish" in silver and gold foil. I think a lot weren't immediately found; some turned up years after. Even so, some boys gorged themselves silly.' It was the greatest fun, not yet repeated, as ever since Easter has been celebrated during the school holidays.

A Science Laboratory was built by handyman Fred Hughes in the space behind the squash court. This had been used as a Hobbies Room since the late 1950s. The Library was recatalogued by R.H.L.A. and a system of block books for every boy was introduced. The Golf Cup was won by Jamie Summers, who subsequently played for Oxford as a freshman. The star performer at a concert was Iain Little, who later became a choral scholar at Caius.

Library, Autumn 1969. It moved to what had been Barbara Hall's classroom in 1962.

The Summer term was memorable for the celebration of Leader Fairbrother's 50th anniversary as groundsman at Cothill. My parents came over from Henley for the occasion, speeches were made, and the youngest pupil presented a silver salver, with a card signed by every boy. 'We salute a true countryman, a devoted servant and a much-valued friend.' Another excitement for the boys was a visit by the then popular TV personality, Simon Dee (Henty-Dodd), who had been greatly impressed by the School Film. 10-year-old Charles Part described how 'he talked to the new boys and asked whether they enjoyed the school. Whenever he was left by Major Pike everyone crowded round him trying to get his autograph and take a few photographs. Mr Lachlan was very busy developing and printing pictures taken of Simon Dee . . . it seems he is very popular.' He duly sent his son to the school, but as a parent he is remembered shirtless in the heat at a Sports Day, rather letting the side down. He disappeared without trace as quickly as he had risen to fame.

It was in this term that judo was introduced to the school by J. Chambers of Faringdon. He was a short, tubby man, wore thick glasses and proved to be a splendid teacher of what was described as 'an obvious successor to boxing . . . has advantages from a prep school point of view . . . a large number of boys can learn together – it's everyone's turn all the time'. Boxing had by this time gone out of fashion at public schools, several of which had stopped it completely. The judo classes quickly became popular, and I used to watch with amused admiration the way in which J.C. instilled Japanese ceremonial courtesy into some of the more undisciplined ten-year-olds. It was a far cry from L.M.S.'s boxing classes, and I still think that teaching 'the noble art of self-defence' to a small boy is no bad thing, provided that he is not allowed to box an opponent heavier and stronger than himself. Meanwhile bearded K. Bones of Radley completed his first year as a gymnastic trainer. 'He is an expert and enthusiastic teacher . . . all boys benefited from their weekly lesson and many from being taught to swim and dive.' We had been very lucky to get him to come over, for he was in the process of developing Radley gymnastics to a position second to none among public schools. He was undeterred by the fact that we had no gymnasium, adapting the New Hall to suit his purposes and taking classes in the open air whenever possible. Keith is a delightful man, a devout Roman Catholic, whose character was appreciated by the boys as much as was his skill as a gymnast and instructor.

The choir achieved a Merit at the Tilehurst Eisteddfod. According to the adjudicator, 'They sang with such enthusiasm that we would have believed that Summer suns *were* glowing even if it had been snowing outside'. However, more concentration and discipline would be needed if they were to win such a competition. The air-raid shelter was cleared of earth, an operation that Anthony Weld Forester remembers being in charge of. There was in fact little earth left after years of boys' playing, and it was an untidy eyesore. The stark concrete was later softened by flower-beds, and the recent Craft, Design and Technology Centre has been built over it. Jamie Summers wrote a 'Vale' when he left, beginning 'I came in tears, I leave in tears', with a concluding verse, 'And now I have to leave my friends, / And leave the school. I make amends / To those who helped me on my way, / Whether at work, or rest, or play.'

In the Autumn term the 1st football XI had a new modern strip, in place of the traditional heavy flannel shirts and long flapping shorts. The new colours proved to be those of Manchester United, but were nevertheless kept until they wore out and the present maroon shirts substituted. In the Spring term of 1968 the Music Room was completed, designed by Gilbert Marsh and built single-handed by Fred Hughes. Two Russian ladies, representatives of Russian women's organisations, were entertained for the night at the request of the Foreign Office. They came into evening prayers, the elder of the two being in tears when she left the New Hall. Three Russian-speaking males from Oxford were produced by Lord Redcliffe-Maud, Master of University College, to provide help in conversation at dinner. Next morning a photograph was taken. It was published in the next *Magazine* with the caption: 'An *entente cordiale* smiles confidently and perhaps something has been done to help us on the road to international goodwill.' Another sort of road was constructed in the Marsh. Gabrielle had introduced boiler suits for picnicking on Sundays, to help the matrons in their efforts to keep the boys' clothes clean. A.D.R. collected a number of old iron bedsteads and joined-up duck-boards, and with Senior Prefect Martin Taylor, David Heathcote and David Duncombe constructed a path which is still called 'Martin's Causeway' by those in the know, trodden warily by gum-booted walkers. Sports Day was memorable, because it was the last time it was held in the traditional form at the end of the Spring term. Since 1969 it has been organised on a Group basis in the Summer term, with a Group Cup but no individual prizes. Athletic Standards, competed for throughout the term, form the basis of the weekly Athletics which is a feature of Summer activities.

That Summer, 15-year-old Pete Bennett, from the USA, after spending six weeks of the term at the school, wrote: 'Cothill is more than young boys scurrying about, going to their next lesson. It is a conglomeration of people, all working to the same end, and all dependent on each other. It is a sympathetic master helping a small boy with what seems to be a small problem, yet it is ever so large to the boy. It is a kind matron offering aid and comfort to a child of eight who has for the first time in his life been away from home for a week. . . . ' Pete became a firm friend of ours and of the school, visiting Cothill for the next four Summer vacations while working at Austin Reed's in London.

Denis Lauré, aged 12, from France, wrote of his early impressions of Cothill: 'I found my first English lunch a little frugal in comparison with the French lunch which are often the cause of indigestion, but for all that I didn't think I would die of starvation. After this . . . I thought with dread at my first encounter with Cothill boys. . . . Happily that was better than I thought . . . principally because they had nearly the same heads as French boys. . . . A moment after I was curiously watching a cricket match. It is an interesting game, but quite incomprehensible to foreigners. . . . I wanted to be able to explain it to my family, but I tried vainly. Finally, all the problems and questions which I put to myself tired me so much I fell asleep at once. . . .'

A visit from the Royal Navy in the Summer of 1967 involved a helicopter landing on the cricket field. This caused intense excitement among the boys and a great bending of the elm branches from the rotors of the machine. An entertaining naval lecture which followed was much enjoyed. The next excitement was an historic innings. Alexander Gordon scored 100 against St

Home century-makers, 1968 (Gordon) and 1989 (Borwick).

Andrew's. Alastair Aberdeen writes: 'Neither you nor I were present when he scored the first century recorded by a Cothill boy in a home match. [This is not in fact correct. Harold Porter scored 128 not out versus Waynflete in 1900.] I had promised him £5 if he did it – maybe filthy lucre had spurred him on. I remember the evening of that memorable feat; the telephone rang. G: "Hullo Dog, Alexander is here and has something to say to you." A: "Daddy, you owe me five pounds."' (There was a sequel five years later when Alexander, playing for Harrow, hit three sixes.) There were other excitements: a WI fund-raising party was held in the school grounds, the boys enjoyed a late night and the sum of £500 was collected; Rosetta had a foal and Willie Boone started on his road to fame by being in the winning pair of the Centenary Public Schools Rackets Championship.

The Autumn term produced a very successful 1st XI (played 11, won 8, drawn 2, lost 1), captained by Anthony Oppé, who scored a goal from the half-way line to defeat Horris Hill on the old Major Game field, which had puzzled visiting teams for so many years by its slope and shape and smallness. Among the indoor activities we started declamations, in which each class provided solos and ensembles. There had been a Cothill tradition of learning by heart portions of the Bible and *The Book of Common Prayer* on Sundays, and a passage of poetry once a week as part of an English lesson. Originally called 'Repetition' (or 'Rep'), this was not universally popular. Bible Rep gradually faded out, but we kept the learning of poetry, which now developed into declamations. These did not survive many years, but Daniel

Beazer, writing of the late 1970s, mentions 'the once-weekly learning of poems from *Dragon Book of Verse* (and 'David's Lament' too). I am eternally grateful for this because it taught me to appreciate our language. Nothing else is quite so effective, I believe.'

The first *Magazine* of 1969 quoted the inebriated P. G. Wodehouse character who could not remember whether education was a drawing-out or a putting-in. 'Our aim at Cothill is to develop boys to the stage where they can at any rate make a good start at educating themselves.... Our task is to discover what latent talents lie hidden beneath the untidy hair, and then foster them until the boy is able to give of his best.... The message of Christmas is that all of us have an immense dignity and importance. It is in an atmosphere of mutual respect and affection between boys and staff that we shall try to respond to that message.' This year saw the completion of the Didcot Power Station, with its vast cooling towers, which have so altered the view from the cricket field. The father of one of the boys, Mark Osborne, had been responsible for the civil engineering side of its construction, and he arranged for a party of boys to have a conducted tour.

The main event of the Spring term was the winning of a Radley scholarship by Simon Tross Youle, whose cousin Michael Hancock won an exhibition, taken from the school. Another excitement was a battle in the Marsh with village boys armed with airguns. This was described in a page of 'Snippets' in the *Magazine*, ending 'Major Pike seemed very jovial about the affair, but called the police to find out who the "yobs" were.' In the Summer Iain Little won an Eton scholarship, which with the two Radley awards made a gratifying total. I wrote at the time: 'All three boys have intelligence plus determination. They are enthusiasts, with a wide variety of athletic, musical and scientific interests.... We have at Cothill boys of widely varying ability, so that we can fairly call ourselves comprehensive. Only a few can hope to win academic distinction, but all can gain from their example.' In the words of the schoolboy howler, 'blessed are the pacemakers'.

A 10-mile sponsored walk by the whole school raised £200 for the National Deaf Children's Association. Alexander Armitage won the 10–11 age group in the Berks & Oxon Judo Championships. Sports Day was held in the middle of the term. J.S.M. wrote enthusiastically of the new organisation on Group lines, with every boy in at least one event, and boiling heat instead of freezing March. New events included throwing the cricket ball, putting the shot and an obstacle race.

One casualty of the new Sports Day programme was the Fathers' Race, a splendid stampede of thundering feet and jingling coins run over 100 yards past the cricket pavilion. Tim Collins remembers a previous race: 'It was conducted on the most unfair lines, i.e. a handicap of one yard per year of

TOP *Fencing, Autumn* 1969. LEFT *Cross-country runner, Autumn* 1969.
RIGHT *Rugby, Spring* 1981.

difference in age. Then Lord Ronaldshay got about 20 yards, if not more, and walked it every time. One year I was the youngest father and therefore backmarker. I had some allies whose idea was that if the result was a foregone conclusion, at least we could stop a certain father who fancied himself from being placed. So we boxed him in and just before the line tripped him from behind with a perfectly ordinary football tackle and over he went – but unfortunately full length forwards and his nose was adjudged second over the line. This story is not apocryphal. There must be a Latin tag somewhere which would deduce a moral.'

That Autumn term there were 26 new boys. Fencing for 12 boys was started by A. Money of Radley. W. Rule, golf professional at Frilford, gave lessons to six boys under the Golf Foundation Scheme. Cross-country running under K. Bones became a regular feature. The death of H. A. G. Phillimore during the term recalled his last visit to Cothill, some years after his retirement. As Dust came into the yard, with his very distinctive skipping walk, boys converged from all directions, to shake his hand or look wonderingly at him as though at a mythical figure. He was his usual shy shelf, blushing with pleasure at the warmth of his welcome and with a kind word for everyone. T.E.B.J. and I went to his funeral in Hampshire. Unfortunately my car broke down and we hitched a lift in a laundry van and arrived, sitting on pillows, half way through the service, part of which was at that moment being conducted by his old pupil and friend, Father Hugh Barrett-Lennard. Let another former pupil, John Duffield, have the last word: 'I hope you will say only kind things of H.A.G.P. He seems to me in retrospect to have been a wonderful man – totally devoted to Cothill.'

An entertaining innovation was class 1's fortnightly newspaper, *The Cothill Scene*, edited by David Way. Production was made possible by John Stephenson's father, whose secretary typed the contributions. 1*d* per copy was charged and the profit of £1.15*s*.1*d* for the first four issues was given to the Library. The first number (21 May 1969) contained a report of the Library robbery, when about a hundred books, including a set of *Encyclopedia Britannica*, were stolen during the Easter holidays. These were eventually found in sacks in a field on Boars Hill, but the paper had a 'spoof' page of photographs taken by Peter Leanse, purporting to show the gang at work. In subsequent numbers various 'Cothill Personages' were covered. When it was the turn of the teaching staff ('Those magnificent men with chalk on their coats'), the Head Master was reported on with reasonable accuracy and respect. L.M.S., when interviewed, maintained that though outwardly we enjoy a much freer, fuller and more interesting life today than in the 1940s, 'all the way through the Cothill spirit has survived, the general atmosphere has changed little'. In the first instalment of a weekly thriller by Charles Smith, A.D.R. threatened the Head Master at dead of night by the air-raid shelter, and subsequent incidents included C.W.B.C. stabbed through the heart ('No more French verbs'), the charred remains of the 'spy from London' in a burnt-out plane, but 'Mr Richardson's remains could not be accounted for'. One correspondent asked, 'Does Major Pike approve of being bossed around by Mr Richardson?', but no answer was forthcoming. There was a report of a sudden craze for making 'Dens' by boys of all ages, 'one team managed to scrounge 127 bricks'. The Vicar had his leg gently pulled; Leo, the Border terrier, was described sitting demurely through evening prayers; Suzanne Holmes, a very popular and attractive matron, on leaving to get married, was wished 'all success in the future after surviving so many battle-torn terms'. J.S.M.'s introduction of Rugby football to Cothill was noted: 'Mr Malim collected a number of enthusiastic seniors to play twice a week'; Giles Greenwell reported that Christopher Figg ran fast and 'scored a number of glamorous tries', concluding that 'the game is enjoyed by all participants (except a few feeble specimens) and a favourable start has been made'.

When David Way left, John Stephenson took over the editorship, Peter Leanse continued to provide much of the copy, alleging a lack of honesty in the school, and describing the discovery of Polo the hamster behind a cupboard, where it had been mistaken for a tennis ball. When John left, *The Cothill Scene* finally faded. Simon Goodrich, in the last number, bemoaned his unsuccessful attempt to perform his duties as a prefect ('I do try, sir'), ending 'Another Bad Mark and more little tears. Our innocent and saintly hero sobs quietly to himself that night as he descends the fire escape, towel in hand, for his nightly midnight swim.'

The mention of the Border terrier in prayers shows how a dog enlivens a school. When we came to Cothill we brought with us our black whippet, Darkie, who immediately endeared himself to the boys. It was especially exciting to watch him going flat out across the cricket field. One day in 1931 he disappeared and no trace of him was ever found. We were all heartbroken, my parents could not bear the thought of another whippet, but there followed at least two Sealyhams, of which Peter was very much in evidence when Gabrielle and I got engaged in 1941.

In 1947 my mother bought a white whippet from Darkie's breeder. Spike became a great friend of our half-Shetland collie Hudi, who even with a broken leg in plaster would hobble from Marcham to go rabbiting with Spike, both of them eventually returning bright yellow from sand. Spike was

Darkie, with friend, 1931.

Peter, 1939.

Spike, with friend, 1948.

Leo, 1969. 'We don't allow it, but that doesn't stop him.'

a delightful, if incontinent, dog, and when he died my parents did not replace him. When Gabrielle and I took over in 1962 Hudi came too. With him we brought a large Pekinese called Coley, a dog of immense personality. After Hudi's death aged 16, Coley was joined in 1966 by a Border terrier puppy, christened Leo Lonsdale after a local friend.

Leo and Coley had a ritual game on the cricket field. Leo charged Coley from 50 yards. Coley remained motionless until the last moment, then turned like a matador as Leo swerved past at full speed for another 50 yards, turned and charged again. This was repeated until Leo was exhausted. His other delight was to charge round the swimming-pool when the boys were bathing, barking furiously. Whenever possible he would jump in and swim like a power-boat at some unfortunate boy who would get badly scratched unless he had learnt to head Leo off. This performance was observed by a prospective mother: 'I'm surprised, Mrs Pike, that you allow your dog to swim with the boys.' 'We don't, but that doesn't stop him', she replied. Leo went with us into retirement and died soon afterwards. Since then there have been no school dogs.

From 1962 to 1969 I had been to some extent my own Head Master. Afterwards I was to be the paid employee of a Board of Governors. This is therefore the moment to go off the field and reflect on the first half of the game, as I remember it looking back 27 years. From the first the problem of keeping the school going was paramount. Every prospective parent was vitally important. Gabrielle and I tried to appear more confident than we felt, but it was a blow to our pride when we failed to secure a firm booking. It is hard to imagine, in the present Cothill climate, when would-be clients are turned away, and numbers could be doubled in a day, in spite of fees of over £2,000 a term, how one agonised over every small increase in fees for fear of pricing oneself out of the market by raising the fees by £5 a term. This is borne out by Paul Holmer (ex-Ambassador in Bucharest), who refers to 'a striking illustration of what has happened to the pound. . . . In 1955 a difference in basic fees of £60 p.a. was then something which a young First Secretary, with three children and living on his pay, had to consider very seriously.' Certain well-known prep schools on the South Coast went out of business, and we profited from their misfortunes by taking in some excellent boys, but this was only a temporary relief.

Academically, the most important development was the gradual introduction of Science. T.E.B.J. confirms that there was no Science on the curriculum in my father's day. Apparently he was very annoyed when he found that Tom and Julian Shuckburgh had built, in the early 1950s, a crystal set. 'He told us to take down the aerial as he didn't want boys playing with electricity. Neither of us had the courage to explain to him that a cat's whisker is non-electric.' This gap in the curriculum was remarked on in the HMI report of 1963. Soon afterwards T.E.B.J. started to teach Science with the Esso kits, which were provided free. 'Each term a box came from another school (we circulated them), complete with everything needed.... The equipment was very much string-and-hairpins-and-old-tin-cans – absolutely ideal for boys of that age, as it gave them the realisation that science could be done at home (after all, Edison worked under his kitchen table).'

Nuffield Science was then the fashion, and T.E.B.J., after attending a course at Malvern to learn something about it, called on Dr H. M. E. Cardwell, Science master at Radley, to ask for advice on how to equip the former Hobbies Room. H.M.E.C. was so interested in the project that he offered to run it, but according to T.E.B.J., 'He was so high-powered none of the boys understood him, and we gathered that none of the Radleians understood him either'. David Way remembers 'Hugh Cardwell's Great Danes, which used to accompany him on his Land Rover, and which were exercised at half-time in the Science double periods'. It was his successor who was responsible for starting a curriculum innovation. C. J. Scott was teaching Nuffield Science at the John Mason School in Abingdon. In 1968 he agreed to come over to teach Nuffield Chemistry and Physics on Saturday mornings. He was a man in his thirties, spare and athletic, with a sensitive face and thick hair already beginning to grey. In his white coat he exuded quiet authority and professional competence. He says that as a teacher in a maintained school two things stand out in his memory: 'being given a free hand to order all the equipment and apparatus I wanted to begin the Nuffield course (everything from test-tubes to electrical apparatus); and learning that the class size was about twelve. On the other hand, being used to purpose-built laboratories, it was something of a challenge to work in the room I was given.' He remembers that the boys found Nuffield Science baffling at first, 'because I asked questions but gave no (or few) answers. They were to find them ("Is it *your* answer? Does it make sense? Does it fit in with what you would expect?"). The "learning by doing" method, with its open-endedness, was different from their experiences of learning for the most part. The *process* was just as important as the product... working in pairs... they were submerged in an experience which required manual dexterity, the ability to work with others, the ability to make deductions from their results.... There was no laboratory technician to clear up after us, so we had to return everything as we had found it.' Claude and his wife Ethne became friends from the time when they asked us to dinner soon after his arrival and we quickly learnt what an unusual couple they were. He had been brought up in the Belgian

Congo, where his parents were Pentecostal missionaries. Ethne and he combined their strong Christian faith with scientific enquiry, music and much humour. Claude was a useful cricketer and played in Masters' Matches, watched by Ethne and young family, the latest arrival of which had been christened Gabrielle.

C.J.S. left in 1971 and is now Head Master of Thorpe St Andrew's School in Norwich. His place as master in charge of Science was taken by R. J. Griggs and his wife Freda. Raymond had just retired from Aldenham where he had been Senior Science Master. They were a delightful couple, he tall, thin and professorial, she small and animated. As a woman of about sixty she seemed undeterred by having to introduce the teaching of Biology in the school. Raymond and Freda taught enthusiastically and effectively until 1975 when Freda suddenly became ill and died the following year.

Of outdoor activities during these years, I have particular memories of one cricket XI containing two fast left-arm bowlers, Richard Fawcett and Orlando Gough; a good standard was maintained in football; the golf course produced promising players such as Jamie Summers. A female lawn tennis coach gave weekly lessons, and was not amused when one of her protegés was beaten in the final by Wold Palmer, who did not have lessons. The game of Snob gave unique pleasure ('Only today', wrote Wold recently, 'I thought of it as we were throwing tennis balls at someone holding a stump while waiting vainly for the ground to dry . . .'). Picnics and barbecues at weekends, gardening and natural history, Dens and bunker games helped to beguile the unathletic.

Barbecue, Autumn 1974.

Michael Alachouzos was one of these unathletic, the elder son of a Greek shipowner and an English mother. After his first visit to look over the school, 'Big Michael', his father, a squat, fat figure, had said to me, in broken English: 'Major Pike, I like the school very much, I like Mrs Pike very much, I like you very much. But I must ask you, as Michael must go to Eton, are you socially acceptable?' We passed the test, and Michael duly arrived, a tearful little boy, for ever carrying a clean white handkerchief with which he mopped his eyes. He confided to me that his parents had loud public quarrels in the Randolph Hotel whenever they came to take him out. These he took as a matter of course; he also took, as a matter of course, food off other boys' plates – with a fork, in Greek fashion. When still under eleven, he entertained the whole school with an hour's expert conjuring, complete with professional patter. Later he starred in R.H.L.A.'s production of *The Thwarting of Baron Bolligrew*. David Way writes: 'Nobody could match Alachouzos for sheer power of invention and histrionic ability. He brought a sophisticated and grown-up sense of humour which had his 10-year-old contemporaries (and not a few adults, I suspect) amazed.' He went through the motions of playing games, with amused detachment and caustic comments. Of his contributions to the *Magazine*, this gives a flavour of his unusual talent:

'THE CANE
(Parody on "The Ocean" by Lord Byron)

Whack on, thou long and slender cane, whack on!
Ten thousand boys are beaten, all in vain.
Thou markest skin with ruin – thy control
Stops when thy victim howls and screams with pain.
The scars are all thy deed, nor doth remain
A single boy without a broken bone,
When, for a moment, wounded and half slain,
He sinks onto the floor with ghastly groan,
With nothing else to do, save lie and moan.'

Extracts from letters written by David Way to his parents between 1964 and 1970 give a boy's impression of these years. 'We have had snow. . . . We had a wonderful snowball fight with Major Pike. He was on the other side and I hit him five times.' 'I enjoy being vice-captain of my dormitory as I can boss all the dormitory about.' 'It's not worth buying a boiler suit unless you want to.' 'The central heating went bish in the church today so we had to put lots of things on.' 'There was a concert yesterday by the Mrs Fry trio, piano, 'cello, clarinet. It was rather boring, only three people enjoyed it, the rest went to sleep.' 'I joined the Natural History Club yesterday (badger department).' 'Mr Richardson produced a whole school play to entertain Major and Mrs Pike called the Pied Piper of Hamelin. The little boys were all rats, Gordon was the mayor, I was chief citizen, a girl [Joanna Bowman] who was a friend of Mr Richardson was the Pied Piper and the rest were boys and girls. We read it from the original poem and Major and Mrs Pike liked it very much.' 'It does not matter about sending me an Easter egg because when I say I have not got one they all come to me and give me a piece of theirs.' 'My dormitory is as super as usual, this morning [Sunday] we had 4 or 5 pillow fights with the next-door dormitory which took up most of the early morning, and at night we either roll marbles down a special track or tell ghost stories.' 'This Sunday the rector went down with flu, so we were spared his dreary sermon and had church here.' 'Because of the price of milk, we had orange to drink instead, for tea.' 'I and about 25 others went to Dr Barnardo's fête which was being opened by Mrs Pike. We were given 5/– each, which went very well.' 'We are having Science with Dr Cardwell this term, three times a week, which is a much needed improvement.' 'The 2nd XI *v.* Hawtreys drew 2–2. It is a super school, an old Georgian type house with pillars and statues, paintings and antique furniture. It is enormous, and very surprising a school has been made of it. We also had a super tea. But the playing fields are dreadful – our pitch being a near-Passchendale.' 'I think everyone has settled in here, but it's virtually impossible to know all the new boys' names [there were 26]. So they all have to wear identification discs, like Russian political prisoners, and must go round in a daydream.' The concert referred to had caused preliminary panic for one young 'cellist. Daphne Gough has reminded me of her son Orlando's story: 'He saw a notice that Mrs Fry's trio would give a concert, and he thought it meant him and two others who had been playing the 'cello for about six weeks. When after a week or two of desperate rehearsals he came to tell you that they couldn't make it, you marvellously didn't laugh, for which he was eternally grateful.'

For an adult view of the school, Daphne Stewart has written: 'Women on the teaching staff were scarce when I arrived in the Autumn of 1964. There were just two of us. Barbara moulded the new boys in Class 8, and I took them over from her in Class 7. She moulded me too in her kindly, helpful way, and I was endlessly grateful for the initiation. We had a very good relationship with the rest of the staff, morale was high, George and Gabrielle treated us like members of the family, and it was a very happy place to work in. George was greatly concerned for our comfort and welfare, which was demonstrated when he burst into my classroom one morning from the yard shouting anxiously above the prevailing hubbub, "Are you all right, my dear?" "Yes, thank you, Head Master", I shouted back, just managing to restrain a crouching "David" from slinging his missile at "Goliath" and catching George instead, "it's just the Philistines getting a bit excited".

'We used the Masters' Cottage over the road as a Common Room, with a study each, and I was able to park my small dog while I taught. He was taken out for exercise during long breaks by strings of eager, animal-loving boys, who once succeeded in dropping him into the deep end of the swimming-pool by mistake. They were fascinated by the bubbles that came up from the bottom.'

Her outside wooden classroom was either too cold or too hot: 'One Summer afternoon a Latin lesson was in progress. I droned on; no one listened; the classroom slumbered in the heat. Then a wasp flew in through the open door.... The boys sat up, ducking if the wasp approached, shoo-ing it, reporting on its progress.... Aggravated beyond my better judgement, I swiped at it with an exercise book, and to my surprise it fell lifeless at my feet. Instantly, as though by a pre-arranged signal, the whole class burst into tears, or pretended to. They sobbed and moaned and prostrated themselves over their desks. There were tortured shouts of "How *could* you..."; "You're *cruel*..."; "My mother says you must *never* kill *anything*..."; "They are *all* God's creatures...". Latin and I were utterly routed, so we surrendered and spent the rest of the lesson in deep ecological discussion.

'Teaching has its just rewards. The "highs" are rare but glorious when they occur, and you are given proof of comprehension as well as application ability. I had prepared a well-structured grammar lesson, making everything as clear as possible. At the end I beamed at the class and asked for an example of a collective noun. "A vacuum cleaner!" called out a small boy with complete confidence. The "lows" were usually one's own fault.... Anyone reckless enough to let slip the immortal name of Kipling during a boring poetry lesson deserved a barrage of ['Mr Kipling'] confectionery names hurled at her.... Events can occur that are totally unpredictable and even bizarre. I looked up once to see a boy staring at me holding a large pair of cutting-out scissors. Still staring he put the blades into his mouth and opened them out so that his cheeks became alarmingly distended and his eyes almost crossed. "Careful!" I cautioned, fatuously, "you might swallow those scissors". Very carefully he withdrew them. "It wouldn't matter if I did", he said scathingly, "I've got another pair".'

One Friday Daphne was asked to head one of the long tables in the Dining Hall. After battling with carving the infamous 'hedgehog', she sank exhausted on her chair to tackle her own portion: 'After the first mouthful all became clear, as I removed pieces of indestructible material from my mouth. The "hedgehog" was none other than our old friend rolled breast of lamb, jacketed and tied with innumerable clipped knots by a painstaking butcher. An earnest little face beside me watched my dilemma. "Don't you like string?" he enquired sympathetically.'

11

COTHILL HOUSE SCHOOL LTD

During the years 1962–68 we had faced and survived a series of financial crises. It was a period of some difficulty for independent schools, which were threatened by a Labour Government on the one hand and by economic pressures on the other. The problem of keeping up the numbers so as to break even was a permanent headache. We had to economise wherever possible. Gabrielle and I lived off the school, but took no salary. Leonard (who had become Bursar) and Joan Swinbank kept expenditure on the rails by expert budgeting. However, the rent and consultant fee to my father reduced any profits and prevented our building up a capital reserve. Any substantial increase in fees from £110 a term seemed too risky, but meanwhile the roof was in urgent need of repair.

For some time it had become increasingly evident that the best way to ensure a prep school's continuity was to form it into a Charitable Trust. Many of our rivals, such as the Dragon, Summer Fields and Horris Hill, had already done this. There were obvious financial advantages; the responsibility for policy was widened, the ups and downs of private education were shared, and the Head Master no longer bore the total burden of the running of the school. Against these had to be set a certain sacrifice of independence. We managed to satisfy the Charity Commissioners that we were a viable institution. In 1969 we became Cothill House School Ltd. I was able to choose the first Board of Governors, with my brother-in-law, Robin Woods, Dean of Windsor, as Chairman. He it was who got us off to a good start with his exceptional all-round ability, his financial knowledge and his affection for the school, as the father of two Old Boys, Robert and Edward. Hilary Bray was Vice-Chairman. The other Governors were Philip Taylor (chairman of the finance committee), Basil Greenwell, Stephen Ryder, Tom Bowles, Sylvia Gray, Dennis Silk, plus Gabrielle and myself. They formed a well-balanced team and from the first were a great support. Two old friends, Raymond Willis and David Hopkinson, were unable to accept my invitation to join the Board, but continued to give the school most generous help in a number of ways. I asked David, as an Old Boy and parent, to mark the formation of the Trust by writing the 'Opening Remarks' in the Spring *Magazine* of 1970.

He quoted from Raleigh's 'The Passionate Man's Pilgrimage':

'Give me my scallop-shell of quiet,
My staff of faith to walk upon,
My scrip of joy, immortal diet,
My bottle of salvation,
My gown of glory, hope's true gage,
And thus I'll take my pilgrimage.'

'Some may say that talk of quiet, faith, joy, salvation, glory and hope is neither helpful nor practical when facing an educational pilgrimage into the 1970s. They want to know what will happen to the school during the next decade.' He thought there would be more day boys, perhaps girls; children with grants from the local authorities. He foresaw more Science in place of Latin and Greek and 'doubtless someone will cook up new new Maths to take the place of old new Maths. More emphasis may be given to tennis, golf and squash, new buildings may arise and the paint-pot flourish. But these prophecies are concerned only with ephemera. One hopes that Cothill will continue to teach self-confidence, self-respect and self-discipline.... The young seem to have faith in the new developments in our society.... A Cothill boy learns "*Dum spiro spero*" early in life; further, he must learn to be passionate, concerned and positively involved. In order to understand the pilgrim's requirements he must never be indifferent.'

One of the first things the Trust had to do was to sanction the celebration of the Centenary. In the past there had been some confusion as to when the school started, but an old prospectus was found (and subsequently lost), which stated that it had been founded in Meriden in 1870 and had moved to Cothill House in 1879. It was therefore decided to hold Centenary celebrations on Sunday, 7 June 1970. J.S.M. was appointed Centenary Secretary, and thus the success of the whole operation was assured from the start, for he attended to the smallest detail. As he says, 'the germs of the idea of celebrating the event developed with increasing speed'. An organising committee included two Old Boys, who had boys at the school at the time, Walter Somers and Graeme Anton. The former undertook to trace Old Boys and their addresses. After a tremendous amount of work by Walter's secretary, Sheila Williams, and a number of crises which included losing in the post the only list of Old Boys, some 1,300 invitations were sent out. Recipients included Old Boys, Governors, past/present parents, past/present staff, local friends; headmasters of public schools, local preparatory and other schools; and domestics, the last asked as guests and not to work.

J.S.M. further recalls 'much negotiation over the hire of a marquee, tables and chairs; telephoning (and going to see) William Hickey and Peterborough.... We got hold of the British Legion to help with the parking, and I think the Red Cross.... I remember the boys each side of me at breakfast counting the acceptances and refusals, the mounting excitement and involvement of the boys, and the unusually quiet and attentive meeting in the New Hall when I went through all the arrangements.' These consisted of three closely-typed sheets of detailed timetables from Friday, 5 June to the evening of Sunday, 7 June. Every boy was given an area to tidy up, under command of a prefect, on the Saturday afternoon. On Sunday, a special Centenary Service at Dry Sandford Church was followed by final scavenging, putting up 200 hired chairs in front of the temporary outdoor stage and the last-minute laying out of projects and exhibitions. What followed is described in the *Magazine*:

'June 7th dawned sunny ("It was certainly a halcyon day – one of those English Summer days of which one dreams"). It was just as well after the months of preparations. The Governors' decision to earmark money had meant that the original idea of having to charge for tickets could be dropped, and an anonymous present made it possible to end the day with a champagne party. Mr Malim ensured that everything was prepared with Royal Naval efficiency ("I must congratulate you on first-class organisation; noticeable was the lack of any loud-speaker blaring. Every event started on time, the catering arrangements were superb"). The programme was designed to show as many aspects of school life as possible: not only displays of gym, judo and fencing, but also exhibitions of photography, art and hobbies as well as school work. This involved team-work by staff and boys, as did the outdoor entertainment, in which every class took part ("I think boys must be cleverer than they used to be; I am sure I could never have remembered my lines as well as they did in the plays").

'The Band of the Scots Guards formed a focal point, playing tirelessly in the hot sun ("occupational hazard, madam"). The main attraction of the afternoon was undoubtedly the huge magenta-and-yellow striped balloon, into which Dr Teddy Hall [later to be a school Governor for some years] directed a continuous stream of pressurised flame. It looked the most dangerous operation since the flame-throwers of World War II, but it was immensely enjoyed by those who hung on to the ropes or just waited expectantly. Unfortunately the balloon only achieved the inflated upright position, as sudden winds made it too dangerous to risk a take-off over the Marsh. In the meantime, a counter-attraction had started with a fire in the Marsh, which threatened to spread rapidly. However, the Abingdon Fire Brigade arrived quickly and, helped by the water of the swimming-pool and a crowd of volunteers, soon brought it under control. The flame-thrower had by this

Centenary celebrations, 7 June 1970: Dr Teddy Hall's balloon.
Band of the Scots Guards.

Senior Prefect and the oldest Cothill Old Boy cutting the cake.
Chairman of Governors, Head Master, retired Head Master and Senior Prefect.

time burnt a large hole in the side of the balloon, but no one seemed to mind too much.

'From the number of cars it was estimated that there must by now have been over a thousand visitors. These ranged from Harold Porter, the oldest Cothill Old Boy, to last term's leaving boys. Ex-members of the staff included Messrs Waite, Banks, Welch, Ogston, Shelton, Langhorne and Glazebrook ("We missed Mr Phillimore so much; how he would have loved it all"). Sam and Dorothy Pike were kept busy by crowds queuing to shake hands, and they clearly enjoyed seeing so many old friends again ("They reminded me of King George V and Queen Mary at a Royal Garden Party"). Tea had been a moveable feast in the fifty-yard-long marquee, starting with the cutting of the Centenary cake by Christopher Figg, Senior Prefect, and Harold Porter; and there had been a performance of the BBC School Film "The World of a Child". At 6 o'clock Robin Woods made a short speech of welcome, explained how the school was now a Charitable Trust, and wished it a happy second 100 years. The day ended with a large amount of champagne being drunk by all ages, some of the younger ones learning a valuable lesson without lasting ill-effects.

'There were of course some who couldn't make it ("Regret, unable attend celebrations, but representing the Spirit of Cothill in the Putney to Calais power-boat race"), and it was sad not to see Muriel Wright and Arthur Reid through ill-health. However, the special visitors' book, given by Elizabeth Anton, was signed by over two hundred Old Boys. That it was a successful party may be judged by the comments already quoted and the following: "An occasion to remember and memories to treasure – a great bridging of the generations and the joy of seeing familiar faces once more in the same lovely setting of Cothill grounds."' Louise Dunmore, at that time the mother of a day boy, writes: 'I shall never forget watching the firemen with blackened faces, having put out the fire, sitting around being refreshed by the boys handing them bottles of champagne.'

M. J. H. Williams left in 1970 to return to his native Barnsley and become a priest. Martin had been in charge of Music for five years, having been recommended by Hilary Davan-Wetton to succeed him. A short, round, bespectacled man in his thirties, with a rasping voice and a Yorkshire accent, he was an ecumenical Roman Catholic. He did much good work on the music generally, widening the range of Sunday choral singing without offending too much the low-church susceptibilities of the Vicar. He was succeeded by a tall man with a goatee beard, a fine harpsichordist, who broadcast on several occasions. Unfortunately he could not cope with boys, and after a year I had to persuade him to resign. His place was taken by Sue Bitterling, a fair, attractive young woman, who was also a keen gardener.

Another addition to the staff in 1970 was C. R. Barker. He had just left Radley and quickly became much liked by boys and staff. According to *The Cothill Scene* reporter, 'Mr Barker's first impressions were that the school was rather informal, the boys pleasant but not all that easy to teach'. Charles went up to Oxford, where he won a Hockey Blue. After schoolmastering at King's, Taunton, he returned to Radley, where he is now a Social Tutor.

Louisa Vivian, our only girl, Autumn 1970.

Louisa Vivian is the first and only girl so far to have been a pupil at Cothill. Her brother Richard had left to go to Eton when she arrived, aged seven, from a small girls' school in London, in the Autumn of 1970, along with 29 new boys, travelling to school in a Land Rover with a trailer which contained her pony 'Gayspray'. 'During the year I was there, she and I had great fun, including at one time giving pony rides at 3*d* a go in the paddock. I remember getting given a detention for that particular episode, as well as having my earnings confiscated. That is what comes of practising free enterprise and business acumen at school. The boys accepted Gayspray, although I did get terribly teased on occasions. I remember galloping full pelt across the football pitch after she was hit on the rump by a well-aimed football. Gayspray and the school donkey became great friends during the year.'

Louisa slept in a different dormitory each term with three or four of her form; 'for some reason I always used to get most of the blame for all the noise – although now I am sure it was justified'. In her final term she 'managed to sleep through an entire fire practice. I was wakened by the noise of the boys coming back into the room, after the whole thing was over.' She was segregated only at bath time, wore corduroys or jeans, with a flannel skirt on Sundays. 'I thoroughly enjoyed playing cricket and football. . . . I rather wish it was still the custom for girls' schools to play cricket.

'One of my memories is being spoilt dreadfully by yourselves. You both took the greatest care of me . . . and I often spent the evenings in your part of the house, having tea and scones, and being taught how to crochet. . . . The boys tended to bully me at every opportunity, but I had several good, close friends who stuck up for me and fought my fights for me. Although, what with doing judo, I was just as likely to pitch in myself. . . . Daniel Dixon always seemed to be there to rescue me when I got into trouble. . . . It amazes me that most of the boys have not forgotten me, and I am often brought face to face with an almost total stranger at a party in London, who starts talking to me about Cothill.'

For Andrew Loyd, who came as a new boy the same term as Louisa, Cothill was 'a wonderfully happy place and I have so many good and fond memories. . . . I enjoyed a period of peace and enormous comradeship.' Harry Rogers, who arrived a year later, describes the Sunday barbecues: 'Group captain (hair dishevelled, up to elbows in lard, face smeared in grease, eyes completely smoked up and watering having just done thirty eggs), "Hey, squit! How do you want your bacon done?" Timid squit: "Oh, er – medium rare please." Group captain: "Medium rare? medium rare! – *Do you want it burnt or raw*?!" Another part of the bar-b-q etiquette was that squits always ate first and the seniors ate whatever was left at the end – usually some form of "hash up". Also, why was it that the potatoes never got cooked properly? All praise to the day when the Brooks brothers introduced bubble-and-squeak, which was basically a Spanish omelette using all the ingredients in one glorious fry-up. It saved so much time.'

Harry also has this to say about Dens: 'They formed an integral part of the school's social structure. They were like mini-societies. You could only join a Den if all the existing members agreed. Most Dens were stick structures covered in leaves. If made properly the inside could remain quite dry and with a good dry-leaf floor could be comfortable.' These Dens were built in the line of trees, now sadly depleted by Dutch elm disease, and as Tom Harley remembers, 'were often incredibly spacious and their construction

A Den, Autumn 1979.

was usually pretty intricate and ingenious'. They were to boys of the 1970s what Dinky toys had been in the 1950s; an enjoyable use of the trees and undergrowth. Longer-lasting have been the bunker games, such as the construction of race tracks and fortifications for war games.

In a 'Comment' for the Summer *Magazine* 1971, W. J. H. Liversidge wrote of going to school 50 years before, 'in a world blissfully free from transistor radios, jet aircraft and diesel fumes.... It was not all fun, but most of it was and we knew exactly where we were and what was expected of us. By the time we were teenagers we had acquired certain standards of behaviour and a veneer of – whisper it – discipline.... The prep school of the 1970s is, in many respects, a better place, but there is still a lot to be said for much of what is currently regarded as old-fashioned, such as decent grammar and spelling.... A school that can teach application and how to work has put across one of the really important lessons of life – that one cannot always avoid what one doesn't particularly like.... In our efforts to make school enjoyable, we may do the young a disservice by making everything appear too easy.... Discipline, now a more than suspect word, has an important part to play in education and should not be confined to the school.... "Speak roughly to your little boy / And beat him when he sneezes" – the Duchess was only guilty of a little pardonable exaggeration.'

The main event of this term was John Stephenson's top scholarship to Radley (the Sewell). There was a postal strike, but Philip Taylor operated a private postal service through Austin Reed's for London-based boys. 'Old Boys' news' was scarce because of the strike, but at least Bartle Hellyer's accident was reported quickly. He had fallen at the last fence when leading in a point-to-point, had broken his back, and was now in the Stoke Mandeville Hospital. There he was to remain for six months, an example and inspiration to everyone with his courage, cheerfulness and humour. At the time of his accident he was in his first year at Exeter University. Since then he has been paralysed from the chest downwards, but by 1984 he was the leading barrister specialising in claims on behalf of paraplegics.

R. H. L. Armitage departed to become Head Master of Lochinver House, Potters Bar. An inspiring History teacher, with a sense of humour, he left his mark on the school in many ways; by reorganising the Sports, recataloguing the Library, starting holiday trips with some of the boys on the Broads and in Wales. He was an above-average all-round athlete, a keen walker and climber, good with his hands. A great theatre-goer, he produced several school plays, notably one about the prophet Elijah, written by his wife Sue. I remember that he did not agree with everything I did as Head Master, though he was always loyal, and one of his first actions after taking over Lochinver House was to abolish prefects.

Richard Armitage and Barbara Hall, Summer 1967.

It was a disastrous cricket season, the 1st XI failing to win a single match, in spite of some fine fast bowling from Mark Smith-Bingham, who took 34 wickets for 181 runs. In the Sports, Mark Osborne jumped 4 ft $5\frac{1}{2}$ in. The previous record holder, Tim Dillon, had jumped 4 ft 5 in. in 1930 without the benefit of a pit (let alone foam rubber) and therefore had to land on his feet. The most memorable event of the term was described by Tom Holmer as 'a wonderful square dance with the Women's Institute, organised by Mrs Pike, which made a welcome change from dancing with other boys'. It took place on the football field on a hot evening and after a while most boys overcame their shyness and joined in, learning the steps and the MC's patter as they went along. It was a 'one-off' occasion that was enormously enjoyed by boys and adults, the former in blue Aertex shirt-sleeve order, with best grey trousers, acting as hosts.

My mother at the Centenary celebrations, June 1970.

My mother died suddenly at home in Henley in the middle of the term at the age of 81. Although S.A.P. was shattered, he admitted he was thankful she had been spared pain and a long illness. She had remained alert and cheerful, coping well with her disability. V. K. D. Waite had written in 1962: 'Dorothy and Sam were so completely and indissolubly one. . . . She shared to the full his devotion to the school, and her energy, skill and organising ability were combined with a charm and poise which graced so many Cothill occasions.' The last such occasion was the Centenary party, when she was overjoyed to see so many Old Boys. She had kissed them all goodnight as new boys, which was appreciated by most, though not by all. Pat Cook remembers her in his book *Ombudsman* as 'a dear who mothered us all'. Nicky Rootes looks back on her Art classes: 'We used to paint *en plein air* in the rose garden. She always insisted that we should mix our own green from blue and yellow, a habit that subsequently stuck.' Patrick Savage, as a young master at Summer Fields, came over with 'an unimportant XI on a golden afternoon in 1939. . . . After the match was over, there was the splendid ritual of tea, with Dorothy presiding over the silver teapot and kettle. It was the real thing, a proper sit-down drawing-room tea. . . . Even as a spectacle it was magnificent.' My mother remained a pretty woman to the end and she always dressed with style. After her stroke her flow of chat dried up to some extent, but the warmth of her personality was undiminished. She was a wonderfully generous and affectionate mother, and her death left a great gap in our lives.

The Autumn term found A.D.R. studying for his Certificate of Education in Oxford, and his place taken by P. D. Gilbert. Peter was a married man with three daughters, an experienced schoolmaster in his forties. It was a good term for shooting, two boys becoming marksmen and Christopher Brooks scoring a 'possible'. The rifle range had always had its small band of enthusiastic devotees, and now C.W.B.C. was rewarded for the hours of patient coaching that he put in during long breaks and on half-holidays. Francis Burkitt remembers going round looking at schools with his parents. 'Swanbourne had a swimming pool, another did carpentry and Cothill had a rifle range. At seven-and-a-half that was all I saw between them. When my father asked my opinion I plumped for the rifle range. . . . Imagine my subsequent delight on finding when I arrived that it also had a pool and carpentry workshops.'

On 5 November the fireworks display took place for the last time. Anthony Galliers-Pratt recorded the entertainment in the *Magazine*: 'Most boys clutching a torch, wearing gumboots and duffle-coat, waiting in the Big Schoolroom, the Head Master in fur-lined coat and Russian hat. . . . Soon we were all lined up in the dark, cold night, hands in pockets and chatting. The more knowledgeable boys were pointing out to others where the Great Bear formation was and the Pole Star. . . . Then the fireworks started. A rocket was first; it soared up towards the stars, burst into glorious colours. Immediately everyone was shouting "Record!". There were whizzers that sounded as though they were an angry swarm of bees. . . . I liked the mortars best; they were just like the Royal Artillery firing in Hyde Park on the Queen's Birthday.'

A concert was given by the Christianhaus Gymnasium Choir of Copenhagen, described as 'a gifted choir of some thirty male and female staff and pupils'. The programme included folk songs from seven different countries, negro spirituals and some excellent unaccompanied choral singing. The choir was brought over from Radley by R. W. Stoughton-Harris, who had arranged their tour. Two interesting lectures were also given, the first by my sister Audrey's stepson, John Parry, on 'Pollution' (shortly afterwards the Government decided to spend £130m on tackling river pollution in Britain). The second was by Gabrielle's nephew, David Woods, on 'Canoeing in Canada', complete with masses of kit from a rucksack. At the end of term J.S.M. produced his first play, *Toad of Toad Hall*, which was a resounding success.

One reason for the formation of the Charitable Trust in 1969 was the possibility of an appeal. So long as the school remained my father's property and therefore theoretically a profit-making concern, such an appeal could never be made. The Trust held an underlease for a period of five years at a rent of £3,000 per annum, though reconsideration of the rental was possible every five years until the underlease expired in 1987. Now that my father retained only the freehold, the newly-formed Cothill House School Ltd was at liberty to do what it could to raise funds.

The accounts for the year 1969/70 show income at £64,339 and expenditure at £64,375 – a situation of which Mr Micawber would not have approved. In addition, the exterior painting of the school at £949 and the Centenary party at £1,000 brought the deficiency to be carried forward to £1,985. My salary was £1,600 and Gabrielle earned about £500. Allowances for London, holidays and entertainment totalled £650. Fees at the time were £215 per term.

To take advantage of the charitable status, the school solicitor, Alan Oliver of Birchams, originally suggested a scheme for parents to lend monies to the school for reinvestment by the charity, leading to a reduction of fees. A sub-committee was formed to consider this plan. At the same time various members of the Cothill staff had felt that the Centenary should not be allowed to pass by without the unique chance being taken to channel the goodwill in some positive way to the future advantage of the school. Robin Woods felt that it was not the moment to increase the size or structure of the school buildings; there were considerable difficulties involved in the question of the freehold, the lease, capital gains and estate duty. He envisaged the establishment of a permanent Improvement Fund, to which Friends of Cothill could contribute at any time.

Accordingly, a letter was sent out to Old Boys, friends and parents of boys in the school, informing them that a Centenary Fund had been set up, and asking them either to make a secured loan to the school of capital sums in any multiple of £500, or to give a capital sum. The response to this came to some £4,000, of which £3,000 was given by Eleanor Castle Stewart, a great friend and WI colleague of Gabrielle's. The Governors, realising that money was not being received in sufficient quantities, decided to employ professional

Eleanor Castle Stewart, one of our chief benefactors, 1970.

fund-raisers. Richard Maurice Ltd were asked to provide a campaign director. John Rogers writes: 'I recall a meeting at Philip Taylor's flat when they sent along their proposed organiser to meet Philip Taylor, George Pike, Leonard Swinbank and myself, and he turned up wearing a blue suit, yellow tie, orange-coloured shoes and I suspect a little the worse for drink, and Philip Taylor's comment, "John, how do we get rid of this man?".'

Richard Maurice received a tremendous rocket, pulled out all the stops and sent along their top man, Lieut-Colonel P. C. Garrett. He proved to be a most agreeable and efficient campaign director, establishing an excellent rapport with those potential donors whom he visited. An ambitious plan for the expansion of the school had been drawn up by Gilbert Marsh, of Marsh & Woolf, who was also a parent of a boy in the school and a member of the Board of Governors. A new assembly hall, new classrooms and changing rooms were envisaged. Peter Garrett soon reported to the Governors that parents spoken to had shown an interest in different items of the proposed plans and he advised that at this stage these should not be too specific. At the Governors' meeting on 25 October 1971 he forecast that £35,000 would be reached by the end of January 1972. At this point it was decided that the priority was the repair of the roof, followed by resurfacing and improving the existing entrances and the front drive. It was also suggested that the Head

Master should explore the purchase or hire of temporary classrooms to relieve pressure on space.

By February 1972 the campaign director was able to report that £56,764 had been pledged. He forecast an income of £14,500 for the first year, then ranging from £6,500 down to £2,300 in 1980. The average covenant was for £30, the average gift £290, a high figure. He said he had been given a warm welcome by practically everyone whom he had visited; that the Pikes were very obviously held in high regard and affection by both parents and Old Boys alike. Where there had been criticism this had more often than not, and particularly among Old Etonians, been directed at the academic standard of the school, and such criticism had been based on out-of-date impressions also. Peter Garrett said he very much wished to express his thanks to me and my staff. I in my turn said what an asset to the school Peter had been. He and his secretary Margaret Herapath had maintained a friendly and well-organised office in the Masters' Cottage, and would be much missed when they left.

On Shrove Tuesday, 1972, Maggie Lovegrove was found dead in her bed. She was 89, and her whole life can be summed up in one word – service. Having no children of her own, she had showered her affection on my family, especially on me, and also on Gabrielle. We loved visiting her in her cottage in the village, where she would give us wonderful meals and entertain us with her inexhaustible supply of reminiscences and music-hall songs. She loved seeing the 'young gentlemen'. On Tom Harley's first day as a new boy she wrote to his mother Rosie, 'I went across to the school and found Tom and gave him a kiss, he seemed quite jolly'. Many other Old Cothillians will have memories of the warmth of her welcome and her endless bags of sweets, including sugar mice. Charles Bland remembers also being read to in bed as a six-year-old by 'dear old Maggie' when staying at Cothill while on a visit to his elder brother Edward. As she grew older and thinner she seemed to lose none of her energy ('I had two great advantages, Mr George, I was very strong and very quick'), and she was a familiar figure walking in hat and coat with unmistakable brisk step, toy tennis racket in hand, to exercise our peke Coley on the tennis-courts. To us her death meant the loss of a uniquely loving and lovable friend in whose eyes we could do no wrong.

In the Autumn *Magazine* I outlined the changes that had taken place during my headmastership. These included the reorganisation of the timetable and curriculum; the disappearance of school caps and Sunday walks (' "Round the Triangle" being far too dangerous as the volume of traffic increased

Maggie Lovegrove, a spectator at the Centenary celebrations, and Coley, June 1970.
50th anniversary of Leader Fairbrother as groundsman, 15 July 1967.

remorselessly'); the introduction of sub-prefects; the start of Rugby football, so long resisted by my father, who thought it a dangerous game for young boys. Other innovations were lawn tennis coaching, a school shop, Sunday picnics/barbecues, Athletics in the Summer, judo and fencing instead of boxing. In 1965 the first day boy (Michael Wiles) appeared half-way through the term, living locally and unhappy at his school. Finally, the formation of the Charitable Trust. The changes had been made to work smoothly, thanks to the loyalty of the long-serving staff.

The 1st cricket XI was again poor, winning only two matches. A survey of Cothill boys' tastes revealed that cricket, football and swimming were the most popular sports, History the favourite subject, the *Daily Express* read by 40%, war films twice as popular as comedies or cartoons, France the favoured country for a holiday, and milk the most popular bedtime drink. J.S.M. produced *Treasure Island* most successfully. Leader Fairbrother died at the age of 80. He had been an invalid for two years, during which time he had been looked after by his daughter Gwen Kiddle. Fairbro' had been an outstanding figure in the life of the school, a mine of information about boundaries and drains and local history, a real countryman, a stalwart of the Baptist chapel, a kind and courageous old soldier.

There was evidence of journalistic enterprise; Marc Piercey produced his *Sports Special*. He did his own typing and was helped by Chris Gillum, Abdol Faridany, Jacob Brunner and Zandy Anton. Marc writes: 'I produced a total of 13 issues of the paper, but I recall that before I could bring one out I had to get permission from you – and if my work had not been up to scratch in the previous week, I stood no chance at all.' He had been helped in the production of *Sports Special* by J.S.M., who the following term went on a year's teacher-training course at Culham. His place was taken by J. C. R. Burbank, initially for one year. John proved to be a good teacher of History, a sound disciplinarian and a willing colleague, When J.S.M. returned I had difficulty in keeping J.C.R.B. on the staff, as he was supernumerary. However, N. S. Lachlan was due to retire in a year's time, and the Governors agreed to let John stay. He has been at Cothill ever since, the longest-serving male on the teaching staff, a familiar, dark-haired, bearded, rather shambling figure in a Barbour coat. This delightfully humorous and gentle man has loyally identified himself with many aspects of the life of the school, though caustically critical of some of them. He has run the Library, taken school photographs, official and candid, supervised most games, having sympathy always for the needs of the individual boy. His three young sons, Benjamin, Joseph and Samuel, have all been at the school, where they have caused their father considerable pride and a minimum of embarrassment.

The foundations of the new classrooms had been laid during the Summer holidays of 1972, and this necessitated moving the Major Game from the pitch that it had played on since 1894. The greater space of the new pitch on the golf course had immediate beneficial results: good, fast football was played, the 1st XI won seven matches, and there was something of a football epidemic in the school.

An Old Boy wrote to say that he hoped that in spite of new buildings and other alterations, 'the old spirit of the place had not made a swift exit'. This produced a reply in the next editorial: 'We aim for progressive conservatism . . . whereby the best is kept, change is not made for its own sake, but new methods are examined and opportunities seized.' One of the most successful developments had been the Stamp Club, which met on Sunday afternoons in Gabrielle's sitting-room. There were 35 members, the chairman and secretary were elected by secret ballot each term, minutes were kept and members were taught procedure. In her capacity as a member of the Stamp

1st XI football on the new pitch, Autumn 1975. The only school to beat us that season was Horris Hill.

Advisory Committee, Gabrielle was able to arrange various expeditions. In March 1973, for example, the club visited St Martin's Le Grand, the PO underground railway and the Postal Museum. Afterwards the Canadian High Commissioner, Jake Warren, and his wife Jane, whose son Ian was a member of the club, entertained the party to tea, with dancing afterwards to old Mrs Warren's excellent jazz on the piano.

Another disappointing cricket season, with only two 1st XI matches won, was mainly due to poor batting. The highest total was 69, and there was only one really good individual performance, an innings of 40 by Richard Steel against Horris Hill. Tom Barker's bowling was splendidly hostile throughout the term, at the end of which there was an historic climax, a tie against Summer Fields in the final match. I am indebted to Richard Porthouse for an account of the match in the Summer Fields *Magazine*: 'Cothill batted first and faced a torrid welcome. The first five batsmen were dismissed for 10 . . . then stands between Dixon and Harley and Dixon and Van Denberg altered things. Dixon batted with stubbornness leavened with resource. Van Denberg, an American, was less orthodox. . . . They had their luck, but courage should beget good fortune. Their efforts brought Cothill to the respectable but undaunting total of 62. Summer Fields's batting foundered on an all too excellent wicket. Cothill had in Barker an excellent bowler, who bowled unchanged. From a long, loping run he kept a good length, and his off-cutters were hard to play. At the other end a very slow bowler [Harley] teased and taunted us. This bowler had his reward when he caught a hard, straight drive which dismissed Morris who had middled everything. Our revival was based on a splendid stand between Morcom and Dent. . . . Morcom was bowled by a fast bail-high full toss, his confessedly least favourite ball. Dent's dismissal was crucial. He hit hard and high an off-drive, which easily could have won the match. It was brilliantly caught by silly mid-off [Hussey] at full stretch. Dent's score of 24 was diminished by "one short", a lapse which cost us victory. The final overs brought together Davies and Morrison, two of Summer Fields's most diminutive players, but two of the bravest. In a silence which could be felt they levelled the scores, before Davies was bowled by a splendid ball from the tireless Barker [who took 6 for 20]. A great match. . . . Our captain said to me during the closing overs, "and to think that there are idiots who say that cricket is a boring game".'

Sixty-seven boys received tennis coaching and four boys again took part in the IAPS tournament in London. *Sports Special* was enlivened by 'Sportsman of the Week' and 'Man of the Match'. The GPO Oxford organised a Schools Design Competition. Five Cothill boys had their designs selected for the final judging in an exhibition held in the Town Hall which was much enjoyed. The school was further identified with the community when it held a wine and cheese party in aid of the Music Centre in Abingdon Old Gaol. (This historic building, thought to have been designed in part by Gabrielle's great-great-grandmother, Elizabeth Fry, had recently been saved from demolition.) A senior and junior concert, a jazz band from Abingdon School and an auction attracted over 500 people and more than £1,000 was raised. Harold Porter died at the age of 87. He had been the first Cothill boy to score a century; a famous mountaineer and friend of Mallory, he had a climb named after him in New Zealand.

In the Autumn term 1973, Fred Hughes, the handyman, retired after ten years of expert building, and instruction. An appreciation of this quiet and friendly man speaks of his being 'ubiquitous – here replacing a window, there mending a fuse, everywhere patching and painting; yet he found time to build as well as maintain. . . . Three times a week he gave lessons in carpentry to classes of ten or eleven. That there were always other boys waiting to begin speaks for the quality of his instruction.'

The most important event of the term was the official opening, at the start of Long Leave, of the new buildings by John Belstead, Parliamentary Under-Secretary of State for Northern Ireland, who had started as a boy at Cothill in 1941. These buildings, now known as the Complex, had been temporary timber insurance offices in Tunbridge Wells. Gilbert Marsh had successfully arranged for them to form six classrooms, a staff room and stores. Not a

Gabrielle, her brother Robin Woods, Chairman of Governors, and Philip Taylor, to become Chairman in 1976, at the opening of the Complex, 26 October 1973.

single new wall-panel was needed and no part of the old structure was wasted. The price of this operation was under 40% of the cost of new construction at the time, some £10,000.

The opening ceremony began in a packed New Hall, with John Belstead, Robin Woods, Chairman of Governors, now Bishop of Worcester, and the Mayor of Abingdon. I started off by saying, 'Bishops live by Faith, Politicians by Hope and Head Masters by Charity', before going on to thank all those who had contributed so generously to the Centenary Appeal. John Belstead recalled coming into the Head Master's study as a new boy, sitting down and saying, 'I think I rather like this place'. He expressed confidence that 'Major and Mrs Pike will ensure that Cothill still has the same welcome for other new boys, . . . but no school can stand still, . . . keeping up to date has necessitated these new classrooms. . . . It is vital that prep schools should flourish, complementary to other schools as part of the total stock of schools from which parents can choose in this country.' To the boys, his chief message was that 'whatever captures your interest, it really is important that you pursue it as energetically as possible, because the whole world you are growing up in is changing very rapidly. . . . This country will need from a school like Cothill highly trained soldiers, scientists, doctors, businessmen who can speak foreign languages, even politicians if they can find the right answers.' Afterwards 'the crowd bubbled forth to watch Lord Belstead insert a key in the door of the new Complex, which he then declared officially open, to the puzzlement of the many boys who had been using it for weeks. Everyone surged into the building, then collected in the New Hall to drink sherry and chatter. A lot of humorists thought the Complex would collapse with the

Our last group with me as Head Master, Summer 1976. Staff, from left*: A. D. Richardson, Sue Bitterling, Joan Swinbank, L. M. Swinbank, Miranda Brignall, G. P. Brignall, P. D. Gilbert, C. W. B. Costeloe, S. P. Blackmore, J. C. R. Burbank, T. E. B. Jackson, Ruth Viner, Jo Belcher, Barbara Hall, Bridget Worthington;*
foreground: *Leo and Mr Thompson.*

A new classroom in the Complex, Autumn 1973.

weight of so many people (they had just seen a Norman Wisdom film on that theme). They were not far out: the ceiling came down a week later.'

The school returned after Long Leave to get on with more mundane, routine matters, but J.S.M.'s production of *A Christmas Carol* was not one of them. In spite of the fact that certain of the cast had to have last-minute sessions with me to make sure that they knew their lines, all was well on the night and the performance was enthusiastically reviewed by Arthur Hearnden, a parent. After that it was the Carol Service, accompanied by recorders and guitars, and the class 8 Nativity play, produced by Barbara Hall.

Robin Woods, in a *Magazine* 'Message' in April 1974, wrote: 'Cothill is not just a prep school, it is a way of life. . . . Either we are to become a rather uniform pack of Englishmen, or we are to grow into a diverse and varied community of people with widely different interests and widely different responsibility. It is because we believe Cothill provides this last kind of education that many of us have faith in it.' The following term, Rolla Edwardes-Ker, another ex-parent, was asked to write the editorial: 'Both my sons have adored Cothill . . . because all the boys are happy being at

Cothill ... they have the spirit of enjoying life and making life enjoyable and rewarding for others. The spirit has to be fostered and each boy taught to develop good nature, self-reliance, humour, compassion and determination. I have seen the Pikes and their wives try to instil this Cothill spirit, the envy of less happy schools, and I hope that Cothill boys will continue to rise to the challenge.'

However, we did not seem able to rise to the challenges of the cricket field, and the 1st XI won only one match (though three others could well have been won). Clearly there was a lack of confidence, born probably of poor batting technique which may have been compounded by Snob. Swimmers did better, performing creditably in a Prep Schools Swimming Gala at Westminster College, Cumnor, organised for the first time by the Head Master of Christ Church School. Our success was largely due to the coaching skill and enthusiasm of K. Bones. T.E.B.J. organised a sponsored swim, which raised £300 for the Dry Sandford Scout hut. Meanwhile the school had at last been put on the main drainage. This was paid for by Eleanor Castle Stewart, a wonderfully generous action following her gift of £3,000 three years before. So it was goodbye to 'Sewer Valley', that smelly, forbidden territory where generations of boys had dared each other to play illicitly, and to which the local authorities had so obligingly turned a blind eye ever since R. Tomkinson had installed the 'entirely modern' drainage system.

Main drainage arrives, Summer 1984. So goodbye to the 'entirely modern system' and 'Sewer Valley'.

Old Boys' Day was attended by well over 50 from various public schools. Christopher Figg brought over the Eton contingent and wrote a very appreciative account of the proceedings. I had had difficulty in persuading the Head Master, Michael McCrum, to let them come, but luckily his knowledge of Christopher's responsible character just tilted the balance. The occasion was greatly saddened by the news that Sebastian Horn had been electrocuted by faulty candelabra at a charity dance in London. We had stayed with his parents Geoffrey and Marjorie, in England and in Spain, 15 years previously, and ever since had grown increasingly impressed by Sebastian's outstanding qualities while at Cothill and Eton.

At the end of the term N.S.L. retired after nine years at Cothill. Though handicapped by deafness, he managed to enthuse the top class with his love of Classics, though he had his difficulties with the juniors. David Way says that very soon after N.S.L.'s arrival an alarm clock was put in his high teacher's desk. This duly went off in the middle of a lesson: 'That's the bell, sir.' 'Right, you'd better go.' Needless to say, this did not work a second time. (Within a few years, David was to return as a member of staff himself for a term.) Tom Harley remembers throwing chalk at N.S.L.'s bald patch and missing; Francis Burkitt and Mark Aldous 'stole tobacco from his pouch during lessons in Latin – the poor man was so old and never noticed (by the way we always put 5p in his pocket to pay for the tobacco) – and then made ourselves clay pipes in the art class and smoked them in the donkey hut one Saturday Summer evening. I don't think either of us has ever felt as sick again, and I've never tried the experiment since.'

Noel's Photographic Society was popular with a number of boys, and he himself took all the team photographs. Known to the boys as 'Lacky Band', he was the gentlest and most delightful of men, whose influence was wholly beneficial.

'*Dum spiro spero*' was the theme of the first editorial in 1975. After quoting from Churchill's speech to Harrow boys ('We shall not falter or fail, we will fight on . . .'), I wrote: 'In a spirit of hope we must set ourselves ever higher standards of work and conduct, quietly getting on with our respective jobs. . . . *Floreat* Cothill, *floreat florebit*.' Later in the *Magazine*, I described going on the Brighton run in a 1903 Oldsmobile, owned and driven by John Allen, the father of two Cothillians. It was a Head Master's day out which was greatly enjoyed in spite of numerous breakdowns, pouring rain and a very late descent into Brighton after all the other competitors had gone home. The prefects visited the *Times* complex, by invitation of Dukie Hussey, via a conducted tour of Boodles. The Stamp Club visited Harrisons of High Wycombe, security printers. The school golf team beat Summer Fields $5\frac{1}{2}-\frac{1}{2}$; James Wade, David Humphreys, Douglas Montgomery and Charlie Brooks were all very promising players.

J.S.M., the Editor, wrote in the next issue, expanding S.A.P.'s ideal, quoted in the Centenary *Magazine*: 'To produce first-class Christian leaders of the country they love.' J.S.M. ends: '. . . above all, leaders must be able to understand and communicate with the ordinary people who are affected by their decisions. A predominantly boarding school seems an ideal place to foster just such ideals of tolerance, example, fortitude and selflessness.' This is illustrated by Daniel Beazer's memory of 'a certain red-eyed boy, who cried incessantly, surrounded by a circle of sympathetic friends. I don't imagine the cause was connected with the school and this was a gentle and touching sight.' The following term there were quotes from two Old Boys. The first, Michael Whitcomb, aged 18, from the USA, had written: 'Cothill was a turning point in my life. I came there an animal and left civilised. My memory of Cothill has been so special that it has become a sanctified ideal. . . . The "education" you have given me has directed me on a whole new way of life. As I write this letter of gratitude I hope that one day I can return to Cothill, a journey which to me would be a pilgrimage.' The second, anonymous, extract is more down to earth: 'Without being sentimental, I still have the most vivid and happy memories of Sunday evenings reading, cries of "fore" on the golf course, and the splendid picnics with Rosetta.'

It was sad to be without J.S.M. for my last year as Head Master, but he had been offered the post of Senior Master at Brambletye by Donald Fowler-Watt, and I encouraged him to accept. Just as he had been the most loyal of colleagues he has remained the most devoted of friends. He visits us every term, with the latest East Grinstead gossip and reassurances that he is giving his present pupils the Cothill treatment.

After J.S.M. left, he was replaced by two young married men, G. P. Brignall and S. P. Blackmore. The former was a competent teacher and games player, and for the next six years he and his wife Miranda were to be invaluable members of the staff. Graham was tireless in every sort of administrative detail, kept endless lists (in true A. C. Phillips tradition) and was described by A.D.R. as a 'walking computer' because of his phenomenal memory for boys' initials and dates of birth. Miranda became a much-valued assistant clothes matron.

Simon Blackmore, youthful, smiling and energetic, quickly showed that he

LEFT *Simon Blackmore, 1990.* RIGHT *Bill Liversidge, Mayor of Abingdon, 1975/6.*

was an exceptionally promising schoolmaster and all-rounder. At Cambridge he read Archaeology and Anthropology. He speaks French and Italian, got a Gymnastics Blue and is a competent football coach. His chief hobby is printing and he was quick to re-found the Printing Club.

Two golf matches were played: against Pinewood, Charlie Brooks, the captain, described the Cothill team 'venturing out into the mist to brush the greens, pulling on as many clothes as possible'. Pinewood arrive 'in their grand Morris Oxford, four very large boys with extremely smart clubs'. Cothill won comfortably. Against Summer Fields, however, the team was beaten $1\frac{1}{2}$–$4\frac{1}{2}$. A Royal Artillery detachment paid a visit as part of a recruiting drive. There were mock battles and models in the New Hall, real guns and equipment outside. The Abingdon Old Gaol was opened on 29 November, and the Cothill choir took part with 14 other schools in a performance of 'Thames Tidings', specially written by Simon Park, a parent. At the end of term A.D.R. produced an edited version of *Julius Caesar*, in which Philip Howard 'exuded authority as Caesar'.

W. J. H. Liversidge retired in 1976. He was in many ways irreplaceable, and was much missed for his excellent teaching and common sense. James Calvert remembers a Geography lesson during the 1976 drought: 'Squidge got angry with a boy and slapped his (own) thigh in anger. He had a box of Swan Vestas in his trouser pocket, and he managed to set himself on fire. He said, continuing the job of educating, that it showed how dry it was.' From now on he devoted his energies to the affairs of the Borough of Abingdon, notably as a Governor of Christ's Hospital and member of the Vale of White Horse Council. He had become Mayor, and I asked him to present the prizes at the end of term. He came in full rig, complete with mace bearer. He appeared to one boy to be 'about twelve feet tall', and made a tremendous impression. He described a mayor's three main jobs as taking responsibility for the day-to-day running of the borough; taking an interest in everything that goes on; keeping up the traditions. In the 'Opening Remarks' of the Spring *Magazine* of 1976, I adapted these points to school life: '(1) Prefects and sub-prefects, realising that duty comes before privilege, can help by doing jobs that help the exchequer, like turning out lights. (2) They can take an interest in everything that goes on in the school, from Latin to Lollipops. (3) They can keep up the Cothill traditions: looking after "squits", being good losers while trying hard to win, treating others as you would like to be treated, making jokes, being "amateur" in attitude, but professional in performance.'

The Spring term was spoilt by influenza, but not before Jim Scott gave a memorable Waterloo lecture. I wrote in the *Magazine*: 'The two armies were drawn up facing each other across the hall, each chair named and its occupant given an envelope (by a uniformed ADC) in which was a typed description of who he was, his immediate superior and the troops under his command. With this was a map of the battlefield and a pencil. Mr Scott outlined the events leading up to this famous confrontation and then fought the battle, moving the formations on a series of large maps, providing the opposing artillery with Chinese pyrotechnics with which to poop off at each other, causing "casualties" with a starting pistol ("Picton, at this point you were killed I'm afraid, bang bang!!"). The last great set-battle came alive, as though by magic, with muskets, swords, tunics and hats for Napoleon [Robert Aldous] and Wellington [Alexander Budworth], all genuine articles from families or museums. Those of us who thought we knew it all were made to think again – and all ages had their eyes opened as to what a lecture could become, given enthusiasm for the subject and an infinite capacity for taking pains – many thanks, Jim, it was super!' For Jim's son Anthony and his contemporaries history was never quite the same again. For the next 13 years Jim Scott was to battle with ill-health, and at his memorial service in 1988 one of his great friends recalled hearing how, during this lecture, Jim's wife Christabel 'had to console a small boy because he had been conscripted into the Imperial Guard and was therefore on the losing side'.

There were few Rugby fixtures, due to illness, but 'ingenious practices worked out by P. D. Gilbert were invaluable'. A Tree-climbing Club was formed by Richard Kay, who described how he was 'caught climbing a tree by Major Pike, he sent for me in his study, and asked me to form a Tree-climbing Club'. The Photographic Society, reorganised after N.S.L.'s retirement, printed photographs for the *Magazine*. The prefects and the top class were taken to see the Constable exhibition at the Tate, picnicking en route with my father in Henley and later exhausting Boodles's supply of coke. 'One of the best days I've ever had at school', wrote Francis Burkitt.

The Summer term of 1976 was my last as Head Master. A year previously I had given notice of my intention to retire when 60, for I had always been determined not to outstay my welcome and become too distanced in age from the parents of the boys. My father, naturally enough, found it quite incomprehensible ('funny chap, George'). The problem of the succession had been resolved. A.D.R. had been my first appointment in 1962, he had served his apprenticeship in two other prep schools, Arnold Lodge (Royal Leamington Spa) and Ashdown House (East Grinstead), and he had obtained a Certificate of Education. His enthusiasm and dedication, combined with natural powers of leadership, persuaded the Governors to agree to my hunch that he was the right man for the job at the age of 33. Two years previously he had been appointed Deputy Head, and had already begun to take on increasing responsibility.

P. D. Gilbert wrote of the 1st XI cricket: '1976 will be a season to remember. Almost uninterrupted sunshine, rock-hard pitches and straw-coloured grass combined to produce an illusion of foreign lands. Headgear of all kinds (and some that defied description) appeared on the field, as participants sought to counter the heat. But the game thrived, and a strong cricketing sense pervaded play on the Major Game ground. The dependable batting of Peter Montgomery, the captain, contributed much to the team's good performances (5 won, 3 drawn, 4 lost). But he was well supported by the rest of the team, almost all of whom reached double figures at least once. Christopher Nash bowled his heart out for 35 wickets... and the fielding was always keen.... Charles Brooks shared in a remarkable last-wicket partnership with David Collinge which took the score from 58 to 115 against Hawtreys – who made the runs with two wickets in hand....' The swimming-pool was in constant use, but 'we failed to get the half-holiday for everyone passing the A test'. The tennis team had a 'clean sweep' against Summer Fields. Peter Montgomery won the under-14 high jump in the Prep Schools Athletics Meeting.

The Car Club had been started the previous term by A. S. J. White, the handyman, who came over on Sundays: 'I have endeavoured to teach something of the mechanics, plus some knowledge of the Highway Code.... I think we shall be turning out some good stock-car racing drivers.' Francis Burkitt remembers how much he enjoyed 'driving around our slalom course built by the Complex [the other side of the stone wall]. We painted and mended some old make of car . . . and spent countless Sunday afternoons driving until Rory Watson crashed it into a tree.' In the Natural History Club, Jonathan Busk noted that 'three well-developed young green woodpeckers were found dead apparently from dehydration. Fourteen kinds of butterfly were seen in good numbers. A pair of coots nested in the sewers.' A Conservative rally was held in the school grounds, and was addressed by Lord Hailsham; Douglas Hurd and John Patten, prospective MP, also spoke. Hailsham's little Jack Russell sat at his feet, which were encased in black boots.

Finally, Sports Day on 10 July was the occasion of a presentation to Gabrielle and me, to mark our retirement. According to the *Magazine*: 'After Mrs Vernon had presented the Athletics Cup to the Greeks – their sixth successive year – Miss Sylvia Gray, CBE, on behalf of the Governors, welcomed the guests and introduced Major Roger Humphreys. Major Humphreys surveyed the period of George's headmastership. The atmosphere of happiness was the particular quality which George and Gabrielle had fostered and for which parents past and present felt such gratitude. Mrs Humphreys then made the presentation of a cheque and 12 prints of "Eton Life" [in the 1860s].'

In reply I said: 'I feel like Florence Nightingale, after she had been given the Order of Merit: she could only murmur "Too kind, too kind". . . . As some of you know, Gabrielle and I took over the reins in 1962. We were not entirely unprepared, and not completely ill-qualified. Gabrielle was National Chairman of the NFWI, and had just returned from an official visit to the USSR. I had been second-in-command to my father for 15 years, since 1947, when Compton and Edrich had just finished scoring thousands of runs in weather like this; when Dinky toys were all the rage in that line of trees over there.'

After thanking special members of the staff and Governors for their loyal support, I concluded: 'Finally, and most important, I thank all parents who have done us the honour of entrusting their sons to our care. Gabrielle and I have tried to inculcate the habit of happiness and good manners. We have tried to produce a few "magic casements opening upon the foam of perilous seas in fairy lands forlorn". The nightingale has sung in the woods to help us, and always the boys have been humorous, straightforward and appreciative. Now it is time to step down. I leave the future of the school in Adrian Richardson's capable hands, confident that a member of the younger generation will give it whatever fillip is necessary.'

12

NEW DIRECTIONS

A.D.R. found being 'a new-boy Head Master' great fun. He wrote in the *Magazine*: 'I don't suppose that people will ever again be so quietly generous and forgiving.' He thanked the Governors, of whom Philip Taylor was the new Chairman, for their 'warm trust and strong support'. The teaching staff had shown him that 'they are doing their level best to teach the boys their lessons, guide and direct their enthusiasms and abilities, and keep them in the way of truth, courtesy and good manners'. The domestic staff 'work in support of the smooth running of the lives of the boys, and like the Governors, much that they do goes unacclaimed. Finally the boys themselves, by their good behaviour and hard work, have pledged themselves to struggle forward under my leadership. . . . Christopher Nash as head of the school showed courage, leadership and diplomacy. I will never forget my indebtedness to him. . . . It is bitterly cold here, . . . diseased elms crash to the ground, but the groundsmen and I talk of new trees and Spring planting.'

The 1st football XI had an unusual season; unbeaten at half term, after losing to Horris Hill they did not win another match. An outstanding golfer, James Wade, broke the Pinewood course record with a one under par. A.D.R., full of energy, produced a cut edition of *Macbeth*, with costumes by Barbara Hall in what Christopher Nash, in a speech of thanks, called her 'free time'. I reviewed a 'fast-moving production'. Edward Way was congratulated on 'getting inside the character of Macbeth'. James Moore's Lady M. was 'a formidably ruthless schemer. . . . In the sleep-walking scene, even the youngest and most fidgety boys were frozen into immobility – "fancy being able to silence this lot" a colleague was heard to murmur.'

In July 1976 Gabrielle and I had moved into Dry Sandford Old School, built, as already mentioned, in 1870 by the Rev. H. C. Adams. It had continued to function as a village school until 1940, when a modern primary school was opened in Lashford Lane. We had bought it for £2,500 from the Church Commissioners, on condition that it was restored to a standard approved by John Reynolds, Vicar of Dry Sandford. It was a listed Grade 2 house, and unfortunately the modernisation of what was little better than a ruin coincided with the oil crisis and inflation. It was a worry for us to have to buy a house at the age of 60.

A.D.R. had asked me to help him by joining the staff as an assistant master. This 'demotion', though theoretically unsatisfactory and full of problems, worked out surprisingly well in practice. I enjoyed being able to concentrate again on teaching and taking games, though I found it quite testing to be a Duty Master again without a Head Master's authority. Gabrielle and I settled happily into the Old School, but it took time to accept the financial constraints of living on an assistant master's salary and the absence of responsibility for running Cothill. While I worked full time and remained on the governing board, Gabrielle had to adjust to being suddenly cut off from a life that she had found absorbingly interesting for the past 14 years, and to which she had contributed so much by her remarkable energy, originality and vision. She made a great impression on the boys. David Way has voiced what many will probably echo: 'I remember Gabrielle's marvellous reading to the early beds. She would come in, dressed for dinner, smelling of scent, and spend fifteen minutes with us, reading, for example, Walter de la Mare's poems.'

Sue Bitterling left and was replaced as Director of Music by J. S. Oxlade. John is a fine organist and pianist, who was to leave his mark by inspiring and accompanying three Gilbert & Sullivan productions with A.D.R. S. D. Swan was another new member of staff to arrive in the Autumn of 1977.

With Adrian Richardson and Robin Woods, 1976.

Commenting on his first term straight from teaching in Canada, he noted that 'there is a particularly cheerful aura about Cothill. . . . I have found the day-to-day atmosphere relaxed. Yet performance in class does not seem to be adversely affected by this. . . . I have noticed the well-balanced curriculum in which Music, Art and hobbies all play a significant part. In games, a healthy will to win combined with dignity in defeat.' S. P. Blackmore, on leaving to try his hand with the Crown Agents, emphasised that 'there is little division of "us" and "them" and a master's job is not one of lecturing and regimenting nameless ranks. . . . Cothill encourages individuals with their own ambitions and hopes, and as the motto suggests, tries to instil the determination to realise them.' Another member of the staff to leave was the young and beautiful Biology teacher Anne Blair Gould. Paul Constantinidi must have been particularly appreciative of his one-to-one periods of extra tuition with her. She became a successful BBC radio producer of 'The Living World' and other programmes before marrying and going to live in Bangkok.

Writing of this time, Francis Burkitt says he enjoyed his last Summer term with Mark Aldous and Rory Watson, 'spent either climbing trees or doing our solar project, which was on the flat roof overlooking the yard, and was I suppose slightly scientific, but certainly great fun. We got water up to 65°C. . . . In the Winter all would find themselves gangs to make leaf Dens along the row of elms that have sadly been felled. Mark Lloyd and I had five rooms and electric light by the time we had finished. . . . Overall I simply have an impression of a supremely happy, friendly and cheerful school, which I still think about.'

Fifty years of Pikes was celebrated by T.E.B.J. in verse in the *Magazine*, and by Hugh Barrett-Lennard who invited me to dine at the Brompton Oratory ('It's 50 years since we first met, playing Snob'). After a delicious dinner, eaten in silence to the accompaniment of the reading aloud from various authors, sacred and profane, Hugh regaled the company over dessert with his Cothill reminiscences, including the singing of the 'School Song', written by V.K.D.W. in 1929 (*Appendix IV*), which only Hugh remembers. It starts, 'At footer, golf or cricket / We play as hard as nails', and each verse ends, 'There's no time for slacking or moping / At the best School, our School, COTHILL'. As Hugh wrote later: 'I think Rumbo sang the solo in a school concert and I sang in the chorus of "*Dum spiro spero*". It's very typical of its time and full of the spirit of the age. There is one verse I have to omit because I cannot remember it. I wonder how many of those who sang the song actually lost their lives in the war.' Keith Rumbo did, in fact, lose his. For whatever reason the song never caught on.

On official business with Eileen Fagent, 1975.

Hugh has contributed so much to this book that a description of him is overdue. After leaving Cothill he went to Radley, where he became a Roman Catholic. After the war, in which he served as a company commander in the Essex Regiment and was mentioned in Despatches, he was ordained a priest. Since 1946 he has been at the Oratory, a spare, tough figure of medium height, with grizzled hair and charming smile. He inherited the family baronetcy in 1977, but this made no difference to his life-style. When he was younger he would pay us unexpected visits, bowling to boys in the nets in his rather grubby cassock and telling them stories of his schooldays. Latterly he has come less frequently, but it was delightful to see him at the opening of the Pike Building in 1985. He is one of my oldest friends, and it was he more than any other who first encouraged me to write this book, by sending me a long, entertaining and spontaneous tape about his Cothill days.

That Autumn term there were electricity blackouts, with candle-lit teas and nervous prep masters. A bright moment was the defeat of Horris Hill at football for the first time in many years. However, the 1st XI was twice defeated by Summer Fields, who lost heavily to Horris Hill. The school suffered a sad shock when the secretary, Eileen Fagent, died suddenly during the term. She had succeeded G.S. when the latter retired, and had proved an intensely loyal if somewhat formidable personality, devoted to the school and particularly to Leo, the Border terrier.

In the Summer *Magazine* of 1978 A.D.R. explained for the benefit of parents the traditional system of Good Marks, V-badges, Weekly Reports and Work Cards. These last were now given to a boy 'not mentioned' on a work list. 'Each of the seven daily lessons and the prep is signed and commented on, and at the end of the day the boy brings the card to the Head Master, who gives a Good Mark for every "Good" on the Work Card. In this way a constant check is maintained, and immediate reward given for each tiny success. Many boys who feel themselves failing slightly ask for voluntary Work Cards, so there is no stigma attached.' In the same *Magazine* Giles Howson, aged eight, describing 'A Day at School' writes: 'I got "Bad" on my Work Card every time. . . . I rag in prep every night and get about eight Bad Marks every forty-eight hours and two Good Marks every month. . . . I lose my books every lesson, never bring a pen or bring a book if it's a reading lesson. If I do it's always trash and it gets confiscated.'

A new master this year was Old Rugbeian Zandy Anton, aged 18, wearing his 'Butterflies' tie. In 'Return to the Fold', he wrote of his wondering what it was that induced him to return to the place which he had been so happy to leave. 'It is, on reflection, due to the many happy memories which Cothill conjures up to all who pass through its gates, and the ever-present smile and warm welcome which are the trademark of all involved with the school.' His introduction to the boys in the dormitories the first night passed uneventfully, but the next morning one of them 'discovered my name on the boards and was heard to exclaim, "But, he's only a boy". . . . Becoming a master relieves all my previous anxieties of what masters mean when quoted as saying "I'm off to the post" or "Marking". Such code words are as essential as the Cottage is as a retreat. Not much has changed. . . . But what better criticism of the school is there than was recently heard on the New College touchline: "Cothill are just too polite", as we went down smiling.'

The Summer term of 1978 was an especially eventful one for A.D.R.; he had to cope with a major fire. On 8 June painters were busy redecorating. At about midday one of them came down a ladder from outside the spare room to recharge his blow-lamp. While he was doing this, an old bird's nest in the eaves began to smoulder. I was teaching in my classroom overlooking the sunken garden. Suddenly Giles Howson put up his hand: 'Please, sir, I think the school is on fire.' Smoke was rising from the roof. At first I thought it was only the chimney on fire, and then realised that there was no fire in the study grate on a warm June day. At that moment, A.D.R. was talking to prospective parents, walking on the lawn. They were suddenly aware that something was amiss. Furniture, clothing, all A.D.R.'s possessions, were being moved

The fire, 8 June 1978.

hastily out through windows by his secretary and others inside. The prospective mother, not sure what to say in the circumstances, volunteered – 'I can see that this may not be a convenient moment. Shall we come back another time?' A.D.R. could only agree that this would be the best thing. They drove away as the fire engines arrived; needless to say, not to return.

The Fire Brigade had arrived within ten minutes. To me it seemed an age. T.E.B.J. went round, telling masters to keep the boys in their classrooms, and so only my class and the one next door had a ringside view. Soon six fire engines were trying to prevent the fire spreading. According to Ben Burford's account in the *Magazine*: 'They set up ladders so as to get up on the roof. . . . Two more ladders were put up, and two firemen climbed up with hoses until four others came with oxygen bottles on their backs to hack through the tiles, so that the hoses could reach the fire beneath. Two firemen went up in the crane with a hose, and with two other hoses extinguished most of the fire, until only small flickers were left, and these were later put out. Unfortunately the canes were saved.'

Ken Welby was lucky enough to get a wonderful view of the fire. 'I had mumps and was stuck in the sick-bay, not far from where the fire started. I had to be carted round in isolation, which meant that I actually saw all the firemen all round the building, which few others did. I remember that my main concern was that all the "trash mags" kept in the sick-bay would be consumed in the fire, but luckily the Fire Brigade prevented such a calamity from happening.' Mark Wordsworth, another member of my class, remembers how at the end of the morning's lessons 'we were all moved out to the 1st XI cricket pitch area, where we stood [behind the wall], amazed'. During this time the kitchen staff had been evacuated, but this did not prevent Pat Fairbrother, Mary Whittington and the kitchen staff producing lunch for the school round the pavilion, with the man from the *Oxford Mail* taking photographs of the boys queuing for stew.

In the event, the damage was mainly confined to the first floor. Ben Burford goes on: 'Dormitory 3B ['Granny's Room'] has no roof; Mr Richardson's bedroom and a spare-room were the worst damaged rooms; and there is a hole in the roof of the Senior Common Room [next to the study], but the matrons' sitting-room and the dispensary were only slightly damaged.' Mark Wordsworth remembers 'when the fire was out, looking into the early beds' dormitory and seeing the charred beds and walls and particularly a badly-burned teddy bear'. This and all other cuddly animals lost in the fire were quickly replaced by A.D.R.

As the *Oxford Mail* reported: 'The fire caused thousands of pounds worth of damage, but no one was hurt. Firemen helped staff to carry out books, pictures, furniture and equipment from the blackened end of the school.' It was indeed providential that the fire broke out at midday and not at midnight, and that it affected the private side and not the dormitories. Luckily, too, the school was fully insured.

On Sports Day the Cup was presented to the winning Group by Bob Drayson, Head Master of Stowe. He had more than once intimated that he would like to talk to the boys in church, and he now took the opportunity to make a short speech. He said that the five Old Cothillians at Stowe had told him of the freedom and friendliness of Cothill, that 'The boys talk to the masters, everyone knows everyone else. There is a good deal of leniency, not many terrible punishments. There is a lot of drive and involvement. The Head Master gives the prefects a feeling of responsibility.' He himself during his short visit had immediately got a feeling of the friendliness and the warmth of the place and could go back to Stowe and give a good report on Cothill.

This Summer term was also notable for two sporting performances. A fine 50 by Tom Faulkner helped the 1st XI to beat Summer Fields, always a source of satisfaction. At Iffley Road Henry Strouts became the National Prep Schools Under-13 400-metres champion. By contrast, Harry Calvert made Cothill history with a long-playing 12-inch record entitled 'Harry Sings: The Golden Legend', accompanied by J.S.O. At the end of term the same boy 'brought the house down' in a French farce, *La Bôite Miraculeuse*, when he was miraculously transformed from a shrewish wife into an angel, complete with wings.

The previous January A.D.R. had become engaged to Rachel, daughter of Philip Goodhart, Conservative MP for Beckenham, and Val, the niece of John Winant, American Ambassador in London during the war. Rachel was at that time only 20, and Adrian was 15 years her senior. They had met skiing with her parents, and I remember his describing Rachel to me as 'the kindest person I have ever met'. They were married in July 1978 at the tiny church in Besselsleigh by John Reynolds, using the old 1662 service. Rachel's youngest brother Daniel, who was still in the school, acted as best man. Rachel has been a beautiful and efficient addition to the school as well as the mother of Thomas, Vicky and Edward.

The brothers Peel have already been mentioned as Cothillians under M. J. Dauglish. Roger's grandson, Robert, had arrived in 1974 to carry on the family tradition of all-round prominence and left at the end of 1978. 'The abiding impression one has of Cothill, and the point that is frequently stressed, is that it is such a happy and friendly school.... In my first two seasons in the Under-10s and Under-11s I remember being trounced, particularly by New College. It was always remarkably heartening to hear G.L.S.P. and T.E.B.J. booming "Up Cothill", but rather more disheartening to them when I let in yet another "soft goal" before our two most vociferous supporters. In my last year, however, nearly the same team succeeded in beating Horris Hill away.... My memories include the midnight feasts, the [hair] delousing sessions, the early-morning parades and the ever-popular midnight swims. A school depends on its masters and all Cothill masters carried great enthusiasm to their thankless tasks. T.E.B.J. was a great favourite with his (in)famous "A water-eating...", a reflection on bad table manners; his long-standing bet of a bicycle for anyone who found a trap in Maths; watching the telly, his "creaking bones" were always asleep within five minutes. Then there was L.M.S., on whom all the typical schoolboy pranks were played, and C.W.B.C. with his very ambiguous invitation "Would you like me to shoot you?".'

L.M.S. wrote the next editorial at the beginning of 1979. He outlined his job as the Bursar, summarising it in the words of the Delphic Oracle '*Meden Agan*'. 'Translated literally, "No excess".... A Bursar would choose to put it in the same way as C. B. Fry or Pele might have done to an aspiring athlete, "Keep your balance".' S. P. Blackmore had rejoined the staff. S.A.P. had his 90th birthday, and was delighted that the 1st football XI beat Horris Hill for the second year running, that the Under-11s went through the season undefeated, and that the Under-10s beat Summer Fields twice.

Winter swimming at the Old Gaol pool had begun as a regular weekly event for all ages. The 14 new boys were encouraged by Alexander Jeffs, who wrote: 'This is my second term and I still like Cothill very much, especially now I am writing in ink.' A.D.R. and J.S.O. added further to the fun by producing *The Pirates of Penzance*. The reviewer, a parent, described it as 'very successful . . . staging excellent . . . dressed with great ingenuity . . . every word clearly audible.... Honours must go to David Hannah's Major-General – beautifully dressed, excellently sung and most amusingly acted.' Mark Wordsworth remembers 'the tremendous fun we had, what with "Pirate King" Brunner, "Chief Policeman" McGhie, "Mabel" Burkitt and "Major-General" Hannah – the very Model of a Modern Major-General, as he continued to remind us on a recent skiing trip when he kept branching off into song.'

Rugby and hockey teams had a successful season, but Rupert Oswell put the non-games-player's point of view. After describing his bolshiness at getting ready for soccer and playing it: 'I ran back feeling glad the game was over. I skipped showers and left the changing-room quickly to go and fight for the Snob stick. I obtained the stick and a sensation of warmth and happiness went through me. At last I was enjoying myself and playing a game.' Rupert was to become a very keen and promising golfer, following a chance lesson from me on the spur of the moment.

Mary Topham left and was thanked in the *Magazine* by J.S.O. An attractive and charming woman, she had been teaching the violin at Cothill for 17 years, and as head of the instrumental department had built up an ensemble of high standard: 'No detail of a boy's progress escapes her.... Her ability as string player, fine pianist, her encyclopaedic knowledge, her view that musicianship must always be paramount above technique.'

The Summer term's *Magazine* contained a 'Head Master's Comment' on the Common Entrance requirements of Eton, Radley, Marlborough, Stowe and Harrow. The most important question to be answered was 'Can he reach the standard?'. To help answer this question, senior boys had for many years sat mock CE papers, papers sat by the 'real' candidates the term before. In the light of experience and by the same markers assessing the mock papers term after term, it was clear that, on the Cothill scale, Eton required about 65%, the other schools about 60%. At any lower percentage, Marlborough and Radley start to look closely at the headmaster's report and games record. Anything under 50% generally stood no chance, though Harrow might consider someone who had a strong claim in a non-academic direction.

I am frequently asked: 'To what particular public school does Cothill send boys?' A detailed answer can be found in *Appendix I*, which lists all the schools to which 1,813 boys have gone since 1894 up to 1989 – that is, as far as records exist – with numbers for each decade. From this we can see the early bias towards Marlborough, followed by a swing to Harrow through the influence of M. J. Dauglish and F. Knowles. The Eton connection existed from the start, and was perhaps strengthened by my going there in 1929. But it was not until the 1940s and 1950s that Cothill joined Summer Fields, Sunningdale and Hawtreys – according to Arthur Hearnden's biography of Robert Birley, *Red Robert* – as one of the four main Eton prep schools. This was a mixed blessing, for when a prep school suddenly becomes fashionable it can as quickly go out of favour; parents meet each other frequently and stories of failures in Common Entrance or similar blemishes quickly circulate. In my parents' early days Charterhouse and Stowe feature more prominently. Radley has always been closely associated with Cothill, and an increasing number have gone there since 1969 during D. R. W. Silk's Wardenship. In the 1980s Marlborough became more popular. The introduction of day boys in the 1960s brought the school into closer contact with the neighbourhood, with the local pre-prep schools and with Abingdon School, to which an increasing number of day boys went on. It had become independent following the abolition of the Direct Grant.

On 15 July my father died in his 91st year, and was buried beside my mother in Dry Sandford churchyard. Soon the letters of appreciation for his life began to come in. Of these Roger Carrington's is typical: 'My memories of him are extremely vivid; his breaking the news to me, aged nine, that my father had died ("Roger, your father's gone to heaven") – no excess of sentiment and a cheerful pat on the back as I departed.... His judicious mixture of exhortation, advice and occasional homily; the affectionate awe in which he was undoubtedly held; the stentorian "too slow" to the hesitant tackler from the figure prowling the touchline in that green tweed overcoat; the rousing little talks at prayers as to what we were to make of our futures;

With my father at Northfield Cottage, Henley, 1976.

the formidable chunks of Old Testament he set us to learn on Sundays; the apprehension among the boys as to whether he had had a good day at Newbury.' Franko Seymour remembers a man 'who had such a gusto for life and instinctively knew what appealed to us boys'; Dick de la Hey recalls 'his wonderful ability to converse with senior boys as equals and not talk down to them'. L.M.S. writes of him: 'He said to me, "Always keep young in spirit; never allow yourself to become middle-aged" '; and adds, 'He succeeded in following his own precept quite admirably'.

His long and happy life had been clouded by my mother's death, and latterly he had suffered much pain in his legs. This confined him to his chair for most of the day, but every evening he forced himself to go upstairs to change into his green velvet smoking-jacket. He kept his zest for life, and enjoyed his dry martini, mixed in a jug by Ernie. He retained all his mental powers and loved being visited by old friends and former pupils. I used to lunch with him once a week, and tried to keep him up to date with school gossip and developments. We had had some very difficult and painful moments soon after he retired, chiefly over money, but I like to think that we had put all that behind us before his death.

After my father's death I inherited the freehold of Cothill House and sold it to the Trust in 1980, having exercised the option to buy out Diana and Audrey for the sum agreed under the original lease of 1962. As I had no pension from the school, it was arranged with A.D.R. and the Governors that I should continue working until 1981, when I would be 65. I had resigned from the governing board at the start of the financial negotiations. I was given a sabbatical term that Autumn, and Gabrielle and I went to Australia and New Zealand. We stayed with Old Cothillian George Portarlington in his splendid modern house overlooking Sydney Harbour before flying home in a somewhat battered condition after a late night and a trip next morning round the Harbour in George's speedboat. Our absence meant that we had missed a successful production by A.D.R. of *H.M.S. Pinafore,* of which a parent wrote: 'As Captain Corcoran, Charles Burkitt, with his clear voice, provided the lynchpin around which others built an exhilarating performance.'

Rachel Richardson recalled, in the *Magazine*, her two years as the Head Master's very young wife, remembering particularly the warm welcome she received from so many people: 'David Hannah, Head Boy and young diplomat who mirrored the "boys' world" for me'; Pat Fairbrother in the kitchen, Gwen Wallis and her ladies, Ruth Viner, the Head Matron. All these helped her to learn the ropes, and since those early days she had learnt that 'the joy of Cothill is that it is one big house. ... I value the classroom contact I have with class 8. ... I try to keep 7 o'clock free to read to the early beds. ... I join the prefects' Sunday evening meeting with the Head Master and we discuss the proposed menus. ...'. It was gratifying for Gabrielle and me to realise that so much of what we had initiated was being continued and that Rachel realised, as we did, her debt to 'the experience and hard work of Barbara Hall, Tom Jackson, Joan and Leonard Swinbank'.

For a boy's view, Nishy Wijewardane provides a Sri Lankan memory: 'The school atmosphere was much akin to a large family, and yet a friendly, competitive element remains in my mind. ... Coming as I did from abroad, with no prior knowledge of English life to guide me, it was something of a challenge; ... entry tests with the encouragement of Mr Jackson and yourself; ... surprising Mr Richardson late on my first night with my version of "Song Sung Blue". ... It was football that gained me friendship and integration with the boys ... and with the support of staff helped me to bridge the gap. ... I recall with amusement the weekly trips down to the local sweet-shop for the 30p(?) rations, ... church-going on Sunday, Biology lessons with Miss Blair Gould, the kindly eye of Miss Viner and Mrs Wallis, beating Horris Hill, the surprise of getting a History prize from Mr Burbank.'

The first elms to come down, Summer 1976. All the others in the background were to follow.

A great sadness in 1980 was the felling of the elms, all of them infected by Dutch elm disease. It greatly altered the skyline of the cricket field, deprived boys of a play area for Dens and car games, and isolated the pavilion. Luckily there were plenty more trees, chestnuts and limes in particular, that now stood out and were fully appreciated for the first time. A programme of tree planting did something to fill the gaps, and alongside the footpath opposite the Fleur de Lys a hedge was laid, winning second prize in the senior class of a schools project run by the CPRE. S.P.B. wrote a *Magazine* article 'Is there Life after Lessons?' about the extra-curricular activities of boys out of school; the various clubs and 'the pastimes and hobbies that the boys themselves invent are numberless and constantly changing'. A Backgammon Club was founded, but soon foundered for lack of boards. Charlie Hoare Nairne became Rubik-cube champion. Grant Richmond and William Skelton put in much hard work to help S.P.B. produce a French newspaper, *Le Cothillien*. The first computer was bought and a printer to go with it. T.E.B.J. was put in charge and commented: 'Apart from the joy of being able to play Space Invaders and other such games, it is hoped that boys will learn to program it.'

Skateboarding, Spring 1986.

Of the extra-curricular activities referred to by S.P.B., one of the most popular is the Printing Club. In the Autumn of 1963 the Bradbury family had given the school an Adana. C. J. Boothroyd formed the first Cothill Printing Society, and soon its nine members were producing headed postcards and addressed writing-paper in an upstairs room beyond the sickrooms. The following term the programmes for the concert were printed by the Society for the first time. When C.J.B. left, their activities lapsed, to be revived briefly in 1966 by Harry Wedderburn, Rupert Foxwell and Peter Motion. They received much help and advice from Jeremy Cullen of the Abbey Press.

After Harry's departure there is no mention of printing in the *Magazine* until 1976. S.P.B., with Francis Burkitt, John Assheton and Mark Aldous as original members, reconstituted it as the Printing Club, which operated in a clock-tower classroom. Soon there were 24 members, at various stages of learning. A gift of Linotype by the Abbey Press made possible the printing of the Sports Day programme and the six-page school-list booklet, resulting in 'standing type' for future lists. Pictures were also printed from linocuts. During S.P.B.'s absence with the Crown Agents, Jonathan Stephenson took

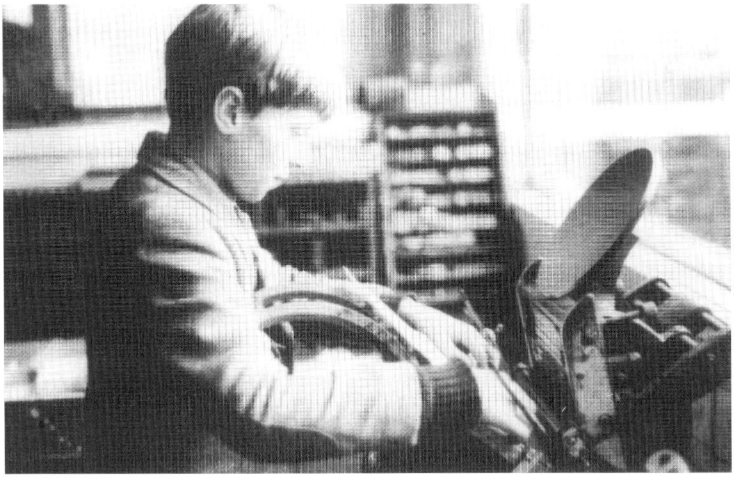

Cothill House Press, Spring 1985.

over, and when he left Ken Welby carried on the production of letter-heads and change-of-address cards. When S.P.B. returned in the Autumn of 1978, the Press moved into the centre of the Complex, where it remained until 1987.

In 1980 the Club reported that 'ex-members Jonathan Stephenson and Kenneth Welby have succeeded in forming their own businesses in Abingdon, the Rocket and Ensign Presses'. Five years later Sean O'Hara at Westminster had his Harp Press. Meanwhile S.P.B.'s enthusiasm has continued unabated: 'Sir, can I join the Printing Club?' 'Of course, all you need is patience.' He points out that 'those who are taken with printing are a remarkably patient breed. Hand-setting is a lengthy process.' In 1985 he detected 'a new generation of printers . . . with a more business-like approach; . . . even files and records are reorganised and rearranged'. The Multilith printed at a rate of 6,000 an hour, with Good Marks, Christmas cards, Carol Service covers among the items produced. Since 1987 the Press has operated in the old Geography Room, where 'the galleys . . . are full of jobs at various stages, some about to be printed, some waiting to be dissed'. Many Cothillians have every reason to be grateful to S.P.B. for giving them such a good early start and inspiring them to continue their interest in printing. Such a flourishing print-shop is unusual in a preparatory school.

At the end of the Summer of 1980 S. D. Swan had returned to his native Canada after three years teaching Geography. Stuart was a delightful, large, teddy-bear-like man with a limp, but this did not prevent his raising the standard of Rugby and taking parties of boys to the Lake District on 'outward bound' courses. I was particularly sorry to see him go because I had to take his place and try to teach his Geography classes. This caused me many headaches, but the boys made light of my deficiencies. It struck me that Common Entrance Geography papers were extremely long and testing, involving knowledge of farming, soil erosion, marketing techniques and the making of motorways. I spent a disproportionate amount of time on map reading, and somehow survived the year.

On my 65th birthday A.D.R. gave a party in the rose garden to which a large number of old friends came, with the prefects acting as waiters. Later

My 65th birthday celebrations in the rose garden, 12 June 1981.

on in the term I played in my last Masters' Match, scoring 23 runs and feeling very stiff afterwards. Then it was goodbye to schoolmastering and the beginning of retirement at the Old School. As I wrote at the time, I counted myself lucky to have lived and worked in such pleasant surroundings; being an 'ordinary master' for five years after being Head Master had not only brought me down to earth, it had made me realise how lucky Cothill had been in the tradition of friendliness among the staff. There was no possibility of a '*Mr Perrin & Mr Traill*' situation in our Common Room.

At the same time as I retired, Leonard Swinbank went into semi-retirement, while Joan retired completely. He had been Bursar and Secretary to the Trust since the school adopted charitable status in 1969. Joan had not only been Head Matron, but Housekeeper, domestic adviser, comforter and general counsellor to Gabrielle and then to Rachel. As Joan has written: 'It's incredible that it's twenty-five years ago that the quartet set forth on its tasks.' During those years Gabrielle and I increasingly realised our great good fortune in having such a stalwart pair as Leonard and Joan to support us. Joan adds: 'What fun it was, and didn't the years go quickly?'. She remembers 'boys of all shapes and sizes, all individual personalities, all requiring different handling.... Marvellous to watch them grow from not much more than babies to about the edge of manhood.... Wonderful moments of unconscious humour – the boy with separated parents, when asked by the optician if his parents wore glasses, "Oh yes, all four of them".'

Science received a shot in the arm from a young master, M. R. Evans, who started a Science society which he called Zenith and which met on Wednesday and Sunday afternoons. Mark left after the Summer term 1981, and was succeeded by Mrs Birkhead, better known as Maggie. She it was who during the next five years transformed a Cinderella subject into a successful part of the core curriculum. 'At first', she says, 'I made lots of mistakes which everyone forgave far more readily than I deserved. To my delight I quickly settled in, felt accepted and loved the place.' The Science Lab, in what had originally been the gym, was soon filled with grass snakes, pet hamsters, locusts, tropical fish and a tarantula which proved a great attraction: 'despite the fact that it never moved, winked or vibrated even one of the hairs on its downy legs, boys would cluster earnestly around its cage'. A grass snake got loose, frightened one of the daily cleaners out of her wits and was eventually found in the butterfly cabinet where it had eaten all the preserved specimens.

Maggie Birkhead continued until 1987 to inspire Zenith with her enthusiasm: 'All sorts of things were tried out as guinea-pig runs for proper class lessons. Once we scooped 308 frogs from the local pond. One term Zenith made a film on the video camera about first aid; all went well until the stretcher (a couple of poles and a blanket) was produced. The injured . . . was hoicked on to the stretcher and carried at a gallop across the field. Half-way the stretcher collapsed and the boy was jettisoned on to the field in a heap.' Visits were paid to the Oxford University Museum and to the BBC Television Centre. There were at least two camping trips. 'One year we walked twenty miles along part of the Ridgeway; . . . the sun shone and we ran short of water.' On another occasion Maggie 'decided it would be more fun to do without tents and rough it in the open air; . . . it rained non-stop all night and all day; . . . the first night we sheltered in a wood and dried out over an enormous bonfire.' The weather finally got the better of them, and they were rescued by the school minibus.

Bill Stockton, returning to Cothill as a parent in 1982, was at first shocked to see that boys no longer wore grey suits and shorts; he also missed the knickerbockers and caps. At the same time, he approved of the sweaters and trousers as being more practical and popular. School groups look sartorially similar from the 1920s up to the 1960s. Then began the fashion for sweaters instead of tweed jackets, with an emphasis on greater comfort and informality. Grey sweaters changed to navy blue in the 1980s. Sunday suits, originally of blue serge and then dark-grey worsted, have now disappeared, replaced by a special school tweed jacket and dark-grey trousers. Shoes and sandals fight a rearguard action against the ubiquitous 'trainers', except for games.

The Falklands War in 1982 once again brought into prominence Francis Pym and John Belstead, Foreign Secretary and Minister of State for Foreign and Commonwealth Affairs respectively. (A decade earlier they had served together in the Northern Ireland Office.) I wrote to both, and got immediate replies; Francis added 'you and Sam have much to answer for'.

Meanwhile A.D.R. outlined in the *Magazine* the changes that had taken place during his six years as Head Master. 'The Big Schoolroom has gone and been replaced by a Middle Common Room and overflow dining-room. The squash court has been given a new front, a new floor and a gallery. The boot-room has been changed into a Computer Room and the boots have returned to their original haunt next to a new and enlarged changing-room. The dormitories have been painted, carpeted. . . . There's a brand-new laundry [under the clock-tower]. . . . The huge hollows left by the departed elms have been filled. Add to this a flourishing, well-organised Music

Department [under the recently arrived S. A. H. Johns] and a wide variety of interesting clubs and societies.... 150 boys, no spare-room, fourteen full-time and five part-time teachers, four matrons, two groundsmen and a whole army of cheerful, willing ladies who do all the cooking and cleaning. ...Enormous energy, goodwill and co-operation are evident in a working partnership between staff, boys and their parents.'

There speaks a confident and successful Head Master, who has enjoyed being an innovator. He has, for example, introduced a 'personal report' form on which each boy records his achievements at the end of term. He says this is invaluable for his own reports, and it produces some surprising examples of self-analysis. I am particularly delighted that he has carried on most of the Cothill traditions and has justified my feeling that it was wise to appoint as my successor someone who understood and loved the place.

He has been well supported by S.P.B., whom he appointed Deputy Head Master in 1981 and who became a member of IAPS. Simon and Adrian complement each other, and both are married with young children – Carolyn Blackmore has a BSc in French and Education, while Rachel Richardson is Montessori-trained. Short French plays continued to be produced by S.P.B., following my retirement. He went one better than me by writing his own, *Chez le Dentiste* and *Les Cowboys*, whereas I had relied on Mayall's *Jouons la Comédie*, now out of print.

Nine computers were installed in the refurbished boot-room. T.E.B.J. was in charge: 'Why do we need computers at all?', he wrote. 'Because the world is being taken over by them, or, to be more precise, because we are getting them to take the drudgery out of life. How often have you heard me say "Never do any work unless you have to!".... It is very much in your interest to learn how to operate them, and that's why we need them at Cothill.' One thing computers could not do was teach Art, and we had been for years very fortunate to have the delightful and sympathetic Bridget Worthington to inspire the Art Club as well as teach drawing and painting as a class subject. She retired at the end of the Autumn term 1982, and was warmly thanked in the *Magazine* for the considerable improvement in the facilities of the Art Room, and 'for the development of the pottery side into quite a feature'. She was succeeded by pretty, dark-haired Angela Radcliffe, who has further developed the boys' enthusiasm and skill.

Ladies loomed large at this time. Rachel Richardson, Carolyn Blackmore and Val Burbank produced Vicky, Robert and Sam, respectively. Moya Lee joined the staff and showed what charm, good looks and keenness can add to the teaching of Latin. Kate Lindgren and Susan Wiltshire, matrons, described

Matrons, after the Christmas Feast, 1989, reminding us to wash behind our ears.

their job as 'rather like having 150 aloof children. . . . Apart from giving them clean clothes and nursing them when they are ill, we become involved in their social, emotional and intellectual development. The boys themselves would be the last to realise this and probably the first to disagree. . . . A shoulder to cry on; . . . comfort for homesickness and physical injury; . . . help even for one struggling to understand his French prep; . . . the love letters that are slipped under our doors and the hate campaigns we suffer contribute to the process known as "growing up" and as such we suffer them gladly. . . . Perhaps in years to come we shall be conjured up, a distant memory.' One Old Cothillian of 1975 vintage does indeed remember: 'Affairs with matrons, believe it or not'; and another of the late 1960s, who was 'one of the select few to enjoy a number of midnight feasts with two of the matrons. We used to be woken up, and then chatted, listened to records and had something to eat in their rooms.' Joan Swinbank recalls 'a large girl who rode a large motor bike who had a crush on a boy; the only time I ever saw it happen to a matron; still she was very young'.

One matron who would not have been involved in such goings-on was Ruth Viner, who in 1983 left to get married after 14 years of wonderful service. She came of a local farming family near Faringdon, had been top nurse at the end of her training, and was a 'natural' with boys, sympathetic but firm, tall, slender and kind-eyed. She had been assistant matron to J.S. until 1976, when she became Head Matron. She was so hard-working that I was more than once telephoned and even visited by her mother, who complained that she was doing too much and was exhausted. Certainly she looked pale, and she slept with one ear alerted for any boy in distress. She identified herself completely with the school. Her Christian faith was apparent in her life, and her 'Good night, God bless' comforted new boys especially. Mark Wordsworth remembers her 'standing at the top of the stairs every evening, conducting spot checks and preventing smuggling into the dormitories – occasionally without success because I remember several wonderful midnight feasts'. There was other insubordination in that era. Angus Gordon-Lennox wrote, as a 12-year-old, of his first night at school: 'The curtains were drawn and the lights turned off. The matron said there was to be no talking. As soon as the matron walked away, Dalgety said, "Well, what shall we talk about?". I thought he must have been deaf.'

In the 1983 cricket season, seven of the 1st XI's ten matches were drawn, including an unusual one against Summer Fields. Our oppontents declared at 120 for 9, and we drew level with the last ball of the match. This Summer was also memorable for some very hot weather at the end of term, senior class plays in French and Latin and the restart of tuition by the Frilford Heath professional under the Golf Foundation Scheme. It was P. D. Gilbert's last term. Since 1971 Peter had been coaching 1st XI cricket and football with great enthusiasm and varying success, as well as teaching Latin and English. In appearance he was the double of Ken Rosewall, and it was natural that he should be an organiser of the annual IAPS lawn-tennis tournament at Hurlingham. He took up golf and practised on the Cothill course with such assiduity that he rapidly became a competent player. An old-fashioned schoolmaster in many ways, he did not at first find the Cothill free-and-easy style altogether to his liking, and perhaps he lacked the light touch in his dealings with the boys. On the other hand, he could let his hair down, and many will remember his imitations of Gary Glitter and other pop stars at the post-Feast entertainments.

A.D.R. asked me to come out of retirement to coach the new boys in football. I was flattered and delighted, as I had been away for two years and I did not know the junior part of the school. My eight-a-side game was somewhat surprised to see me. 'Is it really true', one of them asked, 'that you were once Head Master?' 'Yes, I'm 101, and you won't see anything like me again, so take a good look.' Afterwards he said, 'You aren't really 101, so how old are you?' I did not tell him, and the novely of having an 'ancient, ancient man' coach them soon wore off. I found that I had an exceptional lot of natural footballers, such as Edward Steel, many of whom finished up in the 1st XI. The following Summer I greatly enjoyed introducing them to cricket for four days a week, and here too a number of promising players learnt the groundwork of the game before I gave up in 1987.

In the course of 1984 the numbers rose to 170. This was made possible by turning the spare-room and Thomas Richardson's bedroom into dormitories. I thought at the time that such an increase might threaten the family atmosphere of the school, and in fact it did necessitate a further extension of the private side in due course. £175,000 had been reinvested during the past two years. This sum provided refurbished changing-room/boot-room, three classrooms added to the existing Complex, twelve computers with their own separate room, improvements to the outside lavatories and car park, a new Rugby pitch, a school laundry and an additional dormitory on the flat Library roof. Finally, a second Appeal had been launched to raise £120,000 to build new Science Laboratories and a Reference Library.

Work started quickly on this building, to a design by Marsh & Woolf. It was sited where the original two-classroom wooden building had been, beyond the sunken fish-pond. As it began to take shape, it induced a grandfather, who was visiting prep schools for his three grandsons, to say that of all the new buildings he had seen, Cothill's was 'the most adventurous and unschooly'. The Appeal, under the direction of Air Vice-Marshal Charles Moore, was producing the necessary cash, and on 29 May 1985 Robin Woods performed the opening ceremony with a short speech, I replied with an even shorter one, while Philip Taylor, as Chairman of the Governors, summed up the spirit of the occasion. The Editor of the *Magazine*, H. G. Holden, wrote: 'It was undoubtedly the highlight of the term.... The weather during the previous days had caused some anxiety, but in the event the day proved to be one of the finest of the term. How does Cothill manage it? Boys, parents, grandparents, Old Boys and friends of the school mingled on the lawns, ... and were all entertained by the Band and Pipes and Drums of the Scots Guards Beating Retreat on the cricket ground. It was an evening to remember.' A.D.R. had written previously: 'These buildings and the ideas behind them are dedicated to the Pike family who have given almost fifty years to the aims and ambitions of this school.' To me it was an exciting and humbling experience to see the large stone slab outside inscribed 'THE PIKE BUILDING', and to read the dedication inside the main doors.

A.D.R. was pleased with the result: 'Our designers have achieved that very difficult marriage between the aesthetically and environmentally pleasing and the practical and functional. The teachers are delighted by its flexibility, its operational convenience, its light, its air and its warmth. Even the boys like it: I clearly heard one say to another, "Science isn't bad... now!". The Library, enormously expensive to stock, makes a magnificent study room; calm, comfortable and dignified, with an indefinable feeling of learning in the air. It is also gathering pace, under Mr Lynn's careful supervision, as a refuge

Opening of Pike Building, 29 May 1985:
Pipes and Drums of the Scots Guards Beating Retreat.
Western aspect of the school, with the Pike Building on the left, 1989.

from the cold, or soccer or rugger – or boredom! It is becoming a sanctuary for those seeking knowledge and for those learning to delight in books. Numbers of visitors increase steadily as boys discover how it works and what it can provide.'

1985 was the year when Cothill expanded further, for in response to pressure for boarding places the main building was extended southwards over the front drive and up to the stone wall of the rose garden. This has altered the façade and substituted two side entrances for the old front door. The 'join' between the old and new has been skilfully disguised, and two turrets balance the end of the building over the new private side. The confident outlook for independent schools after nine years of Conservative government under Mrs Thatcher contrasted with the uncertainties of the early 1960s when we agonised over increasing the fees by £5 a term under governments that threatened our existence. A.D.R. acknowledged this: 'Rachel and I count ourselves lucky to be able to enjoy life at Cothill during such a flourishing period of its history.... dependent upon the enthusiasm, drive, imagination and dedication of a team of 73 souls.... This gives me a welcome opportunity to recognise publicly the efforts of each and every one and to thank them profoundly.'

While all the excitement of new building was taking the limelight, two great Cothill figures were quietly slipping away into retirement in the wings, a double event to which A.D.R. gave prominence in the Summer *Magazine* of 1984: 'Tom Jackson and Barbara Hall both go back over thirty years in their association with Cothill. Both have given it every ounce of their professional strength, and both have enjoyed the respect, admiration and affection of generations of pupils and staff. Many bottles of excellent hock and much humorous wisdom were dispensed in an upper room as I sat at the feet of Gamaliel Jackson as a very "cheeky young swine" who was learning his trade from the dormitory master, as T.E.B.J. then was, and I was just one in a long series of "young men" whom he has helped to set upon their way. Mrs Hall has started well over six hundred eight-year-olds upon their way, and what strikes me most particularly is the instant kindly memory that lights the face of a prospective Old Boy parent who hears that she still teaches here. There is no hesitation in their smile or exclamation – "Oh I remember her, she was a brilliant teacher and always so kind when one was feeling miserable". Neither is there any hesitation in their sadness when they learn that she will not be able to be to their child what she was to them. Both Tom and Barbara have given whole-heartedly in that old-fashioned, completely unselfish way; it is too trite to say that they will be "much missed", as to me they signal the retirement of a whole attitude and ethos which our generation will find hard to equal.' Farewells from their colleagues took the form of end-of-term reports in the *Magazine*. Thus, of Barbara: '*Maths:* She has shown a certain plus factor, . . . demonstrated time and again that she deserves her place in the "Hall of Fame". *Science:* Always felt at "ohm" . . . magnetic personality. *Geography:* Her warm front has melted many hearts. *Scripture:* Has led her flock through green pastures. . . . I hope she has been comforted by the staff next door.'

The cricket XI of 1984 was reported in the *Magazine* as 'the best balanced for a long time and this enabled the team to set up a very fine record, being unbeaten and playing some absorbing cricket' under its captain Alexander von Meister. Nicholas Chalmers won a scholarship to Harrow, Jonathan Barton to Oundle; Matthew Greenham gained an exhibition to Marlborough and Henry Skelton a Music scholarship to the same school. Among Old Boys, Willie Boone became World Rackets Champion. In 1985 we attended the funerals of V. K. D. Waite and Nelson Battell. C. W. B. Costeloe retired at the end of the Summer and I wrote in the *Magazine*: ' "Cozzy" has given 22 years of selfless service to the school. His humility, conscientiousness and quiet efficiency have been such a feature of Cothill life that the

In the nets, Summer 1984.

Orchestra, 1986.

school will not be at all the same place without him. Who will spend endless long breaks teaching boys to shoot? Who will paint the scenery for the plays? Who will encourage natural historians, especially the bird watchers? No one is indispensable, we know, but it will be a long time before Cothill has such a stalwart all-rounder of the "old school" to set a comparable example to all ages.'

Cozzy and I found ourselves churchwardens, he of Wootton and I of Dry Sandford, at a time when both churches were sharing the Vicar of Wootton, the Rev. Adam Smith, whose son Christopher had just won an exhibition to his father's old school, Haileybury. I took the occasional half-hour school Sunday service, with a new-style liturgy which had been used for the past year. One such was at the end of the Autumn term. I asked the boys if anyone could continue the rhyme beginning 'This time next week, where shall I be?'. No one could. Nor did anyone know of *The Pilgrim's Progress*. I enlightened them on both. 1985 was the first year the school Carol Service was held at Dorchester Abbey, to accommodate the large numbers who wanted to attend. One of the lessons was read by Gabrielle's great-nephew, Charlie Benson, great-grandson of Edward Woods, Bishop of Lichfield. Gabrielle wrote afterwards to her brother Frank in Australia: 'Charlie read a lesson to a packed house – should think there were five hundred squashed into that Abbey. He was audible (others weren't), looked up, paused at the right moments. I thought "He's not his great-grandfather's great-grandson for nothing".'

The musical life of the school was developing apace under S. A. H. (Hellier) Johns, a slightly-built, bearded Welshman, and his assistant, D. G.

(Graham) Howell, extremely boyish-looking and a very fine organist, who was to take over from S.A.H.J. in 1988. A third choir – the middle – was added, and a brass group formed. A concert was given in Marcham Church, and for the first time it was possible to invite all parents instead of just those of boys taking part. The senior choir, with eight instrumentalists, was invited to give two concerts at Denman College, Marcham, to ladies on WI courses. Richard Sterneberg, the flautist, wrote of the second concert: 'The audience of about thirty-five ladies was very appreciative and the performers once again enjoyed the experience. After a smashing tea of Coca-Cola, sausage rolls, pork pies, cakes and biscuits, everyone relaxed and Martin Binyon took over the piano and rattled off some Scott Joplin ragtime and the James Bond themes. Mr Johns and a lady from the audience sang the Welsh national anthem together, with Nicholas Rogers conducting badly, and the evening was rounded off with the ladies singing their anthem "Jerusalem".' The senior choristers also visited the Dragon for a performance of *The Mikado*, about which Richard commented, 'Although there were a few girls in it, the main parts were all played by boys'. The Dragon have had a long tradition of producing Gilbert & Sullivan (Joc Lynam was a memorable Judge in *Trial by Jury*), but Cothill productions stopped with J.S.O.'s departure. S.A.H.J.'s musical strength lay chiefly in choral teaching, and he raised the standard of the choir to such an extent that the weekly anthems in church had a cathedral sound about them, especially when the choir was augmented by visiting tenors and basses.

The Spring term of 1986 produced a great freeze, with no more Rugby after 8 February, by which time the 1st XV had played 3 and won 3. Hard ground meant more cross-country running; the hockey XI improved under David Liversidge's captaincy, beating the staff 4–3. A Colts Rugby Group tournament was held for the first time, while the Under-9 six-a-side soccer inter-school tournament shield was won by Cothill for the third time in four years. Swimming sessions in the Radley pool took place on a regular basis, with a match against Summer Fields lost, but with some thrilling finishes. A golf competition was held at Ludgrove between Ludgrove, Cothill, Lambrook, Sunningdale, Summer Fields and Horris Hill. Our team of four all scored over 40 in the 18-hole Stableford.

Indoors, the new Reference Library was used for the Common Entrance examinations and it also housed an updated standing exhibition of paintings and collages from the Art Room. The Debating Club included the motion, 'Girls should be allowed to study at Cothill House': 'Despite frequent accusations from Nicholas Hole against other members for sexist and chauvinistic speeches, the motion was soundly defeated.' Another motion, 'Jelly is better than ice cream' was overwhelmingly carried, thanks to James Knight's 'humorous descriptions of melted ice cream and the great virtues of wobbly jelly'. The reporter noted that some junior members needed reassuring that the topics debated by the Club and the votes taken had no bearing on the future of school life. The *Magazine* also reprinted a long and detailed account of a Cothill debate on the Channel Tunnel of 1932. In the end-of-term school play, produced by A. H. Lynn, *1066 and All That*, 'Nicholas Rogers, the Common Man, was the lynchpin', and the reviewer appreciated 'the patrician superciliousness of Julius Caesar, portrayed by James Grant'. In this short Spring term, traditionally given over to infectious diseases, there had been plenty to 'occupy the troops'.

Several milestones were noted by A.D.R. at the end of the Summer: my 70th birthday and the fact that Gabrielle and I had made 'a pawn's move' southwards from the Old School to 199 Dry Sandford, an incomprehensible address for a semi-detached with an orchard leading to the Berkshire, Buckinghamshire and Oxfordshire Naturalist Trust (BBONT) Nature Reserve; that Rachel, Thomas, Vicky and he had 'moved into a splendid new pinnacled extension'; that the school office had moved from under the clock-tower, making space for four music practice rooms. Most important of all, that L.M.S. and T.E.B.J. had finally retired.

The cricket 1st XI played 9, won 4, drew 5, 'Guy Shepherd captained the side with calm good sense and great imagination on occasions', according to A. J. Ellwood, who left after four years on the staff, during which he coached the 1st cricket and hockey XIs as well as teaching Scripture and English. A serious-minded, good-looking Old Marlburian, he was a committed Christian and a strong influence for good in the school. Another member of the staff to leave was Jill Elliott, after teaching individual boys violin, 'cello and guitar with great patience and directing an orchestra which grew from a small string group into quite a large body of players, including B. Challenor on the viola. It was this term that S.A.H.J. reported 'We've reached a century! The number of boys learning to play instruments continues to rise and exactly 100 instrumental lessons are now given each week at Cothill.' It is a sign of the shift of emphasis in the *Magazine* that the musical reporting was now printed first under the general heading of 'The Arts', ahead of the boys' contributions and details of the various sporting activities. S.P.B. wrote, 'Athletics became computerised, . . . the best performances of each boy were recorded on disc and were regularly updated. At the end of term the awards were added up by Groups.' Referring to the close proximity of the Computer Room, which he had now taken charge of, and the Cothill House Press in its new premises, he made the point that 'we try to be Progressive, expanding into new fields and developing new ideas, while at the same time we are Traditional, respecting well-tried methods and long-established values'. In

Hackers in the Computer Room, Spring 1989.

the Spring term of 1987 a Play-reading Club was started at the same time as an Electronics Club. Stuart Kyle won the Thompson scholarship to Radley. The following term Richard Watsham and Simon Garnett won awards to Bradfield.

When I retired as Head Master there had been 133 boys in the school. Fifteen years later numbers had increased to around 230, including 20 day boys, and the annual turnover was more than £1.5 million. A.D.R. told me at this time that he 'could double the numbers tomorrow', but as he has pointed out, many visiting parents were anxious that 'the small country boarding-school ethos should be maintained, yet at the same time wanting their child to be included among a composition of opportunities, influences and standards which require an ever-increasing budget to support their development. . . . At least £1 million had been spent to improve every aspect of the service which Cothill offers. . . . The school's most important asset is its staff, whose welfare is of constant interest and concern.'

Beryl Haggett has been teaching at Cothill for nearly 20 years. We first met when she and her husband Norman sent their son Matthew as a day boy in 1970. I knew of B.L.M.H.'s skill as an Art teacher at The Manor prep school in Abingdon, where they had won the Preparatory Schools Art Prize for the

The Craft, Design and Technology Centre, Spring 1989.

previous three years, and I was lucky to engage her to teach Art on a part-time basis. This coincided with the Centenary, for which she organised an exhibition.

In 1972, N.L.H., who was a Parachute Jumping Instructor at Abingdon, was posted to Australia. On their return two years later, I rang Beryl up to ask her help over a dyslexic boy, as I knew she was a qualified teacher of what was then called 'word blindness'; she had become interested in the subject when she realised that Matthew had problems. It was back to the Art Room, which now also served as a remedial centre for more than one dyslexic and for those who needed extra help in Maths. Since then B.L.M.H. has taught English and Maths to the one-from-bottom class and from 1982 Maths to the top class. Meanwhile N. L. H. had started coaching French in the evenings to Common Entrance borderliners, and after his retirement from the RAF in 1985, he formed a mathematical team with Beryl. She is an attractive, greying, grandmother, a most gifted teacher, overflowing with energy. He was a first-class cricketer and now coaches the 1st XI. His quiet authority and patient skill as a teacher are greatly valued. In 1983 the Haggetts' son-in-law, M. E. Rusby, joined the staff as a Physics teacher, and has two sons in the school. Mark, tall and aquiline, presides over laboratories that abound in every sort of apparatus and an infinite variety of flora and fauna. Clearly 'The Haggettry', so dubbed by T.E.B.J., is a vital part of present-day Cothill.

R. J. W. Manning, a married man in his forties, is now the Bursar, in succession to L.M.S. The son of an eminent Haileybury House Master, Richard had 15 years' experience at Buckland House in Devon before coming to Cothill in 1984 to teach Latin. He will turn his hand to anything, he has time for everyone and nothing is too much trouble. A somewhat ungainly figure, with a large head and a humorous expression, he forms, with A.D.R. and S.P.B., a highly competent triumvirate. His delightful assistant, Rosemary Perrott, keeps him in good order and the private garden blooming.

A. H. Lynn, tall and amusing, has been the main teacher of English for the last five years. A. J. Romanes, a handsome product of Horris Hill and Winchester, has a ready laugh and is a good games player and coach. T. S. Hodgetts, very young-looking with curly hair, has a wife and child, and teaches Scripture. Tony, Alasdair and Tim are greatly appreciated by their Head Master as enthusiastic and modern in their outlook but old-fashioned in their insistence on all-round high standards. As no one person had been able, with rapidly increasing numbers, to replace Barbara Hall, the bottom class had been split between three married women, Margaret Ricketts, Margaret Harrison and Becky Brown. All are warmly sympathetic to the problems facing new boys, and stimulating in their teaching.

Two distinguished Old Cothillians died in 1986 and 1987 respectively, Sir Godfrey Llewellyn and General Sir Hugh Stockwell. Sir Godfrey was the oldest Old Boy at 93, while 'General Hughie' will be remembered as the commander of the British forces during the Suez crisis, a man whose manner, according to *The Times* obituary, 'was of such engaging friendliness that all who met him found it irresistible'. I discovered this to be true when he attended the school Centenary. Gabrielle and I were invited by his regiment, the Royal Welch Fusiliers, to represent his old school at his memorial service in Westminster Abbey; and when we were told that among those at his graveside was his Border terrier, we felt a further bond with him. These two Old Boys would have found Cothill very different from the small school they had known, but undoubtedly they would have approved of its new look and its modern go-ahead atmosphere. They would have appreciated James Laing's scholarship to Eton and such young alumni as Charlie Brooks, who rode in the Grand National and completed the course on Insure, and Chris Baillieu, described as 'Cambridge's greatest oar ever', who gave the BBC Boat Race commentary.

The Cothill *Magazine* had a new Editor in T. S. Hodgetts. He succeeded H. G. (Hyla) Holden, a delightful man, who, after seven years of exceptional teaching of the Classics and games, had moved to the coeducational Windlesham House with his wife Jane (the campaign secretary for the Pike Building Appeal) and their two young boys. In T.S.H.'s first editorial in March 1988, he referred to a copy of the *Magazine* of April 1937 which he had managed to acquire. After singling out its references to the Coronation exeat, the victory over Horris Hill, the lectures and the flu epidemic of that year, Tim concluded: 'One wonders what the staff and boys of the time would make of the school now. A great deal has changed. With the building of the Science Laboratories, Reference Library, and soon a Craft, Design and Technology Centre, Cothill has become a modern and exciting school to teach in. However, one thing remains the same, the boys. Now, as then, the freshness and enthusiasm of the Cothill schoolboys and staff are [to quote from the 1937 *Magazine*] "encouraging qualities with which to deal", and we look forward to our next fifty years with interest and excitement.'

The Craft, Design and Technology Centre, or CDT, referred to, was opened by D. R. W. Silk, the Warden of Radley, on 5 May 1989. Two classes can operate in comfort at the same time; one group painting, drawing or modelling, the other involved in design and construction, 'ranging from the production of simple household gadgets to working models of computer-designed, elastic-band-driven "motor" vehicles'. Messrs Blackmore, Bodimeade and Plowman supply the skill to meet the design needs of every age group. Meanwhile Angela Radcliffe continues to preside over the Art Room, and M. E. Rusby specialises in electronics. A. W. Plowman runs the Carpentry Club, seen at its best on wet Sunday afternoons.

Team games have been improving as numbers grow. In 1989 the cricket 1st XI was undefeated and the season included a historic century by Malcolm Borwick against New College School, only the third to be scored on the Cothill ground. The 2nd XI too had a very successful season and there is plenty of talent among the under-11s. The football and Rugby teams won most of their matches. Six hard tennis courts, built in 1988, have enabled many more boys to be introduced to the game, and in Winter these are used as football and hockey pitches. The golf course, with a new young groundsman to care for the greens, is becoming increasingly populated, and twice in three years Cothill won the 'Stowe Putter'. H. G. Holden looks back on his lining up of the two winning teams as his 'most satisfying moments in teaching'.

'Interest and excitement' have certainly been generated as the result of the latest development. A.D.R. overheard at a dinner party a snatch of conversation between two high-powered industrialists. One said to the other, 'Of course we never employ anyone who hasn't at least one foreign language'. Adrian took this to heart, showed his usual enterprise and decisiveness, and as a result, in the Autumn of 1989, he sent out an illustrated letter announcing that Cothill had bought the Château de Sauveterre, 45 minutes south-west of Toulouse. Under the heading 'Cothill in the South of France', he wrote: 'As from September 1990 we intend to use Sauveterre as an annexe to Cothill. As an integral part of their education, one class per term, together with their form teacher, will travel out to Sauveterre in their penultimate Cothill year. They will live and work with locally-employed staff, where everything they do will be in French and about France. . . . It is planned to make full use of an educational opportunity which will include a study of the historical, environmental and industrial aspects of the area. It will also include an element of exploration and adventure among which may well be skiing, climbing, surfing and camping. The principal reason for embarking upon this ambitious venture is of course the advent of 1992, plus the conviction we hold that the boys being educated now and in the future must have a European dimension to their outlook if we are to give them an education relevant to their needs in the 21st century.'

The venture quickly captured the attention of the Press, including a lengthy colour-illustrated article by Paul Marston in the *Telegraph* Magazine (17 November 1990). Noting that Cothill has been the first British school to set up a permanent teaching base on the Continent, Marston comments, 'One can think of worse locations for a bit of educational pioneering'. Château *directeur* S.P.B., quoted in the article, underlines the importance of the links being forged with nearby schools and the local community, with the sporting emphasis being on co-operation not competition; 'I have fought hard to have mixed teams rather than matches between "England" and "France". It means our boys have to shout '*à moi*' or '*passez le ballon*', or they won't get the ball. Then they start to make friends.' Can one term be enough to make a lasting impact? 'Compared with a fortnight's holiday, 12 weeks is a very long time', S.P.B. replies. 'And it won't end with leaving here. Back at Cothill there is tremendous interest in Sauveterre among younger and older boys. They are talking about France at the lunch table.'

Scenes of Sauveterre, 1990.

Richardsons' group, 1990. *Staff*, from left, standing: *Jenny Bainbridge, Debbie Parslow, Annabelle Scholfield;* sitting: *Jean Barton, T. S. Hodgetts, Valerie Crook, P. J. Barton, Liliane Permingeat, J. F. G. Cook, Becky Brown, R. A. Winstone, Kirsty McCrone, N. L. Haggett, Beryl Haggett, A. J. Romanes, Angela Radcliffe, A. D. Richardson,*

Rachel Richardson, D. G. Howell, M. E. Rusby, Margaret Harrison, D. G. Fullerton, Margaret Ricketts, A. H. Lynn, Anna-Karina Baylis, P. A. Rice, Jenny Grieve, J. C. R. Burbank, Moya Lee, R. J. W. Manning; standing, right: *Manda Parker, Anne Byrne, Susan Mahon,* N. *Bodimeade.*

A fear that, with all its modern developments, Cothill might be losing its special qualities has been expressed by more than one Old Boy. These qualities are seen to be: a small community in a rural setting; a country-house atmosphere where a new boy can immediately feel secure after the trauma of leaving home; and a happy school in which learning and leisure are stimulated by the Head Master and staff, while the boys teach each other how to become good citizens and take responsibility.

It is 15 years since I retired as Head Master, and Adrian Richardson has already been in the driving-seat as long as I was. Just as after 1927 much of the Dauglish/Tomkinson small-school ethos remained as the numbers increased under the new management of the Pikes, so today the Richardsons have set their stamp on the school by building on the traditions that they inherited. I have watched the growth of Cothill with pleasure and pride, and perhaps a little envy. The purchase of the Château de Sauveterre has certainly put the cat among the prep-school pigeons, and the foresight and courage of A.D.R. and his fellow Governors is to be admired. Meanwhile the familiar buildings are still recognisable, even if there have had to be some sacrifices made on the private side. The boys remain the same as ever – friendly, polite and enthusiastic, full of fun and mischief, waiting to 'take the micky' out of any member of the staff whenever possible. *Plus ça change. . . .*

After the latest of my periodic appearances to take the school Sunday service in Dry Sandford Church, the following conversation took place between A.D.R. and a new boy:

'Who was that man?'

'That was Major Pike. He was Head Master before me.'

'Oh, so that's who it was. I'd been wondering what had become of him.'

APPENDIX I

Numbers of Cothillians at public schools, etc. 1894–1989

	1894–1899	1900s	1910s	1920s	1930s	1940s	1950s	1960s	1970s	1980s	TOTAL
Abbotsholme				1							1
Abingdon									18	22	40
Aldenham									1		1
Ampleforth								2	3		5
Bedales										1	1
Bedford	1										1
Bloxham					3			3	11	5	22
Blundells									5	1	6
Bradfield		1		3			4	5	7	16	36
Brighton			1								1
Bryanston									2		2
Canford					1	2				1	4
Charterhouse	2	7	2	7	11	16	8	10	3	7	73
Cheltenham		1	1		1	1	2		7	4	17
Chilton Cantelo								1			1
Christ's Hospital									1	2	3
Clifton	2	3	1	4	1	2		1		1	15
Cokethorpe								1	3		4
Crookham Court								1			1
Dartmouth				1	5	4					10
Dauntsey's									2		2
Dean Close									2	1	3
Dover									1		1
Downside		1							1		2
Eastbourne								2			2
Eton	3	9	16	17	35	116	101	70	38	43	448
Fettes	1								1	1	3
Framlingham								1			1
Giggleswick										1	1
Glenalmond						1			2		3
Gordonstoun						2	4	2	10	5	23
Grenville									1		1
Greshams			3						3		6
HMS Conway		1									1
Haileybury	1	5	5	2					1	1	15
Harrow	3	29	5	5	4	18	31	21	25	15	156
Hereford Choir School					1						1
Highgate										1	1
Kelly								1	1		2
King Edward VII Nautical College								1			1
King's, Taunton									1	2	3

	1894–1899	1900s	1910s	1920s	1930s	1940s	1950s	1960s	1970s	1980s	TOTAL
Lancing			1								1
Leighton Park									2	3	5
Loretto	1										1
Magdalen College School									1	2	3
Malvern	2	2	3	4	3			1		5	20
Marlborough	8	9	12	6	6	5	6	6	8	21	87
Millfield								5	3	2	10
Milton Abbey								7	5	6	18
Monkton Combe										1	1
Oratory									2	2	4
Osborne		5	9								14
Oundle		2		2			1	3	4	2	14
Pangbourne					2	1		1	5	7	16
RGS Guildford										1	1
Radley	1	13	8	17	21	7	14	24	30	41	176
Rannoch										1	1
Reed's										2	2
Repton			1		6	2	2				11
Rossall		2									2
Rugby	1	1	2	4	11	6	2	1	6		34
St Edward's				3	4	1			3	12	23
St John's, Leatherhead		2									2
St Lawrence, Ramsgate			2								2
St Paul's					1						1
Seaford									1		1
Sedbergh			1			1	2				4
Sherborne				1		1	1	2	3	4	12
Shiplake								1	2		3
Shrewsbury				6	3		3	2		3	17
Stanbridge Earls								7	1	3	11
Stowe				1	17	14	4	11	18	10	75
Tabley Hall								1			1
Tonbridge	1										1
Truro Cathedral School								1			1
Uppingham	1				1	1	2	5			10
Warwick								1	1		2
Wellington	2	1		7	5	1	2	7	3	2	30
Westminster			1	2			1	2		2	8
Winchester		4	5	8	3	10	7	6	4	5	52
Worth										1	1
Wrekin									1		1
MAINTAINED (inc. Fitzharry's, Abingdon, King Alfred's, Wantage)								2	11	4	17
MISCELLANEOUS (inc. schools abroad, died, left early, expelled, no record)	3	19	10	20	22	24	19	24	35	21	197
GRAND TOTALS	33	117	89	121	167	236	216	242	299	293	1813

APPENDIX II

Awards – scholarships and exhibitions – to Cothillians 1895–1989

1895 ROBERTSON, E. D. S. (*Fettes*)
1898 PORTER, F. S. (*Charterhouse*)
1899 HEBERT, A. G. (*Harrow*)
1900 PORTER, H. E. L. (*Charterhouse*)
BLANDY, E. N. (*Clifton*)
BERKELEY-HILL, H. E. W. (*Wellington*)
1902 POWELL, E. (*Rossall*)
LONGLAND, A. C. (*Radley*)
1903 NORMAN, R. E. (*Radley*)
NEWMAN, R. E. G. (*Marlborough*)
1904 WILLCOCKS, H. F. (*Radley*)
TYRRELL, H. G. (*Malvern*)
1905 SHAW, E. A. (*Marlborough*)
LAW, G. E. (*Winchester*)
1909 BROUGH, P. H. L. (*Charterhouse*)
ADAMS, G. H. C. (*Radley*)
1914 SUTTON, H. E. (*Malvern*)
PEARCE, L. S. C. (*Marlborough*)
1915 HOGARTH, W. D. (*Winchester*)
1916 HARWOOD, B. A. (*Charterhouse*)
1917 ADAMS, M. C. (*Radley*)
1918 HICKMAN, J. B. (*Marlborough*)
1919 BARMBY, J. (*Radley*)
1920 SHAKERLEY, P. F. (*Clifton*)
1923 DAWSON, G. V. F. (*Rugby*)
1924 KEMBALL-COOK, D. B. (*Shrewsbury*)
1926 KEMBALL-COOK, B. H. (*Shrewsbury*)
1927 REYNARD, A. F. (*Harrow*)
HANFORD, F. W. (*Marlborough*)
1929 KEMBALL-COOK, R. B. (*Shrewsbury*)
1931 RUMBO, K. H. N. (*Radley*)
PALMER, R. M. (*Shrewsbury*)
KEMBALL-COOK, B. M. (*St Paul's*)
SAUNDERS, R. C. H. (*Marlborough*)
1932 DE PIRO, A. C. H. (*Repton*)
1933 DYKES, G. F. W. (*Clifton*)
1934 DE PIRO, R. A. (*Repton*)
1935 HARDIE, W. D. C. (*Stowe*)
1937 BALFOUR, C. J. (*Eton*)
HARDIE, M. C. (*Charterhouse*)
1938 DEMAREST, M. H. S. (*Rugby*)
1939 NAYLOR, D. H. (*Repton*)
RAMBAUT, J. F. M. (*Repton*)
HOPKINSON, D. H. L. (*Wellington*)
1940 NEALE, G. C. (*Stowe*)
1941 GOOCH, R. C. W. (*Marlborough*)
QUANTOCK SHULDHAM, R. C. (*Eton*)
WYKEHAM-FIENNES, A. P. T. (*Stowe*)
1942 ROGERS, R. S. B. (*Charterhouse*)
ILIINE, A. M. S. (*Winchester*)
1945 BUDGEN, J. D. (*Clifton*)
CREWDSON, W. R. I. (*Harrow*)
STOCKTON, W. J. (*Uppingham*)
1946 ARNANDER, C. (*Harrow*)
BAILEY, R. L. C. (*Charterhouse*)
1947 HELY-HUTCHINSON, HON. M. (*Eton*)
1948 DUFFIELD, G. E. (*Harrow*)
BAILEY, M. L. G. (*Charterhouse*)
VALENTINE, F. A. B. (*Eton*)
1950 KEMP, C. A. H. (*Harrow*)
1953 DUFFIELD, J. L. (*Harrow*)
BERENS, D. J. C. (*Eton*)
1954 WIGAN, D. (*Eton*)
1955 WOOLMER, J. S. T. (*Uppingham*)
1959 CHAMBERLAIN, R. A. (*Radley*)
1961 BEECHAM, H. J. B. (*Winchester*)
1962 GOUGH, A. J. (*Uppingham*)
1964 BRADBURY, D. (*Radley*)
1965 SWINBANK, W. R. (*Bloxham*)

1966 GOUGH, O. M. L. (*Harrow*)
1969 TROSS YOULE, S. A. L. (*Radley*)
LITTLE, R. I. K. (*Eton*)
HANCOCK, M. J. W. (*Radley*)
1971 STEPHENSON, J. M. (*Radley*)
1975 EDWARDES-KER, C. (*Harrow*)
FRASER, F. M. (*Bradfield*)
1978 ROBSON, J. E. (*Abingdon*)
1980 ROBSON, R. W. (*Abingdon*)
1982 WELLS, C. G. (*Sherborne*)
1983 THORNELOE, R. S. M. (*Radley*)
1984 CHALMERS, N. J. P. (*Harrow*)
SKELTON, H. (*Marlborough*)
BARTON, J. J. (*Oundle*)
GREENHAM, M. I. (*Marlborough*)
1985 ELAND, P. J. W. (*Abingdon*)
SMITH, C. J. (*Haileybury*)
1987 KYLE, S. D. (*Radley*)
WATSHAM, A. R. (*Bradfield*)
GARNETT, S. J. (*Bradfield*)
1988 LIDSTONE, D. J. (*Charterhouse*)
LAING, J. M. (*Eton*)
WARD, A. W. J. (*Abingdon*)
1989 WHITE, W. R. G. (*Eton*)

APPENDIX III

In Memoriam

The information below is taken direct from the two memorials concerned, and for that reason each one is set out differently.

1914–1918

Entered school		
1905	ADAMS, G. H. C.	2/Lt. Suffolk Regt.
1906	BLACKER, J. R.	2/Lt. Coldstream Gds.
1898	BRANFILL, C. L. A.	Capt. Glamorgan Yeo.
1902	CHAPMAN, C. M. B. (MC)	Sqdn. Comdr. R. F. C.
1905	CHAPMAN, W. W.	Lt. Buffs. Attd. R. F. C.
1905	COLLINSON, G. E. C.	Lt. Cameron Highlanders Attd. R. F. C.
1895	CONSTABLE, A. T. W.	Major. Essex Regt.
1906	COOKSEY, K. B.	2/Lt. R. W. Kents Attd. R. F. C.
1905	FORREST, R. C.	Private. London Scottish
1906	GRAVES, A. G. J.	Lt. Canadian Mtd. Rifles
1901	GREEN, C. W.	Capt. Royal Berks Regt.
1906	HEATON-ELLIS, D. (MC)	Capt. Rifle Bde.
1898	HENERY, G. T.	Private. Liverpool Scottish
1898	HENERY, H. W. L.	2/Lt. K. O. S. B.
1899	HOLLAND, T. E. (MC)	Capt. Rifle Bde.
1900	HOLLAND, V. E.	Capt. 7th Hussars
1903	HOMFRAY, J. R.	Lt. S. W. Borderers
1899	INSOLE, G. C. L. (MC)	Capt. Welsh Gds.
1894	LEATHER, H. J. O.	Trooper. Canadian Mtd. Rifles
1902	MURRAY, E. D.	2/Lt. 19th Hussars
1896	POWELL, R.	Capt. Royal Field Artillery
1904	SHAW, E. A.	Capt. Ox & Bucks L. I.
1900	SICHEL, G. M. J.	Lt. Middlesex Regt.
1902	SICHEL, O. W.	Capt. Royal Warwicks Regt.
1900	STOGDON, H. C.	Private. Royal Fusiliers
1902	STRAUSS, B. L. (MC)	Major. The Buffs
1908	THESIGER, HON. F. I.	Lt. Royal Field Artillery
1905	WHITESIDE, M. B. D.	Lt. H. L. I. Attd. R. F. C.
1903	WILLCOCKS, H. F.	Major. Royal Field Artillery
1898	WYNTER, C. F. W.	Capt. Ox & Bucks L. I.
1905	YOUNG, J. F. H.	Lt. King's Own Regt.

1939 – 1945

Entered school		*Entered school*	
1927	AMPHLETT, J.	1924	HAMILTON, D. G.
1932	ATKIN-BERRY, H. L.	1930	HARDIE, W. D. C.
1923	*BAILEY, C. S.	1928	HOLT, D. L.
1931	*BAKER, V.	1932	*JACKSON, R. G.
1926	*BENNETT, J. P.	1928	MARTIN-ATKINS, F. N.
1932	BRAND, HON. R. J.	1930	*PARKER, HON. W. R. C. B.
1917	BUTLER, W. F.	1928	PRIOLEAU, A. S. W.
1925	CARR, A. M. D.	1933	QUANTOCK SHULDHAM, P. J.
1929	CHAMIER, P. A.	1926	RUMBO, K. H. N.
1920	*COLLINS, P. R.	1931	SANDFORD, P. A.
1928	DE PIRO, R. A.	1921	*STEWART, P. K. M.
1934	EDEN, S. G.	1929	*WYNNE-ROBERTS, D. R.
1932	FINDLAY, C. DE C.		

*These names were unfortunately omitted from the tablet in Dry Sandford Church, and in one case the initials were incorrect.

APPENDIX IV

School Song

DUM SPIRO SPERO

At footer, golf or cricket
We play as hard as nails;
At goal or club or wicket
Our judgement rarely fails;
We win the day with pleasure
But yet are in no measure
Despondent when we lose.
For while we are breathing we are hoping
With our heart and soul and will;
There's no time for slacking or moping
At the best School, our School, COTHILL.

And when our work is over,
All Latin verbs are done,
We tolerate no shirking,
The fight is fairly won.
All things are tackled cleanly,
No advantage taken meanly.
We still remember then
That while we're breathing we are hoping
With our heart and soul and will;
There's no time for slacking or moping
At the best School, our School, COTHILL.

Written and composed by V. K. D. Waite in 1929.
Two of the three verses remembered
by Hugh Barrett-Lennard.

BIBLIOGRAPHY

Briggs, David R. *The Millstone Race.* Privately published by St Piran's, Maidenhead. Short Run Press, 1983.

Chadwick, Owen. *The Victorian Church.* A. & C. Black, 1966.

Cook, Pat. *Ombudsman: An Autobiography.* BKT Publications, 1981.

Fifty Years of Sport at Oxford, Cambridge and the Great Public Schools. Edited by Hon. R. H. Lyttelton, Arthur Page & Evan B. Noel. Walter Southwood, 1922.

Hearnden, Arthur. *Red Robert: The Life of Robert Birley*, Hamish Hamilton, 1984.

Hodgkinson, Colin. *Best Foot Forward.* Odhams, 1957.

Leinster-Mackay, Donald. *The Rise of the English Prep School.* Falmer Press, 1984.

Nickalls, G. O. ('Gully'). *A Rainbow in the Sky.* Chatto & Windus, 1974.

Preparatory Schools Review. 'Natural Science in Preparatory Schools', 1898; Bromsgrove, 1899; M. J. Dauglish obituary, December 1922.

Wilkinson, Spenser. *The Nation's Need.* Archibald Constable, *c.* 1903.

INDEX OF NAMES

Bold type = main members of teaching staff.
Italic figures = mention in captions to illustrations.

Abel Smith, Maj. F. J. (Fitz), 199
Aberdeen, Marquess of, 10, 89, 216
Abingdon, Mayor of, 247
Adams, G. H. C. (Geoffrey), 45, 297, 299
Adams, Rev. H. C., 19–20, 45, 258
Adams, M. C. (Michael), 297
Alachouzos, M., Jnr (Michael), 225
Alachouzos, Michael, Snr, 225
Aldous, Guy, 126
Aldous, M. T. (Mark), 10, 252, 260, 271
Aldous, R. J. (Robert), 255
Aldous, T. (Tom), 126, 139
Alexander of Tunis, Earl, 114
Alexander of Tunis, Earl (*formerly* S. W. D. Alexander) (Shane), 114
Allen, John, 252
Allen, J. E. C. (Jonathan), 159
Allen, Mrs Ruth (*formerly* Viner), 201, 248–9, 269, 277–8
Allen, T. F. D. (Timothy), 159
Amphlett, J. (John), 300
Anton, C. G. F. (Graeme), 113, 229
Anton, Mrs Elizabeth, 233
Anton, I. A. (Zandy), 244, 262
Arding, Mr, 113
Argent, Mr, 55, 107
Armitage, A. J. (Alexander), 217
Armitage, R. H. L. (Richard), 200, 209, 212, 225, 237, *237*
Armitage, Mrs Sue, 237
Arnander, C. J. F. (Christopher), 10, 99, 297
Arthur, Lt-Col. J. R. (John), 128, 199
Arthur, Mrs Val, 199
Arton, Mr, 113
Assheton, Hon. J. H. (John), 271
Assheton, Hon. N. (Nick), 10, 208
Atkin-Berry, H. L. (Harold), 110, 300
Atkin-Berry, M. I. (Mike), 10, 30, 80, 206
Aylesford, Earl of, 10

Bailey, C. S. (Christopher), 300
Bailey, M. L. G. (Michael), 120, 128, 297
Bailey, R. L. C. (Richard), 10, 120, 297
Bailey, R. M. (Robin), 154
Bailey, T. (Tim), 10, 58, 60, 63–4, 74, 75–8, 141–2
Baillieu, C. L. (Chris), 288
Bainbridge, Miss Jenny, 292–3
Baines, Bill, 203
Baker, V. (Val), 300
Balfour, Cdr C. J. (Colin), 297
Ball, V. F., 193
Balniel, Lord (*see* Crawford & Balcarres)
Banks, J. C. (Jack), 10, 62, 63, 68, 69, 80, 94, 150, 199, 233
Banks, J. L. C. (Johnny), 10, 192
Banks, Leslie, 174, 209
Barker, C. R. (Charles), 234
Barker, T. E. G. (Tom), 245, 246
Barker, T. G. (Tim), 10, 102, 103
Barmby, J. (James), 297
Barnard, M. P. S. M. (Michael), 209
Barnett, C. S. (Chris), 10, 48, 54, 56, 94, 162, 164
Barnett, Sir Oliver (O. C.), 10, 47
Barrett-Lennard, Rev. Sir Hugh (H.D.), Bt., 10, 52–3, 55, 56, 58, 63, 66, 82, 142, 219, 260–1, 301
Barron, Elizabeth, 203
Bartlett, Mr & Mrs, 67
Barton, Mrs Jean, 292–3
Barton, J. J. (Jonathan), 282, 298
Barton, Dr P. J. (Peter), 292–3
Battell, Nelson, *61*, 118, 169–70, *170*, 199, 282
Baylis, Miss Anna-Karina, 292–3
Beazer, D. N. (Daniel), 10, 216–17, 253
Beck, Peter, 167
Bedwell, Mrs May, 10, *170*, 170–1
Beeby, G. H. (Harry), 127
Beecham, H. J. B. (Henry), 297
Belcher, Miss Jo, 248–9
Bell, N. E. (Nicholas), 196

Bellew, Lord (J. B.) (Jim), 10, 145
Belstead, Rt Hon. Lord (*formerly* Hon. J. J. Ganzoni) (John), 113–16 *passim*, 135, 136, 139, 246, 247, 275
Bennett, J. P. (John), 300
Bennett, Pete, 215
Benson, C. D.'A. (Charlie), 283
Berens, D. J. C. (Henry), 157, 297
Berkeley-Hill, H. E. W. (Herbert), 27, 297
Betjeman, John, 210–11
Betjeman, Mrs Penelope, 202
Bickmore, J. D. P. (David), 75
Bilton, A. J. G. (Anton), 10
Binyon, M. F. L. (Martin), 284
Bird, Lt-Col. R. G. (Richard), 10, 151, 153, 201
Birkhead, Mrs Maggie (*see* Laing)
Birley, Sir Robert, 172, 173, 267
Bitterling, Miss Sue, 164, 234, 248–9, 259
Blacker, J. R. (John), 299
Blackmore, Mrs Carolyn, 276
Blackmore, Robert, 276
Blackmore, S. P. (Simon), 10, 248–9, 253–4, 254, 260, 266, 270, 271, 272, 276, 285, 288, 289, 290
Blair Gould, Miss Anne, 260, 269
Bland, Dr C. J. H. (Charles), 10, 123, 196, 242
Blandy, E. N. (Edmund), 297
Bodimeade, N. (Nick), 289, 292–3
Bolton, Geoffrey, 85, 149
Bones, K. (Keith), 132, 214, 219, 251
Boone, W. R. (Willie), 113, 174, 189, 196, 216, 282
Boothroyd, Mrs Ann (*formerly* Matthews), 168, *176–7*
Boothroyd, C. J. (Chris), 10, 167, 168, 169, *176–7*, 271
Borwick, M. P. (Malcolm), *216*, 289
Bowles, T. G. A. (Tom), 120, 152, 228
Bowman, Mrs Joanna, 226
Boyle, D. S. (David), 167
Bradbury, D. (David), 297
Bradbury, D. R. (Richard), 167
Bradbury family, 271
Bradbury, J. (James), 160–1
Brakespeare, Mrs Lizzie, 183
Brand, Hon. R. J. (Jim), 300
Branfill, C. L. A. (Capel), 299
Bray, Hilary, *188*, 188, 228
Bray, Mrs Jenny, 188
Braybrooke, Rev. O. H. (Oliver), 10, 75
Brett, Hon. C. L. B. (Christopher), 10, 119, 128
Brett, Lionel (*see* Esher)
Bridgeman, R. L. O. (Dick), 113, 114
Brignall, G. P. (Graham), *248–9*, 253
Brignall, Mrs Miranda, *248–9*, 253
Brooks, C. G. (Christopher), 235, 239
Brooks, C. P. E. (Charlie), 235, 253, 254, 256, 288
Brough, P. H. L. (Peter), 297
Brown, Mr, 134
Brown, Mrs Becky, 288, *292–3*
Brown, I. R. A. (Ian), 160
Brunner, C. O. (Conrad), 266
Brunner, J. S. (Jacob), 244
Brunton, N. R. (Nicholas), 168
Bruton, A. S. (Angus), 66
Bryant, H. R. (Humphrey), 93, 103, 111, 114, 117, 119, 121–3, *124–5*, 130, 134, 149
Buckley, S. D. (Simon), 205
Buckley, Maj. W. K. (Kemmis), 10, 28, 29, 64, 68
Budgen, J. D. (John), 297
Budworth, A. D. D. (Alexander), 255
Budworth, Mrs Julia, 10, 89, 120
Bullard, Sir Reader, 154
Bungay, Mrs Sadie, *182*, 183
Burbank, B. H. J. (Benjamin), 244
Burbank, J. C. R. (John), 11, 244, *248–9*, 269, *292–3*
Burbank, J. C. W. (Joseph), 244
Burbank, S. P. R. (Samuel), 244, 276
Burbank, Mrs Val, 276
Burford, B. J. A. (Ben), 263, 264
Burkitt, C. E. C. (Charles), 266, 269
Burkitt, F. W. M. (Francis), 10, 239, 252, 256, 257, 260, 271
Burrell, J. R. (John), 118
Busk, J. F. H. (Jonathan), 257
Busk, R. D., *48*
Butler, E. H. (Edward), *63*, 64, 69, 85, 86, 100, 113, 115, 134
Butler, W. F. (William), 46, 300
Byrne, Miss Anne, *292–3*

Calvert, H. M. (Harry), 265
Calvert, J. R. (James), 10, 254
Cardwell, Dr H. M. E. (Hugh), 223, 226
Carles, C. W. (Charles), ch. 1 *passim*, *21*, 140, 161
Carlow, Viscount (*see* Portarlington)
Carr, A. M. D. (Angus), 300
Carrington, R. C. E. (Roger), 10, 88, 123, 127, 132, 267–8
Carrington, Mrs Vi, 10, 127
Carter, P. G. (Peter), 10, 164
Cartwright, J. H. O. (John), 10, 64, 74, 80, 83
Castle Stewart, Eleanor, Countess, 241, *241*, 251
Challenor, B. (Bromley), 10, 135, 164–5, 285
Chalmers, N. J. P. (Nicholas), 282, 298
Chamberlain, R. A. (Roderick), 10, 123, 160, 201, 212, 297
Chambers, J., 213

Chamier, P. A. (Pat), 110, 300
Chance, N. J. L. (Nicholas), 160
Chapman, C. M. B. (Charles), 44, 299
Chapman, W. W. (William), 44, 299
Charles, H. R. H. Prince, 167
Chattey, S. K. (Stanley), 10, 94, 103
Cheshire of Woodhall, Lord (Leonard), 115
Cheshire, Mrs Audrey (*see* Parry)
Cheshire, Christopher, 115, 161
Cheshire, C. S. (Scottie), 10, 102
Cheshire, Geoffrey, 102
Cheshire, Nicky, *105*, 134
Cheshire, Miss Sue (*see* McArthur)
Cheshire, Tim, 161
Cholmeley, J. R., 183
Clive, C. G. (Colin), 130
Close-Smith, C. N. (Charles), 10, 24, 47
Cocks, M. G. (Mike), 10, 101, 104
Collinge, C. D. R. (David), 256
Collins, P. R. (Peter), 300
Collins, Tim, 10, 217–19
Collinson, G. E. C. (George), 299
Colwell, Philip, 174, 181, *182*, 182–3
Constable, A. T. W. (Archibald), 299
Constantinidi, P. M. (Paul), 260
Cook, F. P. (Pat), 78, 79, 239
Cook, J. F. G. (John), *292–3*
Cooksey, K. B. (Kenneth), 299
Cooper, P. J. (Peter), 10, 205
Costeloe, C. W. B. (Brian), 10, *188*, 188, 189–91, 193, 198, 208, 220, 239, *248–9*, 265, 282–3
Costeloe, Mrs Thelma, 189–90
Couchman, Miss, *124–5*
Craigmile, C. N. (Clive), 10, 111, 152
Craven, H. N. (Nico), 10, 81
Craven, J. (Jonty), 111
Crawford & Balcarres, Earl of (*formerly* Master of Lindsay/Lord Balniel) (Robin), 167
Crewdson, W. R. I. (Richard), 297
Crook, Mrs Valerie, *292–3*
Cropper, C. R. (Charles), 140
Cullen, Jeremy, 271
Cunningham, D. C. (David), 142
Curtis, Miss Mary, 164, 167, 176–7, 189, 196

Dalby, W. B. (William), 21, *21*
Dalgety, 278
Dalglish, D. R. M. (David), 193
Daniel, Mrs Flora, 167, 173, *176–7*, 186, 189, 201
Dauglish, M. J. (John), 17, 22, ch. 2 *passim*, 25, 27, ch. 3 *passim*, 42, 57, 62, 95, 161, 192, 265, 267, 294
Davan-Wetton, Hilary, 199, 233
Davan-Wetton, Mrs Jane, 199
Dawnay, Hon. J. R. (Jimmy), 127
Dawson, A. J. N. (Nick), 10, 114, 115, 151, 152, 209
Dawson, E. M. (Edgar), 47
Dawson, G. V. F. (George), 297
Dawson, T. M. E. (Tim), 10, 115, 151–2, *155*, 172, 209
de la Hey, Maj. R. M. O. (Dick), 10, 83, 98, 99–100, 133, 268
de Piro, His Honour A. C. H. (Alan), 10, 74, 79, 94, 114–15, 154, 297
de Piro, R. A. (Micky), 74, 83, 84, 85, 114, 297, 300
Dee, Simon (*see* Henty-Dodd)
Demarest, M. H. S. (Michael), 96, 128, 297
Denton, Charlie, *61*, 67
Denton, Mrs Violet, 67
Dilhorne, Lord (*formerly* Hon. J. M. Manningham-Buller) (Johnny), 89
Dillon, G. F. L. (Tim), 238
Dixon, A. W. V. (Andrew), 245
Dixon, D. G. (Danny), 207, 235
Dixon, Maj. Hon. T. R. V. (Robin), 126, 196
Dowell, T. E. (Tom), 115, *124–5*, 126
Drake, Col. A. J. M. (Tony), 208
Drayson, Bob, 264
Duffield, G. E. (Gervase), 128, 297
Duffield, J. E. (Elwes), 10, 28, 48
Duffield, J. L. (John), 10, 219, 297
Dulles, W. F. H. (Billy), 142
Duncombe, D. P. H. P. (David), 215
Duncombe, Maj. Sir Philip Pauncefort-, Bt (P.D.), 10, 100
Dundas, Lord David (*formerly* Hon. D. P. N. Dundas), 153, 161
Dundas, Lord (*see* Zetland)
Dunmore, Mrs Louise, 10, 233
Dykes, G. F. W. (George), 297

Eastwood, Mrs Catherine, 10, 43–4
Eccles, R. A. (Robin), 167, 195
Eden, S. G. (Simon), 300
Edge-Partington, Miss Rosanne, 201
Edwardes-Ker, C. (Charles), 250, 298
Edwardes-Ker, M. (Michael), 156, 250
Edwardes-Ker, Rolla, 250–1
Edwards, D. (David), 154, *155*
Edwards-Heathcote, D. M. (*formerly* Heathcote) (David), 215
Eland, P. J. W. (Peter), 298
Elliott, Mrs Jill, 285
Ellis, Mrs Betty, *124–5*, 126, 201

Ellwood, A. J. (John), 285
Enstone, 'Piggy', 34
Esau, Mrs June, 10, 194–5
Esher, Lord (*formerly* Lionel Brett), 131
Estridge, W. E. P., 69
Evans, Harold, 149
Evans, John, 149
Evans, M. R. (Mark), 274
Eyres, Sergeant, 73

Fagent, Miss Eileen, *261*, 261
Fairbrother, Mrs Elizabeth, 196
Fairbrother, George, *190*, 190
Fairbrother, Leader, 60–1, *61*, 117, *118*, 185, 196, 199, 213, 243, 243–4
Fairbrother, 'Moses', *61*
Fairbrother, Mrs Pat, 186, *186*, 190, 198, 264, 269
Fanshawe, Col. D. V. (David), 199
Faridany, A. H. (Abdol), 244
Farnell, J. A. O. (Tony), 10, 24–6, 29, 33–4, 43, 49–50
Farnsworth, K. (Kenneth), 108
Faulkner, T. P. (Tom), 264
Fawcett, R. F. (Richard), 175, 196, 224
Fender, P. G. H., 92
Ferguson-Davie, J. M. (James), 206–7
Fergusson, D. S. B. (Donald), 10, 123, 130–1, 132
Figg, C. H. C. (Christopher), 220, 232, 233, 252
Figg, Sir Leonard (L. C. W.), 84, 109
Finch, Hon. C. H. (*see* Guernsey)
Findlay, Brig. A. G. (Tony), 10, 29, 60–1, 64, 145–6
Findlay, C. de C. (Charles), 300
Fisher, M. N. T. V. (Mark), 153
Forrest, R. C. (Robert), 299
Fowler-Watt, Donald, 253
Foxwell, R. E. T. (Rupert), 271
Fraser, F. M. (Malcolm), 298
Freeman, T. (Tim), 90
Freeman-Attwood, Mrs Marigold, 10, 11, 151
Fry, Mrs Joan, 225, 226
Fuller, Mrs, 164
Fullerton, D. G. (David), *292–3*
Fulton, Mrs (*formerly* Spokes), 43, *69*, 140, 164

Galliers-Pratt, A. C. (Anthony), 239
Ganzoni, Hon. J. J. (*see* Belstead)
Gardiner-Hill, D. P. (David), 10, 57
Garnett, S. J. (Simon), 286, 298
Garrett, Lt-Col. P. C., 241, 242
Garton, Ernest, *107*, 107, 174, 181, 183, 268
Gautier, Monsieur, 194
Gemmell, Mr & Mrs, 90
Georgano, G. N. (Nick), 10, 198
Gerring, Mrs 'Gran', *182*, 183
Gibson, C. H. (Clem), 154, *155*
Gilbert, P. D. (Peter), 239, *248–9*, 255, 256, 278
Gilbey, G. H. (Geoffrey), 44
Gili, Mrs Phillida (*formerly* Stone), 187
Gill, A. R. (Anthony), 10, 80, 89–90, 138
Gill, P. W. (Patrick), 80
Gillum, C. A. (Chris), 244
Glazebrook, P. C. (Peter), 10, 168, 169, 196–7, 233
Glossop, P. G. (Peter), 149
Gooch, C. N. (Charles), 10, 144, 164
Gooch, R. C. W. (Richard), 108, 297
Goodhart, Lady (Val), 265
Goodhart, D. (Daniel), 265
Goodhart, Sir Philip, 265
Goodrich, Hon. Mrs Audrey, 212
Goodrich, Rev. Brian, 212
Goodrich, J. (John), 10, 191, 198, 212
Goodrich, P. (Peter), 198, 212
Goodrich, S. (Simon), 212, 220
Gordon, A. G. (*see* Haddo)
Gordon-Lennox, A. C. (Angus), 278
Gordon-Lennox, Maj.-Gen. B. C. (Bernard), 116, 199
Gordon-Lennox, Col. D. H. C. (David), 208
Gore, Charles, 81
Gore, Mrs Kathleen, 81
Gorringe-Smith, Miss Joan (*see* Swinbank)
Gotch, Mrs, 135
Gough, A. J. (Jamie), 174, 297
Gough, Mrs Daphne, 10, 151, 226
Gough, O. M. L. (Orlando), 201, 209, 224, 226, 298
Gough, P. W. (Piers), 151, 160
Gover, Mike, 10
Grant, Miss Judy, *124–5*
Grant, J. P. A. (James), 285
Graves, A. G. J. (Austin), 299
Graves, Robert, 209
Gray, Harold, 183
Gray, Miss Sylvia, 183, 228, 257
Green, C. W. (Clifford), 299
Greenham, M. I. (Matthew), 282, 298
Greenwell, Basil, 10, 228
Greenwell, G. H. (Giles), 144, 220
Greenwell, S. L. (Simon), 144, 201
Grenfell, Lord (*formerly* Hon. J. P. F. St. L.) (Julian), 126
Grieve, Mrs Jenny, *292–3*
Griggs, Mrs Freda, 224
Griggs, R. J. (Raymond), 224
Guernsey, Lord (*formerly* Hon. C. H. Finch) (Charles), 19, 156, 169

Haddo, Earl of (*formerly* A. G. Gordon) (Alexander), 215–16, *216*, 225–6
Haggett, Mrs Beryl, 286–7, *292–3*
Haggett, M. St. J. L. (Matthew), 286, 287
Haggett, Sqn-Ldr N. L. (Norman), 286–7, *292–3*

Hailsham of St Marylebone, Rt Hon. Lord, 257
Hake, Gordon, 81, 93
Hall, Mrs Barbara, 10, *144*, 145, 146, 167, *176–7*, 198, *213*, 226, *237*, *248–9*, 250, 258, 269, 281–2, 288
Hall, Prof. Teddy, 230, *231*
Halsey, Lt-Col. G. M. Halsey (Guy), 10, 46, 194
Halsey, P. J. (Pat), 10, 33, 40, 42, 46, 47, 192
Hames, Miss, 32–4, *33*, 46, 47, 49, 50, 140, 164
Hamilton, D. G. (Donald), 300
Hamilton, G. J. (Gerald), 10, 48, 194
Hamilton, J. E. (John), 108
Hancock, M .J. W. (Michael), 217, 298
Hand, Miss Diana, 187
Hanford, F. W. (Francis), 297
Hanmer, J. L. R. (John), 164
Hannah, D. M. (David), 10, 143, 146, 266, 269
Hannah, John, 10, 146
Hannen, Nicholas, 116
Harari, P. V. (Philip), 128
Hardie, M. C. (Miles), 297
Hardie, W. D. C. (David), 110, 297, 300
Hargreaves, Miss Nina, *124–5*, 127, 150, 156, 201
Harley, Mrs Rosie, 10, 11, 151, 242
Harley, T. H. (Tom), 10, 78, 151, 235–6, 242, 245–6, 252
Harrison, Mrs Margaret, 288, *292–3*
Hart-Davis, Duff, 157
Harwood, B. A. (Basil), 297
Harwood, Miss Renée, 201
Hatch, Mrs Rosemary, 10
Hay, E. D. J. (*see* Tweeddale)
Hearnden, Dr Arthur, 250, 267
Heath, K. L.'E. H. M. (Kenneth), 27
Heathcote, D. M. E. (*see* Edwards-Heathcote)
Heaton, D. (David), 10, 71
Heaton-Ellis, D. (David), 299
Hebert, A. G. (Arthur), 297
Hedges, Sister, 68, *69*
Hellyer, B. G. (Bartle), 237
Hely-Hutchinson, Hon. M. (Mark), 10, 114, 117, 169, 297
Henery, G. T. (Graham), 299
Henery, H. W. L. (Hewett), 299
Henty-Dodd, Simon (Dee), 213
Herapath, Miss Margaret, 242
Heyman, A. C. (Archie), 154–5, 187
Heyman, Mrs Diana (*formerly* Pike), 10, 11, 57, *58*, 62, 68, *87*, 95, *95*, 101, 108, 154, 155, 187, 269
Heyman, P. C. (Peter), 10, 154–5
Hickman, J. B. (John), 297
Higgins, Lt-Col. F. H. G. (Fergus), 10, 49
Hindell, H. F., 100, 103
Hoare Nairne, C. V. S. (Charlie), 270
Hobson, Dr Fred, 62, 126, 130, 186
Hodgetts, T. S. (Tim), 11, 288, 289, *292–3*
Hodgkinson, C. G. S. (Colin), 110
Hogarth, W. D. (William), 297
Holden, H. G. (Hyla), 10, 11, 279, 288–9
Holden, Mrs Jane, 289
Hole, N. F. R. (Nicholas), 284
Holland, A. D. R. (Tony), 10, 96
Holland, T. E. (Tyrrel), 299
Holland, T. L. R. (Tim), 10, 96
Holland, V. E. (Vivian), 299
Holland-Hibbert, Miss Lavinia (*see* Orde)
Holland-Hibbert, M. (*see* Knutsford)
Holmer, Paul, 10, 222
Holmer, T. H. A. (Tom), 10, 238
Holmes, Miss Suzanne (*see* Meate)
Holt, D. L. (David), 300
Holt, J. H. (James), 10, 115, 145
Homfray, J. R. (John), 299
Hooke, Jack, 10, 148
Hopkinson, A. T. (Adrian), 209
Hopkinson, D. H. L. (David), 228–9, 297
Horn, Geoffrey, 252
Horn, Mrs Marjorie, 252
Horn, S. J. (Sebastian), 171, 252
Howard, Hon. G. W. B. (*see* Morpeth)
Howard, Hon. P. C. W. (Philip), 254
Howell, D. G. (Graham), 283–4, *292–3*
Howson, G. W. (Giles), 262
Hudson, P. A. (Philip), 10
Hughes, Fred, *165*, 212, 214, 246
Hulbert-Powell, E. C. L. (*formerly* Hulbert) (Evelyn), 10, 55, 164
Hull C. J. L. (Charles), 78
Hull, H. C. E. (Hubert), 31
Humphreys, D. J. (David), 253
Humphreys, Mrs Jean, 257
Humphreys, Maj. Roger, 257
Hurd, Rt. Hon. Douglas, 257
Hurst, John, 98, 107
Hussey, Dukie, 253
Hussey, J. A. (James), 246

Iliine, A. M. S. (*see* Sherrington)
Insole, G. C. L. (George), 299

Jackson, R. G. (Richard), 300
Jackson, T. E. B. (Tom), 10, 11, 132, 135–6, 142–4, *143*, 147, 154, *155*, 156–62 *passim*, 167–70 *passim*, 172, *176–7*, 185, 186, 193, 198, 201, 202, 205, 211, 219, 222–3, *248–9*, 251, 260, 263, 265, 269, 270, 276, 281–2, 285, 287
James, A. G. (Angus), 208

Janson, J. (Jonathan), 10, 64
Jebb, Hon. M. A. G. (Miles), 108, 116
Jeffs, A. (Alexander), 266
Jodhpur, H. H. The Maharajah of (Bapji), 10, 147, 148, 157–8
Johns, S. A. H. (Hellier), 166, 276, 283–4, 285
Johnson, Mrs, 199
Jourdain, H. C. (Clive), 157, 167, 168

Kay. R. D. (Richard), 255–6
Kefford, H. K., 164
Keith, N. A. (Alastair), 94
Kemball-Cook, B. H. (Brian), 297
Kemball-Cook, B. M. (Barry), 74, 297
Kemball-Cook, D. B. (Denis), 297
Kemball-Cook, R. B. (Richard), 297
Kemp, C. A. H. (Christopher), 297
Kiddle, Mrs Gwen, 243
Kidston-Montgomerie, Capt. R. A. (*formerly* Kidston) (Alec), 169
Kindersley, G. (Gay), 10, 96
Kindersley, Capt Hon. P. L. (Philip), 43, 46
Kindersley, R. F. (Dick), 43
Kirkby, Rev. J. H., 81–2, 85
Kirwan, Mrs Kay, 194
Knapp-Fisher, J. S. (Jim), 192
Knight, J. W. A. (James), 284–5
Knowles, F. (Foster), 22, 24, 25, 26, 96, 192, 267
Knutsford, Viscount (*formerly* M. Holland-Hibbert), 10, 64, 89, 95, 166
Kyle, S. D. (Stuart), 286, 298

Lachlan, N. S. (Noel), 11, 200, 208, 213, 244, 252, 256
Laing, J. M. (James), 288, 298
Laing, Miss Maggie (*formerly* Birkhead), 10, 274–5
Lakin, M. P. (Mark), 142
Lamprill, M. (Michael), 154, 207
Lang, Mr, 174, 186
Langhorne, R. E. (Robin), 10, *155*, 159–60, 233
Lanyon, W. M. (Bill), 10, 62
Lauré, D. (Denis), 215
Law, G. E. (George), 297
Le Page, A. (Tony), 174
Leanse, P. J. (Peter), 219, 220
Leanse, R. C. (Robin), 10, 143, 196
Leather, H. J. O. (Herbert), 299
Lee, Mrs Moya, 276, *292–3*
Leggett, Dr D. G. A. (David), 96
Leggett, Mrs Shirley, 10, 96
Leigh, Hon. B. C. (Ben), 198
Leigh, Hon. M. J. (Michael), 198
Leigh, R. J. E. (Roger), 10, 78, 88
Leinster-Mackay, Dr Donald, 10, 17
Lidstone, D. J. (Digby), 298
Lim, Dr F. T. K. S. (Freddy), 167, 169, 195
Lim, W. P. K. S. (Peter), 167
Lindgren, Miss Kate, 276–7
Lindsay, Master of (*see* Crawford & Balcarres)
Little, R. I. K. (Iain), 212, 217, 298
Liversidge, Miss Anne, 195
Liversidge, D. H. (David), 284
Liversidge, Miss Mary, 195
Liversidge, W. J. H. (Bill), 195, 198, 236, 254, 254–5
Llewellyn, Col. Sir Godfrey (R. G.), Bt, 10, 31, 288
Llewellyn, J. B. (Jack), 31
Lloyd, M. C. K. (Mark), 260
Longland, A. C. (Austin), 27, 297
Lopes, Hon. H. M. (Henry), 157
Lovegrove, Daniel, *106*, 106–7, 118, 157
Lovegrove, Maggie, *106*, 106–7, 126, 174, 199, 242, 243
Loyd, A. W. (Andrew), 10, 166, 192, 201, 235
Lynam, Joc, 149, 210–11, 284
Lynam, John, 195
Lynn, A. H. (Tony), 279, 285, 288, *292–3*
Lyon, J. F. S. (John), 111

McArthur, Mrs Sue (*formerly* Cheshire), 10, 161
McCarthy, H. S. D.'A. (Stuart), 113
McCreery, C. A. S. (Charles), 141
McCreery, General Sir Richard, 111
McCreery, R. J. (Bob), 169
McCrone, Miss Kirsty, *292–3*
McCrum, Michael, 252
McEuen, 155
McGhie, A. W. (Andrew), 266
McMillan, Miss Vera, 68, 69, 140, 201
Mahon, Miss Susan, *292–3*
Malim, J. S. (Jeremy), 10, 11, 132, 209–10, *210*, 217, 220, 229–30, 240, 243, 244, 250, 253
Manning, R. J. W. (Richard), 288, *292–3*
Manningham-Buller, Hon. J. M. (*see* Dilhorne)
Marriott, Maj.-Gen. Sir John, 172
Marsh, Gilbert, 214, 241, 246
Marston, Pat, 149
Marten, Sir Henry, 13
Martin-Atkins, F. N. (Francis), 300
Massey, D. R. (Dan), 10, 86, 116, 134, 208
Massey, Raymond, 116
Matthew, J. W. (John), 85
Matthews, Miss Ann (*see* Boothroyd)
Matthews, Mrs Jane, 10
Mayall, E. H., 68–9
Maynard, W. T. C. (Waltsham), 10, 85–6, 134
Meate, Mrs Suzanne (*formerly* Holmes), 201, 220
Meinertzhagen, S. (Simon), 171

Mence, Mr, 113
Metcalfe, G. T. (Tom), 96
Millar, A. M. T. (Andrew), 167
Mills, Canon W. R., 116, 121
Milne, A. G. (Andrew), 113, 196
Milne, C. J. (Christopher), 113, 196
Milnes-Gaskell, 159
Mitchell, C. J. H. (Julian), 126, 131, 208
Moffett, R. S. (Simon), 10, 123, 143, 191
Money, A., 219
Montgomerie, R. A. K. (*see* Kidston-Montgomerie)
Montgomery, D. J. T. (Douglas), 253
Montgomery, N. K. J. (Neil), 167, 209
Montgomery, P. A. C. (Peter), 256
Moon, J. C. G. (John), 78
Moore, Air Vice-Marshal Charles, 279
Moore, J. R. B. (James), 258
Morland, D. M. T. (Denys), 44–5
Morley, W. F. (Walter), 21, *21*
Morpeth, Viscount (*formerly* Hon. G. W. B. Howard) (George), 197
Motion, P. R. (Peter), 271
Murray, E. D. (Eric), 299

Nash, Andrew, 196
Nash, C. T. (Christopher), 256, 258
Naylor, D. H. (David), 297
Neale, G. C. (Guy), 10, 101–2, 108, 297
Newman, R. E. G. (Rupert), 297
Newton, Mr. 67, 85, 107
Nickalls, Mrs, 26
Nickalls, G. O. ('Gully'), 37, 75, 78, 191–2
Norman, R. E. (Raymond), 297
Northcote, Mr, 37, 39
Norton, Miss Edith, 201

Ogston, R. A. L. (Ran), 10, *124–5*, 135, 139, 233
O'Hara, S. M. (Sean), 272
Oliver, Alan, 240
Oppé, A. P. (Anthony), 216
Orde, Mrs Lavinia (*formerly* Holland-Hibbert), 95
Osborne, D. M. (Mark), 217, 238
Oswell, R. H. B. (Rupert), 266
Oxlade, J. S. (John), 259, 265, 266, 284

Paine, J. H. (Jack), 10, 31
Palmer, A. A. H. (Wold), 10, 164, 209, 224
Palmer, C. H. (Howard), 189
Palmer, R. H. (Raphe), 10, 162, 189
Palmer, R. M. (Mike), 74, 297
Palmer-Tomkinson, C. A. (Charles), 169
Palmer-Tomkinson, C. D. (Chris), 10, 149
Park, Simon, 254
Parker, Miss Manda, *292–3*
Parker, Hon. W. R. C. B. (William), 110, 300
Parkinson, Miss Pixie (*see* Welch)
Parry, Mrs Audrey (*formerly* Pike/Cheshire), 10, 11, 57, *58*, *87*, 95, 99, 101, 115, 134, 161, 187, 240, 269
Parry, Hugh, 161, 172, 187
Parry, Miss Jane, 161
Parry, John, 161, 240
Parry, Miss Margaret, 161
Parslow, Miss Debbie, *292–3*
Part, C. T. (Charles), 213
Patten, Rt Hon. John, 257
Pearce, L. S. C. (Laurence), 297
Pearson, G. C. S. (Graham), 96
Peel, J. F. R. (Roger), 43, 46–7, 265
Peel, J. R. (Johnny), 10, 89, 123, 133, 146
Peel, R. R. (Robert), 10, 265
Peel, S. W. (Stephen), 43–4, 46, 265
Permingeat, Mlle Liliane, *292–3*
Perrott, Miss Rosemary, 288
Pether, Miss Jenny, 201
Peto, N. J. (Nick), 169
Phillimore, H. A. G. (Dust), *63*, 63–4, *69*, *71*, 74, 86, 100, 117, 118, 123, *124–5*, 129, 132–4, *133*, *137*, 137, 139, 147, *155*, 159, 161, 169, 171, 174, *176–7*, 194, 198, 199, 219, 233
Phillips, A. C. (Alfred), *28*, 28–30, *30*, 36, 37, *38*, 39, 42, *42*, 47, *48*, 49–52 *passim*, 52, *53*, 53–4, 61–2, *63*, 64, 69, 72, 73, 74, 79, 82, 83, 85, 94, 138, 141–2, *142*, 202, 253
Phillips, Miss Fanny, 28, 43
Piercey, M. V. L. (Marc), 10, 192, 210, 244
Pike, Miss Audrey (*see* Parry)
Pike, Miss Diana (*see* Heyman)
Pike, Mrs D. E. (Dorothy), 41, ch. 4 *passim*, *58*, 69, ch. 5 *passim*, *87*, ch. 6 *passim*, *112*, ch. 7 *passim*, *122*, *124–5*, ch. 8 *passim*, *176–7*, 181, 185, 186, 199–200, *200*, 213, 220, 222, 233, *238*, 238–9, 251, 267, 268
Pike, Major G. L. S. (George), 17, 26, 41, 57, *58*, 59, 65, 66, 68–9, 85, 93, 94, 99, 102, 105, 106, 109, *110*, 115–16, 120, ch. 7 *passim*, *122*, *124–5*, *133*, ch. 8 *passim*, *155*, *176–7*, ch. 9 *passim*, *187*, ch. 10 *passim*, ch. 11 *passim*, *232*, 248–9, ch. 12 *passim*, 259, *261*, *268*, *273*
Pike, Mrs M. G. (Gabrielle), 11, 109, *110*, *112*, 121, 122, 123, 126, 146, 171, 175, ch. 9 *passim*, ch. 10 *passim*, ch. 11 *passim*, 247, 248–9, 258–9, 269, 274, 283, 285, 288
Pike, Major S. A. (Sam), 17, 41, 56, ch. 4 *passim*, *58*, 63, 69, *70*, ch. 5 *passim*, 79, *87*, *88*, ch. 6 *passim*, *112*, *118*, ch. 7 *passim*, *122*, *124–5*, *141*, ch. 8 *passim*, 155, *166*, *176–7*, ch. 9 *passim*, *200*, 207,

213, 220, 222–3, 228, 232, 233, 238, 240, 251, 253, 256, 266–9 *passim*, *268*, 275
Pinkney, Philip, 115
Piper, John, 203
Piper, Mrs Myfanwy, 203
Player, W. L. D. (Bill), 208
Plowman, A. W. (Tony), 289
Portarlington, Earl of (*formerly* Viscount Carlow) (George), 269
Porter, B. J. M. (Ben), 113
Porter, F. S. (Francis), 297
Porter, H. E. L. (Harold), 154, 216, 232, 233, 246, 297
Porter, Mrs Margaret (*formerly* Wisnom), 10, 201
Porthouse, Richard, 10, 245
Potter, Miss, 52
Powell, E. (Edward), 297
Powell, H. G. L. (Hugo), 123, 154
Powell, J. M. R. (Jonathan), 160
Powell, R. (Richard), 299
Preston, Mrs Lois (*formerly* White), 134
Preston, R. M. (Michael), *124–5*, 134
Prickett, Mr, 60
Prioleau, A. S. W. (Jimmy), 74, 300
Pryor, G. (Toby), 10, 149
Pym, Rt Hon. Lord (F. L.) (Francis), 10, 65, 71, 78, 81, 86, 169, 275

Quantock Shuldham, P. J. (John), 300
Quantock Shuldham, R. C. (Christopher), 128, 297
Quantock Shuldham, W. F. (Walter), 154

Radcliffe, Mrs Angela, 276, 289, *292–3*
Rambaut, J. F. M. (John), 10, 194, 297
Rawson-Mackenzie, D. W. (Duncan), 10, 126
Rawson-Mackenzie, F. D. (Freddy), 126
Redcliffe-Maud, Lord, 214
Reid, A. K. (Arthur), 136, 139, 141, 153, *155*, 159, 160–1, 168, 169, 171, *176–7*, 187, 201, 233
Reynard, A. F. (Alexander), 297
Reynolds, Miss, 201
Reynolds, Rev. J. S., 153, 220, 226, 233, 258, 265
Rice, P. A. (Peter), *292–3*
Richardson, A. D. (Adrian), 11, 17, *184*, 184, 189, 192, 193, 195, 209, 215, 220, 225, 226, 239, 248–9, 253, 254, 256–7, ch. 12 *passim*, 259, *292–3*
Richardson, Edward, 265
Richardson, Mrs Rachel, 17, 146, 265, 269, 274, 276, 281, 285, *292–3*
Richardson, Thomas, 265, 279, 285
Richardson, Vicky, 265, 276, 285
Richmond, G. T. (Grant), 270
Ricketts, Mrs Margaret, 288, *292–3*
Roberts, J. E. M. (John), 47
Robertson, E. D. S. (Edward), 297
Robertson, F. A. de V. (Frederic), 27
Robson, J. E. (James), 298
Robson, R. W. (Rupert), 298
Rogers, Cdr G. C. B. (Graham), 10, 136, 165
Rogers, H. P. (Harry), 10, 207, 208, 235
Rogers, John, 10, 183, 241
Rogers, N. D. (Nicholas), 284, 285
Rogers, Dr R. S. B. (Robert), 128, 297
Rolt, D. A. (David), 203, 211, 212
Romanes, A. J. (Alasdair), 288, *292–3*
Ronaldshay, Earl of, 219
Rootes, Hon. N. G. (Nicky), 10, 239
Rosher, J. B., 81, 181
Rowley, J. P. D. (Peter), 10, 194
Roxburgh, J. F., 57, 72–3, 83
Rucker, A. G. (Arthur), 141
Rucker, J. N. (John), 10, 90, 94–5
Rule, W., 219
Rumbo, K. H. N. (Keith), 74, 110, 260, 297, 300
Rusby, M. E. (Mark), 287–8, 289, *292–3*
Ryder, Rt Hon. R. A. (Richard), 10, 136, 167, 175
Ryder, Stephen, 11, 228

Mrs Salter, 94
Salter, Rev. H. E., 82, 94
Salter, Miss Tiny, 82
Sandford, P. A. (Peveril), 114, 300
Saunder, J. V. (John), 10, 66
Saunders, Rev. R. C. H. (Richard), 74, 297
Savage, Patrick, 10, *184*, 239
Scholfield, Miss Annabelle, *292–3*
Scott, Archie, 188, 199
Scott, A. C. (Anthony), 255
Scott, A. H. (Andrew), 158, 188
Scott, Mrs Christabel, 255
Scott, Dr C. J. (Claude), 10, 223–4
Scott, Mrs Ethne, 223–4
Scott, I. A. G. (Ian), 188, 199
Scott, Miss Jenny, 198
Scott, J. H. (Jim), 188, 255
Scott, N. C. J. (Nicholas), 10, 171, 188, 189, 195
Scott, Mrs Ruth, 157, 188–9, 199
Selwyn, Rev. E. G., 45
Sessions, R. V., *48*, 49
Seymour, F. H. (Franko), 10, 61, 68, 71, 86, 114, 129, 268
Shakerley, Col. P. F. (Peter), 10, 164, 297
Shakespeare, Rt Hon. Sir Geoffrey, 103
Sharpe, Tom Fred, 203, 205
Shaw, Archdeacon/Bishop, 44, *45*
Shaw, E. A. (Edward), 44, 297, 299
Shaw, Capt R. J. (Robert), 10, 26, 44, *45*
Sheldon, Mr, 37
Shelton, H. N. A. (Hugh), 10, 139, 164, 233

Shepherd, G. B. (Guy), 285
Sherrington, A. M. S. (*formerly* Iliine) (Andrew), 128, 297
Short, George, *37*, 37, 41, 43, 162
Shuckburgh, J. J. E. (Julian), 10, 113, 131, 141, 167, 222–3
Sichel, G. M. J. (Geoffrey), 44, 299
Sichel, O. W. (Oliver), 44, 299
Sichel, Walter, 44
Silk, Dennis, 228, 267, 289
Simpson, Ronald, 108
Simpson, R. M. G. (Robin), 108
Skelton, H. (Henry), 282, 298
Skelton, W. T. (William), 270
Smith, Rev. Adam, 283
Smith, C. J. (Christopher), 283, 298
Smith, C. T. (Charles), 165, 220
Smith-Bingham, M. D. (Mark), 238
Snow, M. M. (Michael), 10, 34, 42–3, 54, 136, 206
Somers, A. C. (Chris), 10, 66, 192
Somers, D. C. (Derek), 192
Somers, F. J. (Jack), 10, 44
Somers, W. (Walter), 10, 53, 65, 66, 199, 229
Spokes, Miss (*see* Fulton)
Stainer, J. R. (John), 10, 49
Stanier, B. D. (Bev), 10, 88 93, 102, 111, 114–15, 201, 206
Stedall, J. H. P. (Jonathan), 10, 78, 127, 129, 130, 139, 144, 172, 203, *204*, 205, 208, 210, 211
Steel, C. E. (Edward), 278
Steel, R. P. (Richard), 245
Stenhouse, Mrs Charlotte, *58*, *105*, 105–6, 107, 195, 264
Stenhouse, Joseph, 59, 105, 195
Stephenson, J. M. (John), 186, 219, 220, 237, 298
Stephenson, J. P. R. (Jonathan), 271–2
Sterneberg, R. H. (Richard), 284
Stevens, Mrs Gwen, *197*, 197–8, 261
Stevenson, D. H. (Dennis), 189
Stewart, Charles, 203, *204*, 205
Stewart, Mrs Daphne, 10, 198, 226–7
Stewart, P. K. M. (Patrick), 300
Stibbard, P. E. (Paul), 10
Stirling, A. M. (Sandy), 95, 116
Stock, Mr, 162, 168
Stockton, J. (James), 146
Stockton, Col. W. J. (Bill), 10, 130, 146, 275, 297
Stockwell, Maj.-Gen. Sir Hugh, 10, 24, 42, 129, 288
Stogdon, H. C. (Hal), 299
Stokes, A. C. R. (Charles), 195
Stone, Mr and Mrs, 32
Stone, E. R. (Edward), 149–50
Stone, H. C. (Humphrey), 10, 11, 89, 150, 164
Stone, Mrs Janet, 10, 149, 150, 202
Stone, Miss Phillida (*see* Gili)
Stone, Reynolds, 149
Stoughton-Harris, R. W., 240
Stourton, M. G. (Michael), 10, 109, 201
Stow, 'Daddy', 149
Stow family, 149
Stratton, Capt C. M. (Michael), 10, 42
Strauss, B. L. (Bernard), 299
Strode, Dr Christopher, 173–4, 186
Strouts, H. G. E. (Henry), 265
Stubbs, J. L. C. (John), 10, 207
Stubbs, M. B. (Miles), 207
Summers, A. J. P. (Jamie), 202, 212, 214, 224
Sutton, H. E. (Hugh), 136, 297
Sutton, M. A. F. (Martin), 136
Swan, S. D. (Stuart), 259–60, 272–3
Swanton, E. W., 92
Swinbank, C. M. (Mark), 10, 126, 191
Swinbank, Mrs Joan (*formerly* Gorringe-Smith), 10, 119, *119*, 126, 186, 201, 228, *248–9*, 269, 274, 277
Swinbank, L. M. (Leonard), 10, 11, 116–19, *117*, 123, *124–5*, 126, 139, 146, 152, *155*, 161, 169, *176–7*, 185, 187, 193, 200, 214, 219–20, 228, 241, *248–9*, 265, 266, 268, 269, 274, 285, 288
Swinbank, R. G. (Robin), 10, 126, 191
Swinbank, W. R. (Bill), 126, 191, 297
Symonds, J. R. C. (Richard), 10, 58, 68, 78, 84

Taylor, M. R. (Martin), 215
Taylor, Philip, 228, 237, 241, 247, 258, 279
Templer, Field-Marshal Sir Gerald, 121
Thesiger, Hon. F. I. (Frederic), 299
Thompson, J. V. P., 181, 189
Thomson, Sir John, 10, 47, 51, 82, 164, 192, 194
Thorneloe, R. S. M. (Rupert), 298
Thorpe, Mrs, 95
Thorpe, Rt. Hon. J. J. (Jeremy), 95, 167
Tomkinson, Mrs Connie, 42, 43, 47, 52, 56
Tomkinson, Miss Marie, 39, 43
Tomkinson, K. R. G. (Ken), 10, 29, 59, 67
Tomkinson, R. (Raymond), 26, 37, *39*, 40, 41, 42, *42*, 43, 47–9, 51, 52, 53, 55, 56, 59, 67, 107, 194, 251, 294
Topham, Mrs Mary, 266
Tross Youle, S. A. L. (Simon), 217, 298
Tweeddale, Marquess of (*formerly* E. D. J. Hay) (Edward), 167

Tyrrell, H. G. (Herbert), 297

Upton, Capt. P. J. (Pat), 169

Valentine, F. A. B. (Jimmy), 128, 297
Van Denberg, H. W. (Hart), 245
Vandervell, C. (Colin), 154
Vassall, Archer, 18, 83–4
Vassar-Smith, J. R. (John), 10, *155*, 168, 169, 171–2, *176–7*
Vaughan Wilkes, Rev. J. C., 130
Vernon, Mrs, 257
Vincent, Hon. Mrs Louisa (*formerly* Vivian), 10, 234, 234–5
Viner, Miss Ruth (*see* Allen)
Vivian, Hon. Louisa (*see* Vincent)
Vivian, Hon. R. A. H. (Richard), 10, 211, 234
von Meister, A. W. P. (Alexander), 282

Wade, J. W. H. (James), 253, 258
Waite, V. K. D. (Vincent), 10, 63, 64–5, 69, 71, 74, 77, 85, 91, 94, 96–7, 100, 108–9, 111, 114, 115, 116, 133, 140, 165, 166, 175, 199, 233, 238, 260, 282, 301
Waller, W. R. (Bill), 10, 55, 199
Wallis, Mrs Gwen, *182*, 183, 269
Ward, A. W. J. (Adrian), 298
Warren, I. H. (Ian), 245
Warren, Jake, 245
Warren, Mrs Jane, 245
Watsham, A. R. (Richard), 286, 298
Watson, Miss, 52
Watson, R. R. D. (Rory), 257, 260
Way, D. D. H. (David), 10, 11, 144, 146, 205, 212, 219, 220, 223, 225–6, 252, 259
Way, E. J. B. (Edward), 258
Wedderburn, H. E. A., 151, 271
Wedderburn, R. D. A., 151, 167, 209
Welby, K. B. (Ken), 10, 263–4, 272
Welch, H. V. (Henry), 113, *124–5*, 201, 233
Welch, Mrs Pixie (*formerly* Parkinson), 113, *124–5*, 126, 201
Weld Forester, A. E. (Anthony), 10, 123, 202, 214
Weld Forester, C. R. C. (Charles), 62, 74, 77, 79, 89
Weller-Poley, N. T. (Toby), 174
Wellesley, R. C. A. (Robin), 10, 102, 111, 114
Wells, C. G. (Christopher), 298
Wells, D. L. (David), 116
West, Lt.-Col. G. A. A. R. (George), 199
Whitaker, Mrs, 51
Whitbread, H. C. (Charles), 10, 101, 104
Whitbread, M. W. (Mike), 10, 104
Whitcomb, M. K. (Michael), 253
White, A. S. J., *162*, 256–7
White, Miss Lois (*see* Preston)
White, W. R. G. (William), 298
Whiteside, M. B. D. (Miles), 299
Whitfield, P. M. (Paul), 10, 113, 208
Whittington, Mrs Mary, 264
Wigan, C. (Christopher), 163
Wigan, D. (Desmond), 10, 123, 144, 163, 168, *176–7*, 193, 196, 297
Wigan, P. (Peter), 154, 163
Wijewardane, D. N. (Nishy), 10, 269
Wiles, M. G. (Michael), 243
Willcocks, H. F. (Harold), 297, 299
Williams, M. J. H. (Martin), 164, 200, 233
Williams, Miss Sheila, 229
Williamson, L., *48*, 49
Willis, Raymond, 11, 228
Wills, Sir Seton (D.S.), Bt, 139, 157
Wilson, C. J. (Kit), 10, 37, 38, 40, 43, 191
Wiltshire, Miss Susan, 276–7
Winn, R. D. A. (David), 128
Winstone, R. A. (Robin), *292–3*
Wisnom, Miss Margaret (*see* Porter)
Wood, Dr L. G. R. (Garth), 154
Woods, David, 240
Woods, Rt Rev. Bishop Edward, 109, 121, 283
Woods, E. W. (Edward), 228
Woods, His Grace Archbishop Sir Frank, 283
Woods, Rt Rev. Bishop Robin, 11, 228, *232*, 233, 240, 247, 247, 250, 259, 279
Woods, R. B. (Robert), 228
Woolmer, Rev. J. S. T. (John), 150, 167, 297
Wordsworth, M. E. C. (Mark), 10, 264, 266, 278
Worthington, Mrs Bridget, *248–9*, 276
Wright, Miss Muriel, *65*, 65–6, *124–5*, 127, 137, 144–5, 146, 233
Wykeham-Fiennes, A. P. T. (Tony), 297
Wynn, C. (Charles), 95, 97
Wynne-Roberts, D. R. (David), 300
Wynter, C. F. W., (Constantine), 299

Yates, Miss, 198
Yorke, J. S. (John), 139
Young, J. F. H. (John), 299

Zetland, Marquess of (*formerly* Lord Dundas), 128

SUBSCRIBERS TO THE BOOK

MR & MRS I. W. ABBOTT
MARQUESS OF ABERDEEN
ABINGDON SCHOOL
DOMINIC ADDISON
ALAN & MATTI ALDERSON
CHARLES ALDOUS
T. ALDOUS
SIR WILLIAM ALDOUS
NICHOLAS ALDRIDGE
A. R. ALLEN
PAUL ALLEN
RUTH ALLEN (NÉE VINER)
CHARLIE ANDERSON
GRAEME ANTON
HAMISH ANTON
I. A. ANTON
STEWART ANTON
EDWARD ARKELL
ALEX J. ARMITAGE
CHARLES ARMITAGE
HON. NICHOLAS ASSHETON
HON R. C. ASSHETON
M. I. ATKIN-BERRY
T. J. V. AUSTIN

DUNCAN & NEAL BAILEY
R. L. C. BAILEY
CDR C. J. BALFOUR
J. M. J. BALFOUR
J. C. BANKS
DR ERIC BANNISTER
MARK BANNISTER
T. G. BARKER
REVD SIR HUGH BARRETT-LENNARD BT
ANNA-KARINA BAYLIS
G. H. BEEBY
J. L. BELL
MR & MRS HARVEY SCOFIELD BENNETT
PETER MACKINNON BENNETT
HON. MICHAEL & MRS BENSON
D. J. C. BERENS
RICHARD BERENS
THOMAS BERENS
MICHAEL R. BETTS
WILLIAM BETTS
LT R. E. BICKERTON
ANTON J. G. BILTON
JUSTIN & TOBIN BIRD
RICHARD BIRD
MRS BIRKHEAD (NOW LAING)
SIMON & CAROLYN BLACKMORE
DR C. J. H. BLAND
THOMAS BOAL
JULIAN BOLES
NICHOLAS BOLES
MAJ. R. BOON
WILLIE BOONE
ANTONY BOORD
ANN & CHRIS BOOTHROYD
NICOLAS BOWATER
D. S. BOYLE
MICHAEL P. R. BOYLE
HON. PAUL BRADBURY
HON. CHRISTOPHER BRETT
HOWARD T. BRINTON
J. G. D. BROCKLEHURST
MRS M. H. BROOKING CLARK
NICHOLAS BROOKING CLARK
CHARLES BROOKS
CONRAD BRUNNER
ELIZABETH LADY BRUNNER
JACOB BRUNNER
MAJ. W. K. BUCKLEY
A. M. BUDGETT
JULIA BUDWORTH
ADRIAN BULL
BENEDICT & QUINTIN BULL
CHARLES E. C. BURKITT
FRANCIS W. M. BURKITT
MRS R. A. P. BUTLER
C. R. BUXTON

N. D. CADBURY
JOHN CARLETON PAGET
EARL & COUNTESS OF CARLISLE
IAN EDWARD CARR
R. C. E. CARRINGTON

D. G. S. CARTER
P. B. & P. G. CARTER
JOHN H. O. CARTWRIGHT
ENID CASSIN
B. CHALLENOR
RODERICK CHAMBERLAIN
NICHOLAS CHANCE
HEADMASTER OF CHARTERHOUSE
STANLEY CHATTEY
C. S. CHESHIRE
CHARLES S. (RUFUS) CHURCHER
HENRY J. CLAY
LORD CLITHEROE
COLIN CLIVE
RICHARD CLOWES
A. J. COATS
SIR JAMES COBBAN
H. A. COBHAM
MR & MRS R. O. COBHAM
DAVID G. COCKBURN
F. T. COLLINS
J. A. R. COLLINS
GEORGE & SHEILA CONSTANTINIDI
PAUL M. CONSTANTINIDI
PETER J. COOPER
C. W. B. COSTELOE
H. E. A. COX
MARK & GUY COXETER
COL. R. A. COXWELL-ROGERS
VICKI L. CRANKSHAW
J. CRAVEN
NICO CRAVEN
LT-CDR R. J. E. CRAVEN
DOUGLAS J. CRAWSHAW
RICHARD CREWDSON
JAMES A. CROPPER
DAVID & ELSPETH CROSSMAN
NICOLAS J. G. CROSTHWAITE
JEREMY CULLEN & TOVE REVENTLOW
DAVID CUNNINGHAM
MISS MARY CURTIS

DAVID R. M. DALGLISH
FLORA DANIEL
WILLIAM J. DANIELS
O. C. DAVENPORT
RUPERT DAVIES
NICHOLAS DAWSON
TIMOTHY DAWSON
LUKE & TOM DE HAAN
R. M. O. DE LA HEY
HIS HONOUR ALAN DE PIRO
DOMINIC DEL MAR
OLIVER DEL MAR
SAM DEL MAR
DONALD DEMAREST

MRS RODNEY DOUGLAS-PENNANT
CAPT P. R. DOYNE
H. P. F. DOYNE-DITMAS
DR JOHN ELWES DUFFIELD
J. L. DUFFIELD
MAJ. SIR PHILIP DUNCOMBE BT
MRS LOUISE DUNMORE
PHILIP G. DUNMORE

MRS E. M. EAGAR
RICHARD DONALD EASTAUGH
A. J. K. EDMONDSON
CHARLES EDWARDES-KER
MICHAEL EDWARDES-KER
FRANÇOIS W. EDWARDS
FRANCES LADY ELIOTT OF STOBS
RUPERT ENFIELD TAYLOR
S. A. J. ENGLISH
JAN MARTIN ESCHBACH
EVANGELINE & TENNIEL EVANS
SIR MARTYN EVANS-BEVAN BT
G. W. EVES

ANTHONY FAWCETT
CHARLES FERRAND
MR & MRS ALVIN T. FERREIRA
DAVID CHARLES FERREIRA
FIGG FAMILY
ANTHONY G. FINDLAY
MR RONALD & LADY GLORIA FLOWER
MERVYN FOX-PITT
WARREN & MARIGOLD FREEMAN-ATTWOOD
CHRISTOPHER FRENCH
WILLIAM K. FREWEN
JAMES & NICHOLAS FROST

H. M. GADSBY
A. C. GALLIERS-PRATT
D. P. & R. C. GARDINER-HILL
NICK GEORGANO
C. A. V. GIBBS
DAVID E. GIBBS
CLEM GIBSON
S. P. GIBSON
THOMAS H. GIBSON
PETER & ELIZABETH GILBEY
JONATHAN & PHILLIDA GILI
ALEXANDER GILKES
ANTHONY R. GILL
PATRICK W. GILL
CHARLES J. ST. L. GILLMAN
PETER GLAZEBROOK
PETER GLOSSOP
CHARLES N. GOOCH
D. L. GOODHART

SIR WILLIAM & LADY GOODHART
DAPHNE & PETER GOUGH
ORLANDO GOUGH
PIERS GOUGH
M. W. A. GOVER
ANDREW GRAHAM
SIMON T. GRANDAGE
E. P. C. GREENE
MISS JENNIFER GREENE
OLIVER R. GREENE
MRS STEPHEN GREENE
EDWARD J. A. GREENHALGH
M. T. GREENHALGH
JAMES GREENHAM
MATTHEW GREENHAM
MRS BASIL GREENWELL
SIMON GREENWELL
MARK B. GUBBINS
BASIL E. GWYN

EARL OF HADDO
SQN-LDR N. L. & MRS B. L. M. HAGGETT
MRS B. R. HALL
G. F. J. HALSEY
JAMES & MATTHEW HAMMOND
MAJ. R. F. HANBURY
R. J. HANBURY
MICHAEL J. W. HANCOCK
JOHN BARNARD HANKEY
TOM HARLEY
SIMON HARRAP
TOBY & RUFUS HARRISON-BANFIELD
S. C. HARTWRIGHT
MR & MRS JOHN HATCH
HECTOR HAWKINS
CHARLES HAYWARD
SIMON HAYWARD
ARTHUR HEARNDEN
DAVID HEATON
DR W. A. L. HEATON
HUGH A. HELLYER
ALISTER & GILES HENTON
DIANA HEYMAN
PETER HEYMAN
ALEXANDER HEYNES
JONATHAN HEYNES
LT-COL. & MRS FERGUS HIGGINS
MR & MRS DEREK HIGGS
GUY HIGSON
PHILIP HOARE
CHARLES HOARE NAIRNE
JAMES HOARE NAIRNE
VICTOR HOARE NAIRNE
E. D. M. R.-HODGES
T. S. HODGETTS
L. HODSON

HYLA & JANE HOLDEN
C. E. HOLDSWORTH HUNT
A. D. R. HOLLAND
D. H. R. HOLLAND
T. L. R. HOLLAND
NIGEL HOLLICK
PAUL & IRENE HOLMER
JAMES HOLT
GOSPATRIC & DIANA HOME
OLIVER HOME
ADRIAN T. HOPKINSON
CHRISTOPHER JAMES HOPKINSON
DAVID HOPKINSON
ROBIN HORSFALL
C. M. HORTON
G. S. HOW
CLIVE & NAN HOWSON
GILES HOWSON
R. P. HUBBARD
MARCUS HUMPHREY
MAJ. ROGER HUMPHREYS

ROBERT & MORAY ILES
CHARLES L. A. IRBY
G. A. P. IRBY
PAUL IRBY
A. R. IZAT

T. E. B. JACKSON
HENRY & MARY JAMES
JONATHAN JANSON
ALEXANDER JEFFS
BENJAMIN JEFFS
DANIEL JEFFS
MR & MRS JULIAN JEFFS
BAPJI JODHPUR
MR & MRS MARK JOHNSON

YASH & LOUISE KADAN
BARRY M. KEMBALL-COOK
C. A. H. KEMP
TIMOTHY A. F. KEMP
NORMAN KITSON
GEORGE HOWARD KITTO
VISCOUNT KNUTSFORD

M. P. LAKIN
MR & MRS R. LANGHORNE
W. M. LANYON
PETER S. LASKEY
P. S. H. LAWRENCE
MRS MOYA LEE
CHARLES LEGARD
MARY LADY LEGARD
MRS M. S. LEGGETT
ROGER J. E. LEIGH

DR DONALD LEINSTER-MACKAY
PHILIP LEY
WILLIAM PETER K. S. LIM
IAIN LITTLE
WILLIAM LIVERSIDGE
M. C.K. LLOYD
HUGH LORT-PHILLIPS
ANDREW LOYD
DAVID W. A. LOYD
SALLY LOYD

DAVID MCEUEN
R. D. MCEUEN
ANDREW W. MCGHIE
NICHOLAS MACKENZIE-CHARRINGTON
RUARIDH MACLEOD
DUNCAN M. MACRAE
DR RODERICK MAGGS
J. S. MALIM
REAR-ADM. & MRS N. H. MALIM
JOSEPH VON MALTZAHN
JOHN W. MATTHEW
MRS J. M. MATTHEWS
R. G. MAXWELL-BROWN
PIERS H. N. D. METHUEN
MICHAEL MICHAELIS
A. M. T. MILLAR
C. J. MILNE
MARK P. MINNS
PETER D. MOLL
MR & MRS A. T. MONTGOMERY
COLIN & PAM MONTGOMERY
D. J. T. MONTGOMERY
GORDON S. A. MONTGOMERY
PIERS & HUGH MONTGOMERY
JOHN MOORES
PATRICK MOORES
SIMON MOORES
W. G. MORISON
DEREK MORPHETT
G. T. E. & W. R. F. MOSS
PETER C. D. MOY
ROBERT BORGERHOFF MULDER

MARK NATHAN
D. J. & R. A. NAYLOR
GUY NEALE
P. A. NEGRETTI
NEVILLE-JOHN NEVILL-GLIDDON
SIMON ASHLEY NEVILL-GLIDDON
R. H. NICHOLSON
NICHOLAS NIXEY
WILLIAM NIXEY
CHARLES NODRUM
CHRISTOPHER & THOMAS NOLTE

EDWARD O'BREE
BRIAN & REBECCA O'REILLY
R. A. L. OGSTON
MAJ. L. F. & MRS PHYLLIS OLNEY
MR & MRS A. F. OPPÉ

A. A. H. PALMER
JAMES, FREDDIE & LEO PALMER
R. M. PALMER
W. A. PALMER
C. D. PALMER-TOMKINSON
M. G. H. PARKES
AUDREY PARRY
†MICHAEL PARRY
MRS RICHARD PARRY
CHARLES T. PART
MR & MRS R. A. PARTRIDGE
JOHN & ALICE PEEL
ROBERT & ANDREW PEEL
TIMOTHY PEERS
NICHOLAS PETO
JAMES PICKTHORN
F. E. PICKWORTH
MARC PIERCEY
JAMES PIKE
M. E. L. PIKE
AL, TIM & NIC PLATT
BILL PLAYER
J. D. PLAYER
HENRY PORTER
MAJ. H. R. M. PORTER
J. V. A. POTTER
DR MALCOLM G. PRENTICE
MR & MRS SHELDON PRENTICE
MR & MRS MICHAEL PRESTON
TOBY & JASON PRIESTLY
R. PRYOR
FRANCIS PYM

RAJ P. RAMPHUL
D. W. RAWSON-MACKENZIE
MR & MRS BARRY REED
A. F. REYNARD
REVD J. S. REYNOLDS
ROBERT RICE
ELIZABETH RICHARDSON
MR & MRS S. B. ROBERTS
SIMON M. ROBERTSON
ANDREW ROBSON
JAMES ROBSON
RUPERT ROBSON
CDR GRAHAM C. B. ROGERS
HARRY PIKE ROGERS
PETER ROGERS
ROBERT ROGERS
MRS C. M. RONALDSON

NICK ROOTES
J. MARTIN ROWLANDS
J. N. RUCKER
H. RUSSELL
CHARLES RYDER
RICHARD RYDER
STEPHEN RYDER

PATRICK SAVAGE
MR & MRS ROBERT SAWYER
BRUNO L. SCHRODER
ANDREW SCOTT
DR & MRS CLAUDE SCOTT
MR & MRS LARRY SCOTT
NUMPH SCOTT
A. J. C. SEYMOUR
F .H. SEYMOUR
JONATHAN SEYMOUR-WILLIAMS
W. G. SHAKESPEARE
ROBERT SHAW
SIMON G. H. SHAW
TIMOTHY R. S. SHAW
JAMIE SHELDON
HUGH SHELTON
JOHN SHIPTON
DAVID MICHAEL SHORT
N. G. SHRUBSALL
SIR EVELYN & LADY SHUCKBURGH
HUGO & OLIVER SHUTTLEWORTH
SINCLAIR FAMILY
ANTHONY SKYRME
COLIN H. H. SLATER
JAMES & EDWARD SMITH
JEREMY SMITH
M. M. SNOW
A. C. SOMERS
D. K. SOMERS
R. P. W. SOMERS
WALTER SOMERS
MICHAEL SPENS
MR & MRS R. M. SPITZLEY
DR & MRS A. I. SPRIGGS
JOHN R. STAINER
BEVILLE STANIER
STEEL FAMILY
MRS BETTY M. STEPHENSON
JONATHAN STEPHENSON
MR & MRS G. A. STEVENS
DAPHNE C. STEWART
PAUL STIBBARD
ALEXANDER M. STIRLING
JAMES STOCKTON
WILLIAM STOCKTON
CHARLES STOKES
JANET STONE
MICHAEL STOURTON
M. J. L. STOW
R. W. M. STRANGE
HENRY JONATHAN SUMMERS
LEONARD & JOAN SWINBANK
MARK SWINBANK

JAMES TALBOT BAKER
JEREMY TAYLOR
JOAN & PHILIP TAYLOR
KIM D. TAYLOR
MARTIN TAYLOR
SIMON TAYLOR
EDWARD THAW
STEPHEN THOMPSON
SIR JOHN THOMSON
COUNT NIKOLAI TOLSTOY
CHRISTOPHER STEPHEN TOMKINSON
JOHN W. TOMKINSON
R. W. TOMKINSON
SIMON TOZER
SIMON TROSS YOULE
EDWARD G. TROTTER
RICHARD TROTTER
ANDREW, HUGO & BENEDICT TURQUET

P. J. UPTON
T. O. UPTON

HART WHELAN VAN DENBURG
JOHN VASSAR-SMITH
ASHIF VERJEE
ZOOLFIKAR VERJEE
W. P. M. VINCENT
HON. RICHARD VIVIAN

JAMES WADE
MRS MONICA WAITE
MRS JAMES WALLIS
CHRISTIAN G. K. WARMAN
IAN H. WARREN
DAVID & GINA WATTS-RUSSELL
ELIZABETH & PETER WAY
ROBIN WEDDERBURN
PROF. & MRS WEINSTEIN
K. B. WELBY
ANTHONY WELD FORESTER
ADAM BERNARD WELLS
D. L. WELLS
SIMON BOWEN WELLS
MICHAEL R. WESTMACOTT
H. C. WHITBREAD
PAUL M. WHITFIELD
S. P. WHITLEY
CHRISTOPHER WIGAN
DESMOND WIGAN

PETER WIGAN
MRS ROBIN WIGGIN
CLIVE & ROWENA WILLIAMS
ROBERT W. M. (ROBIN) WILLIAMS
R. A. WILLIS
SIR SETON WILLS BT
GEORGE & OLIVER WINTERS
ELIAS & FRANCES WOLF
NICOLAS WOLFERS
CHARLES A. J. WOODFORD
REVD & MRS CHRISTOPHER WOODS
DAVID WOODS
E. W. WOODS
ARCHBISHOP SIR FRANK WOODS
RICHARD & JOANNA WOODS
BISHOP ROBIN & HENRIETTA WOODS
P. G. WOOLDRIDGE
REVD JOHN WOOLMER
MARK WORDSWORTH
LORD WRAXALL

HIS HONOUR JUDGE CHRISTOPHER YOUNG
JOHN YOUNG

MARQUESS OF ZETLAND

1
2
3
4
5
7
8
9